In Pursuit of the Slam:
My Year Travelling to Tennis's Top Four
Tournaments
by
Mark Cripps
ISBN: 978-1-914933-11-0

Best Wishes
Hope you enjoy it
Mark

Copyright 2022
All rights reserved. No part of this publication may be reproduced, stored in a retrieval system or transmitted in any form or by any means, electronic, mechanical, photocopy, recording org otherwise, without prior written consent of the copyright owner. Nor can it be circulated in any form of binding or cover other than that in which it is published and without similar condition including this condition being imposed on a subsequent purchaser.
The right of Mark Cripps to be identified as the author of this work has been asserted in accordance with the Copyright Designs and Patents Act 1988.
A copy of this book is deposited with the British Library.

Published By: -

i2i
PUBLISHING

i2i Publishing. Manchester.
www.i2i.publishing.co.uk

To Mum and Dad, Ben and Zoe

Acknowledgements

There are many people included in the pages that follow. In a way, if your name appears below, I need to thank you for your contribution. When all of the events and interactions I have recorded came together, they created the story. However, some people featured more often than others not only in helping to create the events but in helping to shape and then improve the book as it was conceived, drafted and formed into the pages laid out below.

My parents, Terry and Sheila, are sadly, no longer with us. However, as you will find out below, with dad providing solid support for everything we all got up to in the family, it was my mum who was a driving force in my own love of tennis. But as I have written this book, my brother, Ben, his family and my sister, Zoe have been enthusiastic throughout the writing of it. So, a big thank you to them.

My cousin, Frances Gibb, has always been a tremendous supporter of my work editing books with i2i Publishing and extended that positive encouragement to my efforts in writing this one. She has been willing to pass on her considerable experience as a journalist with *The Times* in the position of legal editor for nearly four decades. Her detailed comments on the early drafts were invaluable.

Without author, Bob Mitchell encouragement over twenty years ago when I took my first steps hitting the keys in an attempt to say something about coaching junior tennis, I would not be writing now. As ever, Mitch, a dear friend, offered his wise counsel on how to improve the book in various ways.

Tennis writer and friend, Joel Drucker has been positive throughout in his support of the book and he reviewed the text and provided inciteful comments on its emphasis as well as its detail.

Steve McCormack, my friend and ex-teammate from university football days, not only reminded me about a lovely anecdote to include about Wimbledon but brought his journalistic expertise to bear on the manuscript. He provided me with supporting praise but also really helpful constructive criticism as I was finalising the text.

Steve Contardi read the book and checked the chapter on his marvellous Tennis Fantasies camp which was a highlight of the trip and through the marvellous friendships it has created, including Steve and his family, has now become such an important part of my life.

Former colleagues, now friends, Martin Chillcott, Iain McConnachie, Jim Fraser, Kamal Boushi and Mark LeClercq gave me important advice. Martin helped with the title and the early part of the book's structure. Iain gave me a helpful overview but also a detailed line by line copy edit of the text. Jim gave me some important feedback on the tone of the text and in the editing process, Kamal encouraged me to retain difficult parts of the story I had told from the heart that I was considering deleting. Mark was really positive about the book encouraging me to consider alternative approaches.

Another ex-colleague, Ray Pierce, read the text and gave me interesting stories of his own tennis journey which were relevant to the theme of the book and have been included. My thanks to him.

Writer, journalist and broadcaster, Richard Evans was kind enough to read the book and used his considerable knowledge of the sport's history to correct my errors.

Somehow, all these years later, Simon Ickringill, still coaching at Ilkley Lawn Tennis & Squash Club, managed to find a programme for the Ilkley Tennis Tournament from 1992 which provided the basis of the chapter on my week spent at the club attempting to compete with players many levels higher than myself, Simon included.

Former British tennis pro, Danny Sapsford, spared me the time to talk about his career. He provided fascinating insights about his approach, aspects of a professional's life that would be difficult to find from other sources.

There were other players I watched on my travels who should be mentioned. Debbie Graham, Amos Mansdorf, Brad Pearce Byron Talbot and Michelle Jaggard-Lai provided positive and enthusiastic support and helped in making sure I was accurate when writing anecdotes about them.

Former colleague at David Lloyd Leisure, Steve Matthews, shared some wonderful experiences of his playing days as an aspiring young pro, as well as the antics off the court at County Week in Eastbourne which I have managed to include in the book.

Fabio Platania runs the excellent *Tennis Pro Legacy* page on Facebook. Fabio directed me towards a brilliant website that listed player rankings over the period covered by my trip and this helped give additional accuracy to how I recorded the details of the tournaments and the players. His page also helped to convince me that there might be an audience for a book about the pro game back in the nineties and before. He also spent time helping to check the text, especially the chapter on the Italian Open in Rome.

Another Facebook contact, ex-player and now coach, Craig Webster, who always posts interesting content on his page was kind enough to read the book and give me the thumbs up.

Other friends including Howard Rogg and Kyri Costi have also taken time to cast an eye over the book. Thanks to both of them.

Lawrence Nasralla, one of the authors whose book I edited returned the favour by making some very astute comments about the text in a number of areas.

Over the last three years, the working relationship developed with proprietor and publisher of i2i Publishing,

Lionel Ross has been a special one. His enthusiasm and commitment to the book have been unflinching from the moment I told him of my plans. I thank him for all of that support while I was writing the book and now, for publishing it.

Finally, a mention of my dear friend, Phil Stevens, another teammate from university football days. When sick and in his final days, it was Phil who asked me to work with Lionel Ross to monitor and help with the final stages of the publication of the memoir that Phil had written about his life. Working with Lionel while making a final check on Phil's book led to me working at i2i Publishing. But Phil never knew about this positive development. Without my involvement with Lionel and his company, I would not have written this book. I owe my dear, departed friend a massive and heartfelt thank you. I know he would be delighted at the book's publication.

Contents

Prologue	In-Flight Magazine	1
Chapter 1	Telegram for Roger Taylor	13
Chapter 2	Tennis Takes Over	31
Chapter 3	Fantastico Foro Italico	47
Chapter 4	Sun, Wind and Rain at Roland Garros	65
Chapter 5	Inter-City Epiphany	91
Chapter 6	Joining the Queue in SW19	113
Chapter 7	Ickringilled in Ilkley	143
Chapter 8	Heat and Noise in Flushing Meadows	163
Chapter 9	Tennis Fantasies at Newk's	189
Chapter 10	Remembering Hop	217
Chapter 11	Musch, Milton and Martinez	241
Chapter 12	Return to White City	257
Chapter 13	Happy Slam at Flinders Park	269
Epilogue	Looking Back; Moving Forward	295
Photo Gallery	Sport, the Slam and Me	319
Bibliography	Recommended Tennis Books	335
Index		341

x

Prologue

In-Flight Magazine

A deafening roar
The match had been going on for hours. The momentum had swung one way, then the other. Two top players had given it their all. The Bullring was packed; the crowd primed for every point. Finally, at the end of five, hard-fought sets, Michael Chang hit his forehand volley into the net. It was over. The crowd let out a deafening roar. The winner, Sweden's Nicklas Kulti, did a little jump for joy. Then, respectful of appropriate end-of-match protocols, he jogged to the net to acknowledge Chang. He had won a match that his opponent looked like he would never give up on. This was the third round in the men's singles at the French Open on a lovely Saturday evening in May 1992.

I looked out over the scene from my seat, high up on the perimeter of one of Roland Garros's iconic courts and felt a moment of intense exhilaration. As I sat watching the players shake hands and the spectators applaud, I couldn't imagine being anywhere else. But seven months before, the thought that the following summer, I would be witnessing such a spectacle and sharing the excitement and elation of thousands of tennis fans on a lovely evening in Paris as the year's second Grand Slam tournament worked its way to a conclusion, would have seemed completely crazy.

A chance sighting
Back in late October 1991, the year before, down in Sydney, I was eleven months into a new job in my corporate career in marketing with American Express. I was thirty-five years old and into my second decade with the company, but there was a problem: I was deeply unhappy. However, something inside told me to get out and once that thought had stuck, I knew

there was only one course of action to take. I resigned the next day. Then, as part of my notice period, I was on a flight to Perth in Western Australia and that's when I had a chance sighting. I turned the page of the Australian Airlines in-flight magazine and there he was: Simon Rogers, my good friend from the days when I was a runner in the film industry in London's Soho district back in the late seventies. He was smiling alongside an older man as they both shared a drink, a father and son, possibly? The image was in an advertisement for Johnny Walker whisky. That moment seeing Simon was when I had the thought which would set me on the pathway to attending professional tennis's top four tournaments, the Grand Slam.

Over the last year, I had been one of the marketing directors in American Express's Australian card business. That job, on paper, should have been the best so far in my time with the company. I knew that side of the business well, having reached a senior management position in charge of an area where I had begun as an entry-level salesman just over a decade before in 1980. I had risen up the company quite quickly with a new job every two years, in sales and then in marketing, until July 1986. Then, I took the job of running the card and traveller's cheque marketing for the company in the Middle East. My time there had been a fantastic experience from a work and a social perspective where amongst other things, I was able to play and develop my tennis.

However, as well as being a fascinating place to live, the region was volatile politically. During most of my assignment, the Iran-Iraq War had been in progress, not that far north, up the Arabian Gulf from my location in Bahrain. Also, in August 1990, with that war finished, Saddam Hussein decided to regain what he believed to be Iraqi territory by invading Kuwait. Everything changed for many people that day, including me, effectively bringing my job in the Middle East to an end.

Harsh reality down-under

It was agreed that I would move on and through connections in the company, I was offered the job in Sydney, a step-up career-wise; a higher grade, bigger budgets, more staff, bigger salary and the prospect of living life in one of the world's best cities. What was not to like? What could possibly go wrong?

Unfortunately, quite quickly after my arrival, I realised that I was burnt out from my Middle East experiences, where for a short period at least, all of us located there were not sure if we would become part of a war zone filled with soldiers, artillery, planes and everything that the Iraqi Army might use in a possible domination of more than just Kuwait across the Gulf states. There had been considerable disruption from just about every perspective, including being evacuated under instruction from the company, on a night flight back to the UK, where I was greeted in American Express's large operational base in Brighton as if I was back at home on a normal visit. No-one seemed to know what was going on out in the Gulf.

"You here on holiday, Mark?" I was asked by a colleague as we passed each other in the corridor. Already struggling to deal with what was going on in the Middle East, I didn't know what to say. Saddam Hussein's name was not yet part of common parlance; it was as if I was in some sort of surreal, parallel universe.

In Sydney, the department I took over needed an overhaul. Not only this, but the American Express card business in Australia was struggling in the aftermath of the Chernobyl disaster, which had affected worldwide travel, and a strike by Australia's airline pilots which had seriously affected the domestic travel scene. As I took my departmental hot seat, I had no idea how hot it was. Even on that very first day, an experienced and talented member of my marketing team resigned. He said he'd had enough.

A few days later, the budgets for the following year were approved. But then, meetings were held and all the numbers were changed. Having just arrived, I had no idea about the significance of the figures. I knew what the marketing programmes were, but the Australian version of them and how much money was needed to make them effective was a mystery to me at that stage.

From day one, there was just too much to do. I had been used to working under pressure. Plus, the Middle East market was known to be one of the most complex in the American Express world. But I was now involved in another league of expectation entirely. Looking back, it's clear that I needed a break before taking on a new job, especially one where what was needed was someone raring to go and full of energy, not someone who was effectively burnt out.

After about three months, things came to a grinding halt. I became sick. I lost my voice and this developed into a terrible sore throat. I had to stay home for days, just at the time I could not afford to be away from the mountain of tasks that needed my attention. Just about recovered, I returned to work. But I began to long for the end of each day. The weekends were such a relief. However, not only did I dread going back to work on Monday morning but that dark and depressing feeling began not on Sunday, but on Saturday evening. Here, it was tennis that proved to be my salvation. I loved to play and I spent every weekend at Sydney's picturesque White City playing in club afternoons, once-a-month mixed doubles tournaments, inter-club league matches and practising and playing sets with my new tennis friends. The club became my base, taking me away from the work environment which dominated the week.

That won't do nicely anymore

I soldiered on at work for most of 1991 but when I was assigned the task of changing the way the sales force under my responsibility was run, which would involve making all of my state teams redundant, with the functions they now performed carried out differently, I knew that my time was up. In my worn condition, I could not see myself leading the process which would involve between thirty and forty people being made redundant with significant challenges and upset to them and their families.

I felt increasingly like some sort of corporate zombie as I made presentation after presentation on the subject. Then, one afternoon, a memo was put on my desk. I looked at it, read it and realised that not only did I not know what to do with the problem it laid out but I just didn't care anymore. My personal assistant, Karen, stood at my office door as efficient as she had always been. She had a pile of memos, letters and reports from my in-tray to go through. I just sent her away.

My colleague and good friend, Nicky Markham, who I had worked with in the UK marketing department, poked her head around the door and asked, "Is everything okay?" I looked back at her and said, "No … I can't do this anymore." This exchange led to a brief chat and as it was the end of the workday, we agreed to go for dinner in a nice pub near Nicky's home. After Nicky leant me a sympathetic ear, something I will always be grateful for, I returned home to write my resignation.

The next morning, I handed in the letter to my boss who was so shocked, that at first, she didn't believe me. But from that moment, I felt as if a massive weight had been lifted off my shoulders. My notice period began. While I no longer had a job, I did have enough money, saved up from my years in Bahrain, to keep me going and to buy me some time to decide what to do. Exactly what that would be, I didn't have a clue.

A year-long trip takes shape
A few days later, I flew to Perth as part of the work on my sales teams and as the flight began, I began to mull over the alternatives for me to pursue. Could I start another corporate job in marketing, here in Australia or back in the UK? If I didn't stay in the field of expertise in which I had just spent

over a decade building some experience, what would I do? As the air miles flew by, an idea began to form.

Once I had spotted my old friend, Simon, drinking his whiskey in the in-flight magazine advert, I put work, jobs and careers to the back of my mind. The thought of catching up again with him, now married and living in New York, was really exciting. If I looked up Simon, I could also visit a few other of the major American cities I had read about, the ones at the heart of so much American culture that had been part of my upbringing. I could visit some of the significant places in the nation's history which I had studied at university. I could go to the real-life locations of the wonderful film from the sixties, *How the West was Won*; the site of the battle of the Little Big Horn, the subject of another sixties film, *Custer of the West* and also, of a rather strange board game I was given as a child. I could visit the sites of the big battles of the American Civil War, events which had made such an impact on me when I read about them as a child and collected A&BC bubble gum cards telling the story of that terrible conflict, often in grizzly images. I could travel to Washington D.C. with all its museums. Finally, I could go to many of the iconic sports stadia in American football, both those in the NFL and the huge colleges where the sport had begun, as well as some of the historic baseball fields.

It was only then that I thought of the US Open at Flushing Meadows in New York, a Grand Slam tournament I had read about, followed and watched on the television from the late seventies onwards when the final weekend was shown on the BBC. If I planned my trip for the autumn, I could aim to sit in the Louis Armstrong stadium for the men's final as the sun set and that fantastic image of the Manhattan skyline began to show over the Hudson River. If I began my travels in New York, I could go west. If I finished my trip in California, I could fly out to Hawaii and then on back to Australia, where I could spend some time in the country enjoying it in the way it should be enjoyed, including two weeks spent watching the Australian Open in Melbourne.

The plane continued its journey towards Perth and as I stared out of the window at the expanse of this huge continent, I realised that I'd planned half of a Grand Slam of visits, so why not complete the other half? If I started off what was now looking like a year of travelling, by going around Europe in the spring, I could plan to be in Paris in late May for the French Open. Although it wasn't a Grand Slam tournament, nontheless, I could also be in Rome a few weeks before and visit the famous Foro Italico, the site of the Italian Open.

At the end of Roland Garros, I could head home through northern France and visit the sites of the battles of Verdun and the Somme from the First World War, both of which I had studied at university. I would arrive back at my flat in Wimbledon in perfect time to visit the build-up tournaments prior to the start of the tennis just a short distance from my home. Then, every morning, I could walk up to the grounds between Somerset Road and Church Road and watch the matches. After a short post-Wimbledon break, I would then begin the second part of my travels completing the parts of the trip I had planned earlier in the flight.

I was aware that most people who travelled around Europe often did so by rail. So, I would try and do it that way, assuming I could buy the appropriate rail pass. Also, I knew that before the growth of the airline industry in the US, rail was the way that many people used to cross the continent and now Amtrack were still running many of the famous old services. I decided to travel around the US on the train as well, seeing the country at ground level as opposed to from thirty thousand feet.

On the question of funding, I had built up quite a substantial amount of savings while working abroad, especially in the Middle East where American Express's policies benefitted an expat in my position. Although my work had been a seriously challenging experience in Sydney, financially, the remuneration added further to my savings. At the entry-level of senior management that I had reached, the company expected a lot but they paid you well too. Also, at this juncture in my life, I was single and answerable to myself. After a decade of pressing my nose to the corporate grindstone, it dawned on me that I could do just about anything I liked.

If I used my savings to help pay off my mortgage back in the UK, I would have had to start a new job immediately and I needed time to work out what that might be. What better way to decide my next steps than by taking some time to travel? But why was the Grand Slam such a motivating subject to base my travels around?

Grand Slam: The best of the best
The term, Grand Slam was used first in golf when it was applied to Ben Hogan's achievement of winning golf's major tournaments in 1930. In tennis, various journalists, including Alison Danzig of the *New York Times*, began to use the term through the thirties and it was definitely in vogue when the American, Don Budge, won all of the sport's major singles titles in Melbourne, Paris, Wimbledon and New York in 1938.

Although the four Grand Slam tournaments fitted into the schedule of the ATP Tour and the WTA Tour, it was the International Tennis Federation, known usually as the ITF, that supervised the running of the major tournaments, the Australian Open, the French Open, Wimbledon and the US Open. The tournaments were owned by the national associations in each country except in the UK, where Wimbledon was owned by the All-England Club, the tournament's location.

Each Slam was made up of singles and doubles for men's and women's and mixed doubles too. They all had junior versions and now, nearly three decades later, wheelchair and quad wheelchair versions too. Over-age events including doubles in Over 35 and Over 45 categories for men and women have been introduced as well.

The Grand Slam tournaments were the best of the best for the players especially, as far as ranking points and prize money. Even for losing in the first round, the rewards could keep a lower-ranked player on the tour for many months and there were increasing amounts of money for those who progressed further and a staggering reward for the winners, all funded by the biggest sponsorship and TV rights deals in the sport. As a test of endurance, the Slams were the toughest. The singles events were all one-hundred and twenty-eight player draws, making the competition on the court the biggest challenge. Seven wins were needed to win the top prize and in the case of the men, in best-of-five set matches. Every player sought to be fit for the Slams or to be high enough ranked to enter them automatically.

Also, worldwide media and fan attention was huge. The tournaments had far and away the biggest audiences on television, radio, press, as well as attendances at the site, compared to any other tournaments in the calendar year of both tours, including the end-of-year championships. Finally, each event had a long history which I shall outline later and transcended the sport in their countries. People who did not follow tennis at all for the rest of the year, would follow their Grand Slam tournament avidly for its two-week duration, just like my mum and our family did as we shall see.

Today, there are various incarnations of the Grand Slam other than what might be called the pure one: Winning all four major singles tournaments in the same calendar year. Four titles won in sequence but spanning two years is called a non-calendar year Grand Slam. The four Slams won individually at some point during a player's career is, not surprisingly, a Career Grand Slam. An Olympic Games Gold medal won in singles in addition to the four traditional Slams is called a Golden Slam. The end-of-year tour championships of the ATP or WTA Tours, when added to the Slams, is called a Super Slam. Although the holy grail of Slams is the one achieved in singles, all of these definitions apply to the doubles events too. Indeed, should any player win all twelve Slams in singles, doubles and mixed across their career, they will have won what is called a Boxed Set Slam.

At the time of my proposed trip, only two men, Donald Budge (in 1938) and Rod Laver (in 1962 and 1969), and three women, Maureen Connolly (in 1953), Margaret Court (in 1970) and Steffi Graf (in 1988), had won the four singles titles in the same calendar year. Graf had also won the Olympics thereby achieving a Golden Slam.

The 1992 Australian Open, the first of the following year's Grand Slam tournaments was just over two months away. I could have tried to set up elsewhere in Sydney, but I wanted to see my family, my friends and my flat, which was in Wimbledon, overlooking the site of the tournament at its original Worple Road location. Also, I wasn't sure if my visa was still valid and I certainly didn't want to fall foul of the Australian immigration authorities. My non-calendar year version of a Grand Slam would begin in Paris, take me back to the UK for Wimbledon and then on to the US enabling me to reach Australia again for the 1993 version of their Slam.

You should write a book
Since I completed the trip that I am about to describe, a few people urged me to write a book about it. I was open to the idea but I couldn't see what angle to use. I wasn't convinced by a pure travel perspective. But once I had thought of the Grand Slam theme, especially seeing as it was at the heart of my year out, I wondered why I hadn't seen it before. I had been telling my tennis related stories in various tennis internet forums and the posts had been well received. The Grand Slam approach was a self-contained story with a beginning and an end, so I thought, why not? I could produce something I was excited to

write about and that readers might be interested in. Using my experiences writing a sports memorabilia blog for a decade and what I'd learned as a book editor, where I had helped a number of new authors tell their life stories, I decided to tell mine through the prism of my Grand Slam trip.

As well as tennis fans, I hope the book will be of interest to those who like books about travelling. Also, I hope that the book might give some ideas to those doing a gap year, or taking time out from their regular schedule, whatever their age. People considering an actual change of direction might be interested in how I used my passion for tennis to make such a change. Even for readers who are happy with their jobs and career, maybe they might use my experience to create ways to follow their passion in different and better ways than they are doing currently?

The book concentrates on my tennis experiences which were central to everything I did. The chapters follow what happened chronologically and there is one about the tournament fortnight of each of the Slams, topped and tailed by those relating what I did both before and after each tournament. At the start, I've given readers a taste of how I grew up as a sports fan overall with a focus initially on football and cricket. I relate how tennis was always there in the background, ultimately taking over from my two other main sports.

The book will be a nostalgic look back at tennis from the sixties through to the nineties and will aim to appeal to the many tennis fans out there who love this period of the sport's history. However, looking at the past can lead to a view where everything was better back in the day, as the saying goes. Although an analytical comparison of the state of the sport then and now would be interesting, this is not the place for it. It is the reality that then and now, the sport has never been perfect. At the time of my trip in the early nineties, just over two decades after tennis had become fully professional, there were a number of major issues facing how the sport was run. But this book will not analyse those problems. They have been covered in a number of excellent panoramic looks at the professional tours in books written by fine writers which are all listed in the bibliography.

My story here is a fond look back at the sport when I had a chance in a lifetime to follow it back in the early nineties while I did some thinking about things other than annual marketing plans and how to implement them. For me, things were changing and my trip around the world following the Grand Slam was a time when I could try to work out how to make a fresh start with the next phase of my life.

Chapter 1

Telegram for Roger Taylor

Watch out, Rocket
Mum was excited. "Where should I send it?" she asked aloud to no-one in particular as she began to flick through the phone book. She was about to send a telegram to a well-known tennis player.

It was late June 1970, the end of the first week of Wimbledon. The British No. 1, Roger Taylor, ranked at No. 16 in the world and also the sixteenth seed at this year's tournament, had reached the fourth round of the men's singles. So far, so good, as far as British tennis fans were concerned. What was not so good about the situation was Taylor's opponent at this next stage of the tournament. Back then, in the days when the men's final was played on the Friday of the second week as opposed to the Sunday, the fourth-round matches were scheduled a day or two earlier than now, usually on the Saturday at the end of the first week. Rod Laver, the number one seed and at the top of the world rankings, had won thirty-one matches in a row up until this point. To say that 'Rocket', as Laver was nicknamed, was at the top of his game, was an understatement. So far, in SW19, he had won all of his three matches, only dropping a set to the man with the cap, Frew McMillan from South Africa, a player known to the Wimbledon crowds more as a doubles specialist but one who as a singles player, still reached the quarter-final of the US Open and a career high ranking of No. 39.

Taylor's progress had been a bit tougher. He had survived a match against American, Charlie Pasarell but in pre-tiebreak days, one that involved a very long, thirty-four game second set. Charlie had, of course, been part of an amazing match in 1969 against the forty-one-year-old Pancho

Gonzales. Played over two days, this match had taken one-hundred and twelve games over five sets to resolve, as Pancho came back from two sets to love down. No-one, let alone Taylor, doubted Pasarell's staying power.

But even with Taylor's good form, not too many held out much hope for him as he prepared to face Laver, the Rocket, a name given to him because the great Harry Hopman, who we will hear about later, decided he didn't have any pace. In fact, the press had told Taylor, our man from Sheffield, that he would do better staying at home. However, in our nice house in Hampstead Garden Suburb in North-West London, you couldn't keep my mum's enthusiasm at bay. She was adamant that on our behalf, she would let Roger know that one household at least, was well and truly behind him. Having found where to send her telegram, something which was completed on the phone in those days, she read out the message, 'Good luck today. From the Cripps, your tennis family fans'.

We all sat back to watch the match, the first one up on Centre Court and the BBC's television coverage. I don't know how he did it but somehow, our Roger did the business that day and even though he lost the first set, he came through to beat Rod, 4-6, 6-4, 6-2, 6-1, an amazing result, one I found recently on top of a list of all-time Wimbledon upsets. Once the glow of success faded, the problem was that there were so many great players back then that even though you had beaten the top player in the world, there were other opponents almost as difficult who you might then come up against. At the quarter-final stage, Taylor beat the big-serving American, Clark Graebner, a player sometimes likened to Superman due to his haircut and the fact he played in glasses. Next, he came up against none other than Ken Rosewall in the semi-final. This proved to be a match too far and 'Muscles', as Rosewall was known, because they said he didn't have any, beat the British player in four sets. In turn, Ken would go on to lose to the mighty John Newcombe who will feature again in my story in a few chapters' time.

Sadly, Roger Taylor never reached a final at Wimbledon, coming close, losing in the semi-final again, in 1973, as he had done in 1967, to Wilhelm Bungert. However, that Saturday in 1970 will always remain in my memory as a special day. The anecdote is a perfect example of my mum's love of tennis and Wimbledon, every time it came around, each summer. Indeed, both mum's passion for the sport, especially at Wimbledon, combined with her fascination for Roger Taylor, had formed an essential part of my own developing love for the game. But this growing interest was in the background as football and cricket dominated my childhood years other than for the two weeks in late June and early July each year when Wimbledon took centre stage in our house, as it did in countless others across the nation.

My love of tennis would get released in my twenties as I felt the need to change my sporting priorities. Years later, I would get to meet not only the recipient of our family telegram, Roger Taylor but also, Charlie Pasarell, Ken Rosewall and John Newcombe, as we shall see. However, back then, in my childhood days, tennis had not been my number one sporting preference. Football and cricket had dominated my life through school, at university and into my mid-twenties.

My three sports
Many that know me through tennis might not be aware of my lifelong interest with football and cricket too. My involvement with these national sports, as each winter and summer came around, dominated my early life. But meanwhile, as if it had been creeping behind, waiting its turn, tennis took its place in my life as a third major sport and in a significant way, it took over from cricket initially and then, a few years later, from football too. However, initially, I became deeply involved with

two sports that dominated my life from when I was about seven years old.

Summer of '63

Just after my seventh birthday in the spring of 1963, two sporting events had a fundamental impact on me. The first was the F.A. Cup Final between Leicester City and Manchester United at Wembley Stadium. I remember watching the game live on BBC television absolutely transfixed by the sound of the crowd and the movement of the players as they tried to score. The game was made even more special by my fascination with the name of the Leicester City forward, Mike Stringfellow. What a funny name, I thought. I liked him and I liked his team. I had been hooked. This sport called football was one for me.

A few weeks after the excitement of discovering football, I ran in from the garden on a sunny day and stopped still in front of the television again. This time, something else was going on. The men were all wearing white clothing and some of them had bats in their hands. Other men were sprinting in towards them and a few yards away, were hurling a ball at them. What on earth were those men up to, I wondered? I was watching the First Test match between England and the West Indies. The first thing I did was to go and find a ball and then run back out into the garden and start to bowl. For four summers, I barely stopped. I had been smitten and bit by bit, football, in the winters and cricket, in the summers, began to take over my life.

Footballing winters

In football, the next development of my interest was entirely down to the commitment of my parents. As the following season began, my dad took me to see a local Athenian League match at Edgware Town. I loved it and cared for the matchday programme as if it was a nugget of gold, ensuring that it took pride of place amongst my possessions in my bedroom. Mum got in on the act too and on another Saturday afternoon, she took me to Wingate Football Club at their compact little ground in Hendon where the start of the M1 is now. I fell in love with the stand on the far side of the ground and the colours of the players' shirts.

My first experience of the professional game was also around this time when a school friend invited a few classmates on a birthday treat to be taken by his dad to see Arsenal in a First Division match against Blackpool. Also, once or twice a season, my dad would write to Tottenham Hotspur for tickets to a game. One of these was in April 1965 against Leicester City. So it was that I saw Mike Stringfellow in the flesh.

My brother Ben, decided to start supporting Queens Park Rangers, then a Third Division club, over in West London. He took me along and I remember now, walking up onto the terraces and being stunned by the green pitch under the floodlights. Then, in 1966, during the World Cup finals, my dad took me to England's group match at Wembley against France.

Other visits to Spurs and to charity matches played at the local grounds of clubs like Finchley, close to where I would end up at school and where, a decade later, I would play under floodlights in representative matches, kept my enthusiasm going.

From watching to playing
Although there had been football and cricket played in games lessons at my junior school, my involvement with competitive sport really began when I started going to Finchley County School, when I was eleven-years old. Right from the start, I could tell that there was a commitment to sport, although tennis was not catered for at all.

In my first football match for the U13 team against Hendon County, another small county grammar school and rival, selected at centre-forward, I scored four goals. Walking into school on the following Monday, there were no congratulations offered, just a loud instruction from one teacher, "Keep your hat on, boy."

Through the seven years at secondary school, I played in all the football teams, bypassing the second team as I progressed from the U15 level straight into the first team, so I played for three years at that level. We were weak in football and lost most of our matches, character building fodder for us, as the bigger schools always seemed to beat us 5-0. I ended up being captain of all the teams.

Come back next year
While the teenage years ticked by, other than during the two weeks of Wimbledon, tennis was far from my mind but like so many football-mad teenagers, I developed a desire to play professional football and dreamt about playing for Queens Park Rangers. I wrote to the club asking for a trial and one Sunday morning when I was about sixteen, my dad took me out to QPR's training ground in South Ruislip. From the early minutes of the trial match, I knew I wasn't good enough. There were too many boys, bigger, stronger, quicker and with more skill than me. The staff agreed I could come back the following year but I think we all knew that I was unlikely to follow up.

I didn't let this disappointment spoil my enjoyment of football. I still loved it and carried on practising all week and playing on Saturday and Sunday. In the summer of 1971, I had travelled down to the Bank of England Sports Ground in Roehampton, the site of the Wimbledon qualifying event, to attend a London Schools Football Association summer camp training week. It had been boiling hot and exhausting, although a great experience and at the end of the week, a select eleven played against Chelsea's youth team captained by a young Ray Wilkins.

Also, through the route of Sunday football, I did manage to get selected to represent the Barnet Youth League in an inter-league cup competition. I played, now in midfield, in the final against the Ealing League in a match held at Finchley Football Club's ground close to Finchley Manorhill, which Finchley County School had morphed into as part of the government's commitment to the comprehensive system.

First team in bibs
When I drove up the motorway to start three years at Liverpool University in October 1974, I went there to end up with a degree. I had very few expectations as far as sport was concerned other than to get involved. I just wanted to make the most of the experience academically and sport-wise. Literally, on the first day, I signed up for the university football club and after a few days of trials, I ended up getting picked for the first team to play in a season opening friendly against the youth team of the mighty Liverpool Football Club. The coach had called out, "First team in bibs," and one of the senior players had thrown me one. That's how I found out I'd been picked. I was the only first year to get selected.

Much to my amazement and delight, after surviving ninety minutes chasing future England player, Sammy Lee, around the pitch at break-neck speed while rarely touching the ball, I managed to stay in the side all season and the twice-weekly matches became the focus of my university life in between lectures and tutorials in modern history and politics. As well as all the inter-university matches, we also played friendlies, including one against the 'B' team of Third Division side, Tranmere Rovers.

There were also two training sessions a week to survive and these involved an awful lot of sprinting as the coach would bark out commands, shuttle runs that would go on until you were exhausted.

There were also two excellent weeks spent at Lilleshall in Shropshire, where English Universities held a summer training camp, similar to the London Schools one I had attended a few years before at Roehampton. Attending at the end of my first and second years was a great experience, including playing a training game against Birmingham City's full First Division side where again, in the presence of professionals, I chased shadows for ninety minutes, especially that of my direct opponent in midfield, Malcolm Page, a Welsh International.

By the time my third year came around, I was appointed as first team and club captain for my final year, a job that I was proud and very happy to do but at times, with all the organisation the job entailed, was one that took its toll on my playing performances. Thankfully, as had happened to the team in all three years, where in the first term we struggled, in the second term, everything came together, so my university football days finished on a high.

Cricketing summers
In cricket, it was the middle of the summer in 1964, the year following my discovery of the game. Again, with my brother, accompanied by his autograph-collecting school friend, David, we went off to see another sporting occasion, this time a county cricket match between Middlesex and Yorkshire at Lord's. This day re-enforced my fascination with cricket as I watched professional cricketers playing live with all the sounds, especially of bat on ball, again against the backdrop of a striking green playing surface and huge stands.

A year later, we were at Lord's again to see various games. It was so exciting. One memorable match at the Oval was in the semi-final of the Gillette Cup where sadly for us, Middlesex lost to Surrey. The following summer, in 1966, the school took a group of us to see England play the West Indies in the Lord's Test and as was the way back then, as schoolboys, we were allowed to sit on the grass just the other side of the boundary rope.

Also, dad took me to join the colts sessions at Finchley Cricket Club, then a top club below county level. So began a long association which continues today.

Boys with many bats
My first appearance for the school was significant and in an U14 match, playing with boys a bit older than me – I was just twelve-years old - all those years of bowling practice in the garden paid off against Woodhouse, our local rivals, as I took 7-14, sending stumps and bails flying as batsman after batsman seemed to miss my deliveries.

Through my batting, I won two new bats from the school, presented in assembly, for scoring fifties in games, something which rarely happened in twenty-overs-a-side matches. The second of these bats was awarded after I scored seventy-nine not out in and U15 match, also against Woodhouse, in the days when the whole team would be lucky to reach such a score. I bowled as fast as I could and took lots of wickets probably because the batsmen were a bit scared, as I was, facing any bowler above schoolboy military medium pace.

My schoolteachers put me forward for Middlesex Schools trials and I played once at U15 and once at U16 levels, unfortunately, not with much success. In the first match against Eton School, as I walked with dad across to the pavilion, I realised that there was a boy a few yards ahead of us and it was Mike Gatting, who would go on to captain Middlesex and England. Somehow, he was carrying what I'm sure I counted as six bats, although it was probably no more than three or four.

One weekend, when Finchley were short, I helped out by playing in the Sunday men's first team. I neither batted nor bowled but somewhat crazily, was asked to field at forward short leg, very close to the batsman who just happened to be the former Middlesex all-rounder, Ron Hooker. Ron had retired from county cricket the season before so had not lost much of his edge from the professional game. When he hit a six off our slow bowler, I felt, as well as heard the ball, as it fizzed past my head on the way to the legside boundary. These days, I'd have to put on all sorts of protective gear in order to field in that position.

Run, dad, run
My dad's firm, J.D. & D.M. Watson, the big civil engineering company, ran a team in a twenty-overs-a-side league played in the early evenings in London's Battersea Park. A few times, I played for the team with dad, and opened the bowling with some success. I batted low down the order but on one occasion, was at the crease while my dad was at the other end. Afterwards, outside a local pub, one of the team commented on the Cripps partnership: "You don't half shout at your dad!" one of the young engineers remarked, an observation based on the fact that I had done all the calling. I remember those times with dad very fondly. He was always wonderful as far as providing support for me with my sporting obsession. He never told me what to do but was always there for me to hear my critical self-analysis of how I had played.

At one point, I made the decision to go and play for Arkley Cricket Club with some of my good friends from school, including Brian Andrews and Peter Brown, after Saturday morning school matches were over. Later, the time came to move back up a level, but these seasons with the club will always remain special to me and were important at the time.

Thirty-minutes of silence
When the summer of my first year it Liverpool came around, it was time for cricket. In preparation for the summer, during the second term, waiting for Friday night nets to start with the university cricket team in the sports hall was the only time that

tennis reared its head in university sport. In the hour before our net session, the men's tennis team practised on the fast wood surface that was used for so many different sports.

I watched the players compete for a few minutes as they finished off their practice and some vague memory came to mind of a very long match that I'd heard about in which our family hero, Roger Taylor, had played many, many games to decide a King's Cup match against Czechoslovakia. The indoor court, made of wood, was so fast that neither player could return serve, so the games ticked by at a fair old lick until someone got their racket on the ball enough times to break and then win enough games to take the set. From a participation perspective, tennis was still on reserve for me.

As the summer term began, the cricket teams started playing matches from the first week, so as to get as many completed before the exams took over. In all three exam terms, I played between twenty and thirty matches each year. Somehow, I passed all my exams.

In 1975, my first year, as with the football team, I also got picked straight away for the university first team in cricket which was very strong with lots of good players. Again, I was the only first year to get picked. It was a memorable day when we played Bradford University on the Park Avenue ground which had played such an important part in the history of Yorkshire county cricket.

In my second year, our efforts to win the national UAU trophy came to an end on the field of Christ Church College, Oxford when we were beaten in a semi-final by the eventual winners, Loughborough Colleges, who beat us in the very last over. The Colleges had a few players with county experience, including Alan Wilkins. Alan went on to play for Gloucestershire and Glamorgan and on this ferociously hot day in June, was the match-winner, hitting a four and then a six over my head to secure victory as I fielded at square leg. It was a shocked silence that filled our changing room after the match as my team-mates came to terms with the defeat. No one said anything for thirty minutes as we showered and changed.

The following year, my cricket days at university came to an end with a hat trick against local club side, Sefton Cricket Club. It was almost a perfect sign-off to university sport.

An important fortnight for me too

Back to 1963 and around the same time that football and cricket became essential parts of my life as a child, my awareness and interest in tennis had also begun. For example, I can remember the Wimbledon men's final between Chuck McKinlay and Fred Stolle, and the women's final between Margaret Court and Billie Jean King but prior to that, any knowledge I have is not from watching the matches but from checking the reference books.

In the middle of summer, when Wimbledon came on the television, for the two weeks of the event, I became increasingly aware of mum's love for the sport. However, gradually, I was deepening my interest too. Like many families, when Wimbledon came around, the tennis rackets were produced from the cupboard under the stairs. For us, these rackets were a motley crew of bats. I reckon one of them must have been one of Bill Tilden's old spares and another, with the words, 'Ladies Racket' on the handle, could have been a model from the forties, maybe one of gorgeous Gussie Moran's? Well, only if its colour scheme matched her Ted Tinling-designed lace knickers, edged with frills, which caused such a stir at Wimbledon in 1949. There were three or four of these rackets, a couple of them housed in the old-style frames which you screwed tight to ensure that they didn't warp while they hibernated through the winter months between Wimbledon fortnights. Strung in either old-style gut or some basic form of early synthetic string, I doubt any of them had ever been anywhere near a re-stringing machine. But they served their purpose. These were the days before short tennis or mini tennis with rackets of all sizes to cater for children and teenagers as they grow bigger and taller. As small kids, just like everyone else, we played with adult rackets, doing our best to hang onto them with their thick grips, way too big for small hands.

While living in Mill Hill in North-West London, mum and dad had joined the tennis section of Mill Hill Cricket Club and I remember going there to watch when brother, Ben, younger sister, Zoe and yours truly were all very young. It was when we moved to Hampstead Garden Suburb in 1964 when I was eight years-old, that we made our debut as players. Mum would book us a court at Golders Hill Park, opposite King Alfred School where we all went at the time. I remember the excitement when mum said we were going to play. We always went in the early evening so that dad could play with us after returning from work. The grass courts were incredibly worn but we didn't care. This was our chance to pretend that we were the top stars we had been watching on the television.

These trips to the park were not free of danger and I'm not referring to the odd torn hamstring or twisted knee experienced by top players on slippery grass courts. No, I'm talking about one in the eye. It was my eye that became the target as dad unwittingly smacked a serve and it made its way like a tracer bullet right at me as I crouched by the net pretending to be one of the Wimbledon ball boys. I remember seeing it coming but before I knew it, smack, the ball had whacked me in the eye socket. Surrounded by the family, especially dad, who was mortified at the prospect of bringing my ball-boy career to a halt even before it had begun, mum tended to me to make sure I was alright. Luckily, there was no immediate short-term damage and after a short medical time out as they are called now, the Cripps's version of Wimbledon continued.

I was quite happy to have Wimbledon on the television. I had no idea about top tennis outside of the tournament down in South-West London. If you'd mentioned the Grand Slam to me, I would have given you a very blank look. All of that knowledge was to come. I have a fond memory of watching the matches and then listening to Harry Carpenter announcing the results in his clipped tones, where he would show complete mastery of the pronunciations of the names of all the players, regardless of what country they came from. "In the men's doubles, Alvarez and Mandarino have come through against El Shafei and Ulrich in five sets," he would announce as the result cards were shown on the screen.

I used to love it. Although like so many people then and even now, once Wimbledon was over, that was it as far as tennis was concerned. For me, it was back to cricket and then as the next winter arrived, out came the football boots.

Tickets from the ballot
Every year, mum entered the ballot for Wimbledon tickets and she seemed to win one, if not two pairs on a number of occasions. In the early sixties, when we were all young, she usually went with colleagues from the Citizen's Advice Bureaux where she worked part-time. She would always take her own food and drink, including strawberries in round, plastic Tupperware containers with just a light covering of sugar which a few hours later, by the time she was in her seat in either the Centre Court or Court No. 1, would have turned into a delightful sugary syrup-covered dessert. She would return with a programme - the ones issued between 1950 and 1976 which always had a top player's photo in black and white on the front cover - and tales of the players and matches she had watched. We would then watch out for these names as the tournament progressed from our prime spectating positions in front of the television.

In the mid-sixties, this is how I became aware of not just the top stars who were always shown on the television but the top British players like Bobby Wilson, who hailed from the

Chandos Club just down the road from our school in Golders Green where Davis Cup ties had been held. Then, there was big-serving Mike Sangster and former finalist, Christine Truman. As the years progressed, Roger Taylor rose up to prominence, of course, as did Virginia Wade. But there were many other British players too. In later years, I would have the pleasure of meeting many of them.

As well as having the television on almost permanently through the Wimbledon fortnight, while we watched as much of the men's final as possible, considering that it was played back then on a Friday afternoon, a school day, we all sat down as a family to watch the women's final on the Saturday afternoon. My brother Ben would always keep score on a fresh piece of lined notepaper, writing down the game score after each point like an armchair umpire, noting the completion of the game with the score '50', a detail which when I reminded him about it, he could not remember at all. Not only would the top men and women usually reach the latter rounds of the singles but they would also play doubles and mixed doubles, as was the norm back then. So, you really felt as if you knew them. We became aware of the elite of the sport, players like Margaret Court, Billie Jean King and mum's favourite, Maria Bueno.

By 1966, I was ten years-old and although still a kid, had developed my own awareness, views, likes, dislikes and observations on the players. I remember being intrigued by the German player Wilhelm Bungert's dark-coloured belt when he lost to John Newcombe in the 1967 final. With Wimbledon's all-white rule, how did he get away with wearing it?

In fact, it was around this time that having moved to Finchley County School, mum became aware of a one-week mornings-only tennis instruction course for kids in the Easter holidays over on the public courts opposite my school. Football and cricket were forgotten, one of our rackets was dragged out of the cupboard and off I went to try and play tennis. Although

I was pretty much a beginner, I do remember really enjoying the week and went on at least one other occasion.

Ben and I also used to fill our days in the summer holidays not only with endless cricket games on Hampstead Heath extension but games of tennis in the park at what was called the Market Place. Somehow, the hour was always up just as one of us would be serving for the match. What a shame. Never mind, we'll complete the next match, we'd say to each other, with one of us relieved that we could call on the clock to save us while the other stewed in frustration at being deprived victory.

In 1967, Wimbledon came into view again but this time, following the tournament in June and July, another event was held on the Centre Court and it was televised. This was the Wimbledon World Lawn Tennis Professional Championships and was set up by the All-England Club to exert more pressure on member nations of the International Lawn Tennis Federation, as the ITF was called back then, to vote for open tennis throughout the sport. The tournament, held over three days in August, was televised by the BBC, as a way to celebrate the beginning of colour television. The singles event was made up of an eight-man draw and there was a four-team doubles event too.

The players were all the well-known favourites. The four seeds were Rod Laver, Ken Rosewall, Pancho Gonzales and Andres Gimeno. These seeds were supplemented by Lew Hoad, Fred Stolle, Dennis Ralston and Butch Bucholtz. All matches were best of three sets except for the best of five sets final. I remember that on the third day, a Sunday, we drove down to Wimbledon with the thought that mum and I would try to get in. But when we got there, it was an all-ticket affair and although we might have bought tickets from touts, ultimately, we turned around and went home. At least, we'd experienced a slice of the atmosphere, even if we didn't get in.

Rod Laver won the singles event beating his great rival, Ken Rosewall but not before a long third set which went to 12-10.

However, my turn to go to Wimbledon and actually enter the grounds to see some tennis, arrived the following summer when mum won tickets in the ballot for the middle Saturday. I was almost frozen with excitement as we found our seats on Centre Court. I surveyed everything in front of me. It was breath-taking. The funny thing about the Centre Court is that although it is a major arena, back then holding fourteen thousand people (it holds more today), there was a really intimate feeling when you were watching. It was almost as if you could reach out and touch the players, even if, as we were, you were sitting quite high up towards the back of the stands. I particularly remember the sound of the ball on the racket when the players hit it. There were microphones on the court which picked up the sound of the strike and this was relayed to the crowd via speakers set high up in the stands. But you could also hear the actual contact without the help of the microphones and this meant that there was a tiny delay between the sound of the real strike and the one communicated through the speakers. I found that double sound somehow satisfying. It's not one I have heard in any tennis arena since.

Anyway, we had a marvellous day. The Centre Court order of play had an American feel about it with singles matches involving Nancy Richey, Dennis Ralston and then, Clark Graebner (Superman). To finish things off, there was a men's doubles between Owen Davidson and Lew Hoad against Tom Okker and Marty Riessen, a fantastic match which went to five sets with the Australians coming out on top. I absolutely loved the whole experience and felt very happy as we drove home at the end of a beautiful, sunny day.

After that, it was back to the television for enjoyment of Wimbledon. In 1970, we had the excitement of Roger Taylor beating Rod Laver and in 1973, his long semi-final against Jan Kodes coincided with an evening where mum had invited a friend around for dinner. Always the stickler for showing good manners, she called me to the table when the food was ready. The problem was that this was just as the match was coming to its conclusion in the fifth set with every game a scrap and the result still in the balance. While I knew it would be rude to stay watching, I sat dutifully at the dining room table, eating my meal. However, even as I tried to be polite and take part in the conversation, my head kept turning ever so slowly to my left in the direction of the lounge and the television which was still on and showing Taylor's ultimate demise.

Chapter 2

Tennis Takes Over

A shift in sporting priorities
I started to go to Wimbledon on my own after finishing at Liverpool University. By then, I was fortunate to have mum's old car. One year, I drove down to South-West London on the middle Saturday just after lunch. Those were the days when the roads around the site were still free of restrictions and I could usually find a parking place easily. Also, getting in through the turnstile was easy. Although the famous Wimbledon queue existed, both the size of the site and the attendance numbers were smaller than today and by mid-afternoon, it was possible to walk straight in, something that is all but impossible today. I really enjoyed wandering around the outside courts watching all the matches, especially the doubles with teams of American players, most of whom had been playing in college and were now on the tour full-time.

Occasionally, I would obtain a show-court ticket. In 1978, my school friend Albert Samuel and I were on Centre Court watching Ilie Nastase play the American with the huge serve, Roscoe Tanner. We had great seats on the corner of the court, quite high up where you could get an idea of both the speed of the play as well as the angles used. I remember seeing Nastase's beautiful, French wife, Dominique, watching the match, not from the usual box half-way up the stands but from a simple chair at court level close to one of the corners near where the ball-boys would stand. Also, with Ilie, you were never far away from something happening. After being run off court by Tanner, seeing as he was right next to the umpire's chair, the Romanian stopped for an impromptu drink. As he raised the cup to his lips, he handed his racket to the nearest ball-boy. He then proceeded to take back the racket but with some sleight of hand, totally confused the lad who after the exchange, somehow, still had the racket in his hand as Nastase sloped back to the baseline carrying a cup but no racket. The crowd loved it. Despite Roscoe's serve repeatedly thudding into the back wall, Nastase won the match in four sets.

As far as work was concerned, from the summer of 1977, after finishing at Liverpool, I started going through various different jobs, trying to work out what I wanted to do. It was while I was working at a television production company that I was told of a step up in the organisation. However, in order to take up the job, I had to find my own replacement for the job I was in. One of my colleagues said he knew just the person. The young man was interviewed and offered the job. His name? Simon Rogers.

After my time at Liverpool, I had to decide how to continue with my football and cricket. With cricket, that decision had been made a year before, when I returned to Finchley Cricket Club. I had a really enjoyable five years there. With football, I ended up playing for Winchmore Hill Football Club who played in the Southern Amateur League. This was a well-organised class of pure amateur football on good pitches. My time spent in the first team there felt like it was the right level. On Sundays, I played for Oakwood, the team I had joined as a teenager, a club ran brilliantly by one man, Nick Sonenfield whose commitment knew no bounds. We were now in our early twenties and most of us were playing decent Saturday football. Oakwood was in the Hendon Sunday League and we did well. It was a slightly lower standard initially but just right for Sunday mornings after our demanding Saturday matches.

As the eighties began, in winter, I was still playing football for Winchmore Hill on Saturdays and Oakwood on Sundays. As another summer began, so did another cricket season with Finchley where by now, I was becoming an established first team player in their Middlesex League side.

But 1980 was a challenging year for me as I was struck down with both glandular fever and measles in the same year. Somehow, I found the energy to fight off both.

At work, I had decided to try and get a job with a big organisation, where the working environment would allow me to work my way up as I became used to what was required. Through a recruitment agency, I had interviews with Procter and Gamble, Coca Cola and American Express. I liked the people at Amex and was offered the job despite not having the required experience. It was June 1980. I was twenty-four years old. But I hadn't been there all that long when I was told that I was owed a week's holiday and if I didn't take it, I'd lose it.

Again, mum made her presence felt. Shortly after hearing about my situation, she shouted through the flat to me, "Have a look at this." She had an advert for a tennis holiday week at a place that had the name attached to it of none other than our idol of a decade or so back, Roger Taylor. I liked the idea and after chatting to my school friend, Kyri, whose girlfriend, Rosie, had to take her holiday earlier in the year due to job requirements, we decided to go ahead. We would spend a week at the Roger Taylor Tennis Centre in Vale de Lobo on Portugal's Algarve coast.

It's not a popularity contest
That initial one-week trip to Portugal in late October to use up my week's holiday had important consequences. This was the first time I had been away on my own, or without my parents. Through my university years, I'd tended to work through the summer holidays and I hadn't been away, other than the odd, short tour with Finchley or Winchmore Hill. The first thing I realised, after committing Kyri and me was that I didn't have a tennis racket. Exactly why I went to London's major toy shop in Lower Regent Street to buy one, as opposed to the city's major sports outfitters, a few hundred yards down the road in Piccadilly Circus, I cannot remember, but it was Hamley's I

went to and not Lillywhites. I emerged, the proud owner of a Dunlop Maxply Fort. With the racket and some tennis clothes bought, I was ready.

We flew from Heathrow on TAP, the Portuguese national airline, in a nearly empty plane and very soon, we landed at Faro Airport and arrived at Vale de Lobo. After getting something to eat, we decided to try and find the tennis courts which were located a short walk away from the centre of the resort. I can remember the excitement at finding the courts with the big clubhouse up on the side of a hill and even though there was no tennis going on and the floodlights were off, the place looked fantastic. The following day, we met our coach, Nick Walden. Not only was Nick a fine player and an excellent teacher but his claim to fame was being in the ball-boy crew on the first day of the amazing match at Wimbledon in 1969 between Pancho Gonzales and Charlie Pasarell where, on the second day, Gonzales came back from two sets down to win. Nick had another experience with the veteran pro on another occasion when Pancho lost his cool in a match on Court No. 2. He whacked a ball towards the back fence nearly decapitating Nick who somehow, remained motionless, receiving praise from the nearby crowd for maintaining his composure. The others who had booked up for our week in Portugal were Michael and Rita Bunn from Birmingham. We got on well and had a marvellous time; it was non-stop laughter from start to finish.

A pleasant surprise was the arrival of the great man himself. While Nick was at the centre full-time, Roger Taylor was there at certain times and luckily for us, this week, he was in Portugal to complete a week's training with a top Portuguese junior. By now, Roger was in his late thirties but he was still in fantastic physical shape. He could stay out on the court practising all day and wearing his tracksuit trousers in the heat as well. He hit the ball so cleanly and could control direction, depth and spin at will. His super-smooth service action looked so good close up. He never seemed to miss and his serves still had those wicked sliced curves with the ball always going away from your backhand side, if you were a righty or your out-stretched forehand, if you were a lefty.

Roger also used some wonderful sayings which Kyri and I still use today. We grilled Roger with lots of questions about life on the tennis tour. When talking about competitiveness, at one point, demonstrating the toughness that helped take him into the world's top twenty, he said, "It's not a popularity contest out there." Next, when I complimented one of the local Portuguese players who was practising down on the court below us, he said, "There are thousands of guys who can hit like that." What he meant was that competing at local levels, let alone those at the top of the world game, is so much more than just being able to hit nice-looking strokes when there's no pressure. I would meet him a number of times in years to come and my mum was very envious. I always liked him and I still enjoy watching his matches on YouTube now. He was a really fine player and epitomised my tennis childhood as we experienced all those wonderful moments watching him play on television each year when Wimbledon came around again.

As far as my own tennis was concerned, not for the first time in the coming years, during that week, I would discover that my mastery of this racket sport was not what I thought. But despite the frustration of this realisation, the seed of a new challenge had been planted. I watched those who could play, like Roger, Nick and a few pretty good local players practicing at the centre and found myself wishing that I was able to play like them.

The following summer, in 1981, for the first time in nearly fifteen years, I did not play cricket but played tennis instead. Something had finally clicked for me with the sport. I had been bitten by the playing bug and I think the fact that I was nowhere near as good as I would have liked added to the challenge. I had a new quest. I now knew this was what I had to do but felt awkward about leaving Finchley. I'm not sure my team-mates understood what I was up to, especially, as I was on the cusp of really establishing myself in the first team.

But tennis it was going to be, at least for one summer. However, one summer turned into many more. In fact, I never went back to cricket other than just prior to my knees deteriorating to the point which caused another major change in my life, I returned to Finchley and enjoyed playing in some veterans' matches.

After the change was made, as I moved through my mid-twenties and early thirties, my tennis experience became a function of my work situation as American Express provided me with job opportunities that moved me from one location to another.

Coping with clay

Back in London, Kyri and I decided to join the tennis section of Hampstead Cricket Club, a short drive for me from our last family home in Regent's Park. There were three courts, all clay and we had to get used to the surface, the club and its rules. It was a strange moment when my former Finchley colleagues turned up to play a match against Hampstead and they all walked past the court where I was playing. I could tell that one or two of them were wondering what on earth I was doing.

Kyri and I played at the weekend club afternoons, making many new friends in the process. One of these invited us to play doubles at the Vanderbilt Club in Shepherd's Bush, an amazing place located in what looked like a series of warehouses on waste ground just off the A40, more suitable as a location for filming car chases and shoot-outs in the TV programme, *The Sweeney*. This was my first experience playing indoors on fast carpet. Back at Hampstead, we were also both picked for a couple of third team club matches which again, made me aware of my shortcomings. I strove to get better. We also went on another week at Vale de Lobo and had a good time.

Prince and Pernod
In 1982, I moved down to live in Brighton and Hove after a job promotion with American Express. I was recommended to the Southdown Club in Lewes, a few miles east of Brighton.

I joined and spent four happy years there making many friends, playing loads of tennis, including every club session I could find the time to attend, participation in the winter doubles leagues and in the summer, playing for all three of the club's men's teams. The Southdown Club had many good junior players in its ranks including Clare Wood, Julie Salmon and Sara Gomer, who all went on to play on the pro tour. The coaching team included Clay Iles and Rohun Bevan who had both been good enough to play Wimbledon. The other coach was Tony Clark, a Sussex County player who was a very patient teacher and my partner when I played my one Sussex League first team match against Pavilion and Avenue in Hove, just five minutes from my flat in Wilbury Road, which overlooked Sussex County Cricket Club's ground.

I practised all the time, especially with fellow third-teamer, Paul French, and in all weathers too with me now playing with a larger head, Prince racket. My desire to hit balls was so strong that one evening, even though it began raining, we played, for at least an hour, getting utterly soaked. On another occasion, when I found out that somehow, I had left my tennis shoes at home, I drove all the way back to my flat in Hove, picked up the shoes and drove back out to Lewes and took part in a curtailed session. Any hits were better than none.

In my first winter in Sussex, I played my last season of football and it was a happy one. I travelled north towards Gatwick to play for Sussex County League side, Burgess Hill Town, where I was known as 'Harry' after the Millwall captain, Harry Cripps. After a season in the reserve team at a good standard with a fun set of team-mates and with an inspirational manager, Ken Swallow, I developed a bad pelvic strain injury at the start of the next one. It took a while but once I had recovered, I decided to concentrate on tennis. I was always fit and playing in midfield, I had to be. But the fitness standard at Burgess Hill was at another level and if I'm honest, I couldn't face the work that I would have to put in after my injury in order to reach it. For the first time in twenty years, my motivation faltered. Also, I saw tennis as a sport I could play for the rest of my life. So, at the age of twenty-eight, I hung up my boots. My time at the club had been really enjoyable and I still follow their results to this day. This was a pivotal point in my relationship with sport. Tennis had now taken over as my number one priority.

Things were developing in British tennis. The very first Pernod Tournament in the country was held at the Southdown Club. A ratings event, this meant that every level of player could enter and if you won, you'd go on to play those at the next rating up from you. The men's final was between two top British players. One was Nigel Sears who became a top coach on the WTA Tour and whose daughter, Kim, married Andy Murray; the other and winner that day, was Jeremy Dier whose son, Eric, now plays for Tottenham Hotspur and England.

You're a wizard, Larry

In the summer of 1983, again with Rosie's blessing, Kyri was free again to join me in another tennis holiday. We decided to go somewhere different and I found tennis holidays being offered in Spain's Costa del Sol.

We ended up at a place that would become the Benevista Tennis Centre, a few miles west of Marbella. A British coach called Larry Isherwood was in charge and he ran a good week. Again, the numbers of people attending were small. As well as Kyri and me, there was an ageing former merchant sailor from Australia called Norm and a young student called Nick who hadn't brought enough kit, so was constantly walking into the pool fully dressed in the kit he did have, using it like a massive washing machine. This time, it was Norm that gave us the phrases to remember. When Larry demonstrated to us what he wanted us to do, Norm - impressed by the coach's obvious very good level - would call out, "You're a wizard, Larry." This complimentary approach did not apply to his own game where he was more than self-critical, at one point after a drill which he had not understood nor executed at all well, he shouted, "I'm all over the court like a wild woman's crap." Later, Kyri and I wondered who these wild women were and what was so special about their process when executing a normal bodily function.

We played tennis all day, had numerous coffee breaks and spent some time around the pool of the adjoining hotel where Nick washed his kit while he was still in it, and we met a group of friendly people. Going out for a drink in Puerto Banus all together one evening, I ended up back in the hotel with our new friends while Kyri had gone off to bed in our small apartment, a few hundred yards down the hill towards the courts which were located next to the main road.

Only staying briefly for a quick night-cap, as I walked out through the hotel reception, to continue back down to our place, a rather grumpy night manager unleashed the third degree on me demanding to know my room number. When I told him that I wasn't staying in the hotel but was a resident of the apartments, which were part of the same complex, he went berserk, telling me, "You have no business being here," a statement he repeated at least twice more. I made the mistake of arguing with him after which he threatened to call the police. I stormed out and started marching down the hill. But after a few minutes, I saw a car approaching up the hill from the main road. I panicked, imagining a night in a Marbella police cell and jumped through the hedge into a field. As the car drove by, I had difficulty getting back up onto the road but finally, covered in dust, I entered our place and relayed the story to Kyri. As I went to my room, in an excellent impression of the hotel's Mr Grumpy, he called out, "You have no business ... going to bed." This was another of those phrases which remains part of our friendship all these years later.

Coffee with Lew

Another nice aspect of tennis on the Costa del Sol back then was regular one-day tournaments which were held at various clubs, including one every Tuesday at the club owned by one of the greatest players in tennis's history, Lew Hoad, who I had watched on that very first day at Wimbledon in 1968. In the first week, we had our coaching with Larry but in the second week, after a late night, we dragged ourselves out of bed early, got in the car and drove along the coast to Mijas where up in the hills, what is now called the Club de Tennis y Padel Lew Hoad or, the Lew Hoad Tennis and Padel Club, was located.

The setting for the club was beautiful and the atmosphere very laid back with outdoor yoga classes going on next to the car park as we drove in. Lew was one of the stars of the fifties. He had nearly won a Grand Slam in 1956, prevented by his friend and fellow Aussie Davis Cup teammate, Ken Rosewall, who beat him in New York. Lew won Wimbledon again in 1957 and in men's doubles, won eight more Slams, including a doubles career Grand Slam. He also won a mixed title in Paris. Turning professional, effectively meant disappearing from the main world of tennis and playing in all sorts of towns off the beaten track in one-night events before moving on to the next place on the tour. At least, this way, he earned decent money.

The club was run by Lew's wife, Jenny, and I wasn't sure if the great man would even be there. Immediately, I went to the bar to order two coffees. They were produced and as the first was placed in front of me, a hand came across me and slid the small cup with its steaming brew, back along the countertop. A bit bemused by this, I looked to my left and who should be commandeering my espresso but Lew himself. I smiled meekly and waited for the coffee to be replaced. Lew looked in a state not much better than me, so I resisted the temptation to mention that five-set doubles match on the Centre Court at Wimbledon in 1968. Although seeing as he and Owen Davidson won, I'm not sure why I didn't. Possibly, I thought that this would be like talking shop to a man who was about to have his first coffee of the day in his own bar and therefore, somehow inappropriate.

Beaten by the one-armed man
Not only were Kyri and I a few steps behind that day but we experienced defeat at the hands of a veteran Spanish player who only had one arm. Somehow, this amazing man, well known across all the clubs of the Costa Del Sol, managed to serve by placing the ball on the edge of his racket, resting on the strings, raising his arm up, as if he was flipping a pancake, so the ball would also rise into the appropriate position above his head, as if he had placed it there with his left hand. He would then strike a superbly accurate serve to his mesmerised opponents with all the functions performed by his one right arm. The left arm sleeve of his tennis shirt was pinned.

This friendly opponent was well-known to the holidaymaker tennis community. He travelled along the coast road to all the clubs offering these one-day tournaments and he won most of them. "Beware of the one-armed man," you would be warned at two o'clock in the morning after another beer in the bars of Puerto Banus. You'd think the warning was crazy until you were shaking hands the following afternoon, defeated by the very player that you had been warned about the night before.

Boot camp at Hopman's
When it was time to plan my next holiday, I thought of tennis again. But this time, there was a new opportunity. Kyri had

been hired as an IT consultant to work in Florida in the Tampa area. So, my big, two-week holiday in 1984 was to visit him and his business partner, Mike and while they were at work, I could go and try a day or two at the famous Harry Hopman academy at a place called Bardmoor, not that far from Kyri and Mike's condominium. I enjoyed the days at Hopman's, as it was often referred to, immensely. I knew I would return and the following year, with Kyri and Mike still working on the same contract, as part of my first week, spent another couple of days experiencing the exhausting drills created by the Australian former player, Davis Cup captain and coach over three decades as he made the Australian team the best in the world and multiple winners of the famous trophy.

Another highlight of this 1985 holiday was that in the second week, the professionals came to town. The Florida Federal Open, an event on the Virginia Slims tour, was held at Bardmoor. Some of the top players were there, including Gabriela Sabatini. However, the star of the week was Stephanie Rehe, a player whose career would be blighted by injury. But not this week, as she beat Gabby in the final. Back at home, I was in the process of buying just about every tennis book I could lay my hands on and one which I really enjoyed was *Courting Fame* by Karin Stabiner. The book tells the story about young women players as they made the progression from the top junior ranks into the pros. The book featured Debbie Spence, Melissa Gurney, Marianne Werdel and Shawn Foltz and their stories in some detail but also mentioned Stephanie Rehe and others too. Along with Rehe, Melissa Gurney played in the tournament at Bardmoor and I followed her career with interest afterwards. It's a book I would recommend to anyone interested in the pathway up the levels towards the professional ranks as it was in the mid-eighties, although it's probably pretty similar today. The book is in the bibliography.

That will do nicely
There were also a few tennis experiences which came about through work at American Express. In 1981, I remember a sales meeting at the Selsdon Park Hotel in Croydon. As we all got ready for dinner, many of us had our televisions on and watched the titanic Wimbledon semi-final that was being played in the early evening between Jimmy Connors and Bjorn Borg where Jimbo wiped the Swede off the court in the first two sets playing superb tennis. Not wanting to be late for the meal, everyone left their rooms and their televisions to go downstairs. How surprised we all were to discover later that Bjorn had fought back and won the match in five sets. Of course, that was the thing with Borg. He kept going with his amazing fitness and iron will giving every last drop of effort to come out on top, as he did on this occasion.

Once I had moved down to Brighton and Hove to work in the marketing department, the opportunities with tennis increased as one of the senior executives, who became our head of marketing, Ray Pierce, was a big tennis fan and a really good tennis and squash player too. When we went away for a couple of days for quarterly marketing department meetings, after the presentations were over, Ray and I would play a couple of sets before dinner, although there was never any doubt about the result. Ray was too good for me and my game was still developing. But Ray didn't seem to mind; like me, he just enjoyed being on the court hitting balls.

On another occasion, Ray invited me to play doubles at the Vanderbilt Club. One of the other players was Clifford Bloxham, an exceptionally good player who had played college tennis in the US. After a year trying to make it on the tour, he had decided to try another line of work and had recently started a job in the sports agency called Advantage International. While he may have given up on his dream of a life on the pro tour, on that early evening in Shepherd's Bush,

Clifford's level of play was still outstanding. He played with a precision and intensity that left me in awe.

Another enjoyable experience was when the company sponsored a special tournament held in Brighton, the Cliff Richard Challenge, a pro-celebrity event designed to raise money for Cliff's charity which tried to help identify and develop talented young tennis players. While I didn't play in the event itself, Ray asked me along to the practice sessions beforehand where we hit balls with the likes of Annabel Croft, Sara Gomer and the singer, Shakin' Stevens.

Also, in late 1985, we had a company box at the Albert Hall in London for the year-end Nabisco Masters Doubles Tournament where fans could enjoy watching top pairings like Ken Flach and Robert Seguso, Sergio Casal and Emilio Sanchez, Heinz Gunthardt and Balazs Taroscy, and the eventual winners, Stefan Edberg and Anders Jarryd.

Double-bagelled in Bahrain

In 1986, I took the job in Bahrain, referred to earlier. The position was a step up, with responsibilities for the Middle East and the first rung on the hierarchy of senior management in the company. Immediately, I looked for the tennis opportunities in my new home. These presented themselves across the way from our offices at the courts behind the Regency InterContinental Hotel where I stayed initially, until moving into a flat of my own.

The coach on the courts, Rob Cornell, worked for a coaching company called PBI (Peter Burwash International) established and owned by former Canadian Davis Cup player, Peter Burwash. PBI secured contracts to run the tennis at various hotels, clubs and resorts around the world. The coaches all used the same method of teaching, one Burwash had been inspired to create after a devastating defeat to Arthur Ashe when he felt in what he called 'permanent emergency'. That teaching method was summarised in a book, *Tennis for*

Life. Burwash had also written another book called, *The Vegetarian Primer*, one I read, and after thinking about it, decided to become a vegan, a regime I still follow.

I booked a few lessons with Rob and while at the courts, met a French ex-pat, Geraud Laveissiere, who looked like a particularly good player and when we got to play matches, showed just how good. Geraud suggested that I go with him to play in the Thursday afternoon tennis league for the Bahrain Police, known there as Public Security, whose superb floodlit courts were literally yards away from the flat that I eventually ended up living in on the edge of Manama city centre.

In the league matches, I usually played with Geraud and his game lifted mine rather than the other way around. There were a few useful players in the league's other teams. Frank Sabaratnam had played as a pro and represented Sri Lanka in the Davis Cup. For some reason, in the line-ups for a special cup match against the Gulf Hotel, I was pitched against Frank in singles. He was way too good for me and I lost 6-0, 6-0, an education as well as being embarrassing. There would be other examples of bagelling (losing a set without winning a game), in my competitive match journey to come, as we shall see.

A new development was the appointment of American, Larry Gagnon, as Davis Cup coach for the young Bahrain team. Larry was a very good player and had played on the tour, once beating Jimmy Arias. Larry agreed to give me some lessons and on a Wednesday evening, I drove to the centre where the Bahrain team was based for a two-hour session which became the highlight of the week. Not only did we hit a substantial number of balls but he passed on some really valuable tips to me on how to improve. It was also quite a physical work-out as the heat and especially, humidity, were still considerable, even in the evening. In one exhausting drill, we played points but Larry was allowed hit balls into the tramlines and I had to chase them all down as if they had been hit inside the lines. It was a satisfying moment for both Larry and me when in the

Bahrain Sports Club Open, one of the three tournaments held each year on the island, somehow, I beat a good player called Mike Keating. Mike was a gentleman and gracious in defeat. Larry shook my hand and as he smiled, he said, "I'm impressed." This meant a lot to me, although after the glow of the victory faded, the reality of my next opponent had to be faced. That opponent was none other than Larry himself and his class showed a few days later when he dispatched me in straight sets. Larry's work was realised when Bahrain played their first ever Davis Cup match against Syria out on the same courts that I had trained on. The well-known Wimbledon umpire, Jeremy Shales, was flown out to run the tie.

Survival in Sydney
My time in Bahrain came to an end after the August 1990 Gulf crisis began. On arrival in Sydney to take up my new job, it was always my intention to find and join the famous White City Club which I did after a play-in test.

Every weekend was spent there playing in every type of activity. With a slightly smaller midsize racket, I had a few lessons with club coach, Kelly Durant, who had played at the lower end of the tour. Finally, after realising that I needed to pack in my job with American Express, I played out my last few weeks at the club. Also, after a recommendation, I signed up for a self-help, personal development weekend where participants could review their lives. Although I didn't identify the Grand Slam specifically, the things I wrote down placed special emphasis on making the most of my passions and interests, including my love for tennis. Days after this weekend, I was on the flight to Perth when my plan to travel, taking in the Grand Slam, came together. By early December, I'd said goodbye to American Express, my colleagues, the small group of friends I had made while in Sydney, including all my friends at White City and I was heading home to Wimbledon.

Chapter 3

Fantastico Foro Italico

Back to Worple Road

After arriving home from Sydney just before Christmas in 1991, I breathed a big sigh of relief. It was good to be back in my Wimbledon flat which was a lovely place to live but it also had Grand Slam significance. It was located halfway down Worple Road between Wimbledon and Raynes Park. Those who know their Wimbledon history might be aware that the tournament has been located at the current Church Road site since 1922. Between 1877 and that move, the site of the tournament was at, you guessed it, Worple Road. Actually, my flat looked out on the area which was, by now, playing fields for a local school. But in the hallway of the house in which my flat was situated, there was a photograph of the site as it used to look when the tournament was in full flow, taken probably just after the First World War and showing Worple Road and the roads off it, looking hardly any different at all from what such a photograph might look like even today. But there, at the end of my garden, as if beamed down Star Trek-style were nine tennis courts with a Centre Court with small stands slap bang in the middle, hence its name, players on the courts and spectators surrounding the action. Although I had moved to Wimbledon in 1986 because it was a nice place to live and the home of the tournament, I had no idea when I bought the flat that there was such a historic significance to its location, something I was delighted to discover.

As 1992 began, I had to start planning the details of my Grand Slam year ahead. The first thing I had to decide was when to start my trip into Europe. I knew I needed to be in Paris in late May for the French Open and that while travelling around the capitals of North-West Europe, I wanted to be in

Rome a few weeks earlier for the Italian Open at the famous Foro Italico.

The plan was to visit the northern European countries and then progress south to Rome and then north-west to Paris. After that, it would be back to Wimbledon to attend the build-up tournaments and then, the tournament in SW19. The whole European leg of the trip would be completed on the train and back in Sydney, through American Express Travel, I had purchased a couple of Euro rail passes. A pass would allow you a certain number of trips each one denoted by a small circle. Each circle would be clipped by the ticket inspector on each journey and it would be handed back to you ready for the next leg. Thankfully, there were many more small circles on the two passes I now possessed than the number of individual trips I would be taking. Although you would have to book a seat on most of the trains, the pass made travelling easy and flexible.

In these days before the internet, I made a few trips into London to visit the tourist boards of the countries I intended to visit. Most of these offices were located on Piccadilly. I created a collection of files, one for each country, filled with the brochures I had collected and I supplemented my knowledge by reading the wonderful *Let's Go Europe 1992* travel guide. This was full of all the basic information I needed, including the main places in each major city to visit plus the good bars and restaurants for people on a low budget, as well as recommended small, bed and breakfast hotels.

The decision as to when to start the trip with enough time to take in everything was made for me by another opportunity coming up, one I could not turn down. My good friends from Bahrain, Michael Hosking and Nigel Peters, who had recently extended their involvement in the music business as concert promoters, had been given the contract to promote the pop star, Paula Abdul, on a tour of South-East Asia. They asked me if I would like to tag along. I certainly had enough money to do it and the timing was right. I could arrive back in early April, at about the right time for me to leave for Europe. I spent three amazing weeks in which I was right there as part of Paula's entourage but needing to stay very much in the background as Michael and Nigel did their work.

Time to begin

Paula Abdul's tour was a wonderful experience but very soon, after concerts in Malaysia, Singapore, Hong Kong, China and the Philippines, I was back home again with my departure into Europe imminent. That day arrived and I locked up the flat and made my way to Victoria to board the boat train to Dover. By the evening, I had arrived in Amsterdam. After a week there, I began to wonder if I'd ever be able to leave and complete the rest of my trip. I was having such an amazing time.

But tennis was never far away. One evening in the famous Bulldog bar in the Leidseplein, I was chatting to someone about American tennis stars. As we talked about Jim Courier, Andre Agassi and rising star, Pete Sampras, I was aware that the guy next to us was interested in our conversation. Involving him was the beginning of another long friendship as Peter told me what he thought about the top American players. I would see a lot more of Peter later in the year in New York.

The other bit of tennis news related to a possible holiday which I spotted one morning while reading a copy of the American magazine, *Tennis*, which I had bought earlier. There was an advertisement for a fantasy week, to be held in Florida later in the year, after the US Open, when I would be travelling around America. Participants would play in the company of the stars of the past, including players like Stan Smith. This sounded like the perfect type of activity to fit what I was doing. I phoned the man running the event and committed to a deposit which would secure a place. There would be an interesting twist to this part of the story when I arrived in New York in August.

As I finally broke free from the delights of Amsterdam, I realised that time had become a bit tight and I sat down one afternoon and planned the trip that I would have to complete including all the train times from one city to the next in order to get me to Rome in time for the Italian Open. So it was, that I spent two to three days each in Bruges, Brussels, Luxembourg, Hamburg - where my sister, Zoe, joined me for the weekend - Copenhagen, Oslo, Stockholm, Helsinki and back, via Stockholm and Copenhagen again, down to Berlin. Here, my mum joined me and we spent a few days re-living her time spent in the city after the Second World War when she was a clerk in the British Zone during the post-war reconstruction of Germany. After saying goodbye to mum, it was on to Munich, where, on the train, I met another American, called Gary, also a tennis fan and we enjoyed a night out in the city's bierkellers, drinking strong beer and eating pretzels.

I left Munich and on the Sunday evening before the Italian Open began, I arrived in Rome. This was not my first visit as I had helped run a training course for American Express in the city back in the mid-eighties. It was good to be back. Using my invaluable *Let's Go Europe 1992* guide, I had booked a hotel near Rome's central station, the Stazione Termini. The next morning, with directions from my friendly, Israeli landlady, Abby, I headed off via the underground in search of the Foro Italico.

Reborn with Cino

To be precise, it was the men's event of the Italian Open that I was heading for. Back in 1992, the men's and women's event were played at different times with the women's tournament being played in the week prior to the men's. Although I would attend plenty of women's events and matches in the year to come and enjoy the women's game hugely, as I always had done, somehow, I had made a glitch in my planning. In fact, thinking back, my knowledge of the men's and women's tours, both their tournaments and schedules, would improve throughout the coming years, but at this point, in the pre-internet, pre-Wikipedia days, I'm honestly not sure I even knew that there was a women's version. I had only read about the men's event and that was the one fixed in my mind. Using hindsight, if I went again, I would ensure I could see the women's event, although with the expansion of the Foro Italico site, now both events are accommodated in the same week.

Anyway, scheduling confusion aside, looking at the actual tournament itself, the Italian Open had always been a significant one on the international circuit and other than a few gaps, it had always been a men's and a women's event, although after the initial years, the development of both events would diverge on occasions. The tournament was a key one on clay in the build-up to the French Championships, as they were called initially, then the re-named French Open from 1968, following the start of open tennis. However, it was a tournament which had experienced its ups and downs.

Initially, in 1930, it was held in Milan and in 1935, moved to Rome. However, between 1936 and 1949, the tournament was not held, returning in 1950. In 1961, it was held in Turin. In 1979 the women's event was held for the first time prior to the men's event. The women's event was played in Perugia from 1980 through to 1984 and in Taranto in 1985. There was no women's event in 1986, although it moved back to Rome in 1987, where it stayed.

Back in the sixties, before open tennis arrived and the prescriptive and professional approach dictated by the likes of Arthur Ashe and the new Association of Tennis Professionals, represented by Richard Evans, was introduced on how tournaments should be run, the Italian Championships had a reputation for being disorganised. Examples of this lack of organisation included officials who had fallen asleep during matches, mix-ups in court allocation where men and women were sent to play singles against each other; and examples of where players were seeded when they had no intention of playing the tournament that week. But these examples were a long time ago in a former age. With the rise of professionalism in the sport overall and in how tournaments were organised and run, these glitches went away.

In the eighties, it had taken the commitment of Cino Marchese working for Mark McCormack's sports agency, IMG, to not only save a dying event but to breathe new life into it in a big way. Marchese packaged and sold the tournament aggressively, at one point introducing what turned out to be a masterstroke. He scheduled the women's event back at the Foro Italico in the week before the men but sold many of the sponsorships and corporate packages on the basis of just a twenty per cent increase for both weeks on what the price had been for one. This new proposition was also positioned as a take it or leave it deal. It worked. Bit by bit, interest in the tournament increased and the top players started to return in an era where lucrative exhibitions, as well as juicy guarantees at some tournaments, could be secured elsewhere. By the time of my trip, the tournament had a much-improved image and was being run on a much more secure foundation. As I sat in the burning Rome sun, it certainly looked to me like the tournament was run like clockwork, as you'd expect.

Right back at the start, the tournament's first winner on the men's side was the American, big Bill Tilden who, I had once read, loved his favourite meal of a huge steak followed by a large portion of vanilla ice cream, washed down with a large pot of black coffee. Not for our Bill, the portions of Sushi that some of the top, modern-day players insist on eating within thirty minutes of completing their matches in order to replenish lost energy and nutrients. The women's event was won by Lili Alvarez, an amazing multi-sport athlete who wrote a book about tennis in 1927 but deserves a whole book about her, if one has not already been written.

From there, the tournament has been won by most of the top names in the men's and women's games. Perhaps, not surprisingly, the most wins have been achieved by two clay-court greats, Rafa Nadal and Chris Evert. Amongst the men, Bill Tilden was the oldest winner at the age of thirty-eight and Bjorn Borg was the youngest at seventeen, while in the women's ranks, I was intrigued to find that one of the shortest recorded finals was in 1975 when Chris Evert beat Martina Navratilova in thirteen games, 6-1, 6-0, one of three finals of that duration. Although no disrespect to Miss Evert, Martina was yet to go through her total tennis transformation and there would be some titanic matches on clay between the two players, not least at the French Open in the eighties. A sign of the times, prior to when floodlights had been installed at the Foro Italico, the 1969 men's doubles between four of my favourite players from those childhood days in Chapter 1, Tom Okker and Marty Reissen on one side of the net and John Newcombe and Tony Roche on the other, had been abandoned after two sets due to darkness.

Mussolini's forum
Although periodically, other cities had been used to host the tournament, for most of its life, the Italian Open had been played at the Foro Italico. This complex was originally conceived out of the mania that ruled fascist Italy in the pre-war years. Designed in what is now known as fascist architecture, the Center de Tennis, where I would spend my week in May 1992, was one of four venues on a large multi-sport complex, whose design was littered with neo-Roman statues, many of which had been donated by Italian provinces outside Rome. As well as the tennis facility, there was the enormous Olympic Stadium built to stage the 1940 games

(although it would actually be used for the 1960 version), an athletics stadium and also, a swimming hall.

Mussolini wanted the whole complex to re-enforce his fascist imagery and communicate the message to the Italian people that sport and physical strength would combine together with Italy's military might and help create its dominant place in the world. The mixture of sporting, athletic and martial glory was at the heart of Il Duce's fascism and what his architects attempted to translate into their designs and structures.

In 1992, the centre court, the Stadio della Pallacorda, was where the main showpiece matches were played each day, along with the finals in singles and doubles at the end of the tournament. The other courts were organised in sets of clusters end to end with a small show court where the boundary of the site was located at the opposite end to the Stadio della Pallacorda. Concrete seating wrapped around these courts which were sunken down below the ground level you were on when you came through the main gate. The clubhouse was on the far side of the other end of the sunken clusters and the Stadio della Pallacorda rose up next to it. After that, came some practice courts, but without any seating. You needed a ticket for the centre court but with a ground pass, you could sit where you liked on the clusters of outside courts and move around freely. The whole site was surrounded by swaying, tall trees and made a wonderful spectacle as the players fought it out on the clay courts below. I had loved the image of the Foro Italico conjured up in my head when I'd first read about it before. On arrival, it was every bit as good as I'd imagined.

Seeds and early departures
Although I had missed it, in the previous week, the women's event had been won by Gabriela Sabatini, then world ranked No. 3. She beat world No. 1, Monica Seles. However, Monica

had won the doubles, partnered by Helena Sukova, beating Katerina Maleeva and Barbara Rittner.

As we moved into the men's event, the seeds represented pretty much the top players in the world rankings at that time. It certainly was not as if the seedings or the tournament draw was filled solely with clay court specialists, although there were a few of these. Argentinian, Alberto Mancini was the eighth seed and future French Open winner from Spain, Sergi Bruguera, was the sixteenth seed. Two names that were not there were Stefan Edberg and Andre Agassi, both of whom would play in Paris a few weeks later. Boris Becker, the number three seed, had to withdraw and would also miss Paris. Top seed was world No. 1, Jim Courier. Seven of the remaining seeds would lose in the first round as the tournament got underway, a pretty high number. These departing players were Michael Stich, Guy Forget, Goran Ivanisevic, Aaron Krickstein, Richard Krajicek, Karel Novacek and Alexander Volkov.

Early starts and late finishes
On the first day, I made my way back to the Stazione Termini from my little hotel, a few streets away and bought the ticket that Abby, my landlady, had told me to buy for the underground or Metropolitana di Roma, as it was called. The underground system in Rome was not that extensive, as when new lines were planned, as soon as excavation started, new remains from mediaeval times but especially from the days of the Roman Empire would be discovered and plans for the extension to the system would be delayed. In this way, every building site could become an archaeological dig. Emerging at the end of the line, which was still very much still in the city, I started to walk up a long road at the end of which, I could see the Stadio Olimpico, the home of both Roma and Lazio, the football clubs from Serie A, Italy's top tier. Once at the stadium, I would find the tennis centre.

After a twenty-minute walk, I arrived at the Foro Italico in mid-morning. The place didn't look very busy and I walked up to the ticket window and bought a ground pass immediately. Entering the grounds, it was everything I hoped it would be with the trees swaying above and the courts sunk down below the ground level I was on. Somehow, I picked up that from the following day, things would get busier and if I wanted to be sure of getting a ticket, with the ticket window opening at nine o'clock in the morning, I should arrive earlier.

I had eaten an amazing panini snack with a black coffee from a street vendor whose van had a few seats and tables beside it on the corner of the Foro Italico site. So, for most of the day, other than when having the odd espresso, I sat on the different clusters of outside courts watching the matches. One I remember was between lucky loser, Ronald Agenor from Haiti, playing the Peruvian player, Jaime Yzaga, if only because, although I knew their names, I hadn't seen either player live. They were playing on one of the outside courts where if you were careful where you sat, you could find some shade from the fierce sun which was now well and truly high in the sky and seriously hot. Yzaga won the match in two tiebreak sets but I especially enjoyed watching Agenor.

Born in Morocco, Ronald grew up in Haiti, although lives now in the US. At the time of the tournament, he was ranked just inside the top one hundred but had achieved a career high of No. 22. After his playing career, in which he won three titles, he was recognised in various ways and became part of the organisation Peace for Sport. A few years younger, Jaime Yzaga was of similar playing pedigree to Agenor. In his career, he reached a career high of No. 18 and won eight titles. Both played in the Davis Cup for their countries and earned very good prize money for their efforts. Here were two solid pros just outside the top ten but of a talent sufficient to keep them right up there for a decent career. I enjoyed their close match very much.

Once the tennis was over, I was hungry and my appetite was fuelled by another decent walk, this time back to the underground station the way I'd come in the morning. Using a recommendation from my *Let's Go Europe 1992* guide, I ate a tasty meal in a small restaurant close to many of the well-known old Roman sites in the centre of the city. It was just a bowl of simple pasta with a glass of wine but it tasted exquisite. Then, I made my way back to my hotel where I slept like a log. However, I knew that I had to be up and out early to make sure of obtaining a ticket. So began a routine, helped by Abby bringing in coffee and breakfast really early which enabled me to get back to the ticket window at the Foro Italico just before nine o'clock each day.

On arrival, I immediately spotted the queue but thankfully, it wasn't of Wimbledon-sized proportions, nor did there seem to be any rules, as when the ticket window opened, everyone merged into an amorphous mass and started pushing gently. It was then, as I got closer and closer, that I came up with an idea and it would not prove to be one of my best on this trip. Bearing in mind the effort I was having to go through just to get a simple ground pass, I thought that I'd buy two and offer one to someone outside the grounds later on, in what we would now call a random act of kindness. I felt good with the world. Why not pass on some of these good vibes? This was a great idea and I could bring joy to many. But after two days, I realised that the people I had approached thought that either I was some sort of ticket tout or just a plain weirdo and I abandoned the whole thing by Thursday. I still wince every time the memory comes to mind.

However, walking away from the ticket window with a ticket (or two) presented me with another slight problem as the tennis didn't actually start until gone eleven o'clock, if not a bit later. What was I going to do? Looking back, what I decided to do seemed like a bit mad. I walked back to the underground and went back to my hotel where I rested for a couple of hours, making use of a fan which Abby kindly brought into my room. Then, I'd spruce myself up again and start out on the return journey back to the Foro Italico. However, thinking about these trips backwards and forwards, I am forgetting to mention one important thing, the heat. I knew that over the weekend, unless I could get tickets for the show court and certainly on the Monday after the tournament, I would spend a day or two visiting all the amazing tourist sites that Rome had to offer. But to use up valuable energy and motivation killing a couple of hours of sightseeing each morning before the tennis began, was just not going to work. Actually, with only limited shade at the tennis, it was hard work enough as I had never been great in the heat. I almost wished for the odd cloudy day. So, returning to the tennis anytime just after midday and usually, closer to one o'clock, I was committed to at least six to seven hours of matches until the doubles finished on the outside courts. That was great but a challenge energy-wise in itself.

My routine was set and other than the two-ticket idea, certainly up until the weekend, it is what I stuck to.

Italian players; Italian crowds
Back on the courts, there was an aspect of watching that I was keen to observe. I had read about how passionate the Italian fans were about their own players. But I'd also read that this passion could go both ways. If a player did well and won, all would be well. However, if the player did poorly or upset the fans in some way just because they had lost, then the reaction could be negative and even derisive. So, I kept my eye out in the first few days for the courts on which the Italians in the draw were playing.

Indeed, there were quite a few of them; Paolo Canè, Omar Camporese, Cristiano Caratti, Renzo Furlan, Diego Nargiso, Stefan Pescosolido, Claudio Pistolesi and Gianluca Pozzi. I would see a lot of these players in the months ahead. Wild cards were pre-protected places in the main draw which the tournament director could offer to players they felt deserved them or would attract fans to the tournament. They were often awarded to players of the nationality of the tournament's location. Every tournament on the two tours, as well as the Slams, would have such an allocation. Here in Rome, while some of the Italian group had been awarded wild cards, all the players had decent rankings. These were a group of similar age who turned pro and retired at broadly the same time after at least a decade on the tour. While the tournament wins were relatively scarce, their career high rankings were spread from No. 18 (Omar Camporese) to No. 71 (Claudio Pistolesi) but like a few other players I have mentioned and will mention later, they were the stalwarts on tour in singles and doubles, week-in, week-out for years.

From across a cluster of courts, I watched Renzo Furlan's match against Frenchman, Thierry Champion and the crowds behaved everything like I had been led to believe they would. They were ecstatic when Renzo won. Equally, the crowds were not happy at all either with the result nor, quite possibly, the player, when Claudio Pistolesi lost to Charlie Steeb. Win or lose, things became passionate. Excesses of sadness followed excesses of joy, that's for sure. Claudio was the last of the eight to be knocked out after he and three others had reached the second round.

Too much sun
One excess I experienced was with the beating sun. Right from the start, it was hot, really hot. I wondered how the players coped with it. At one point, I found myself at the back end of the site where Jim Courier was hitting on a practice court in the middle of the day underneath the boiling sun and he had no shirt on. Watch out, Jim, I thought. Get the sunscreen out. But as I was worrying about the world No. 1 and the risk to his fair-skinned complexion, I fell foul of the sun myself ending up with what were probably the first stages of heatstroke.

It began because I spotted one of the game's greats practising. Guillermo Vilas, who was at the Foro Italico to play in the Over 35s event, looked like he still needed the endless supply of practice partners that I had once read about. Here he was on one of the courts opposite the clubhouse, hitting, hitting and hitting some more. I sat on the concrete-blocked, terraced seating paying homage but like Jim Courier, in full view of the relentless sun, although unlike Jim, I kept my shirt on. Some early matches in the tournament's Over 35s event then began and I felt almost an obligation to sit and watch the stars including the likes of Peter Fleming. The problem was that this was one of the two courts besides the clubhouse where at this time of the early afternoon, the seating on the far side court, where anyone wanting to watch close up had to sit, had no shade whatsoever. After a while, I began to feel a bit funny. I immediately walked around the perimeter of the sunken clusters of courts to where I had watched Ronald Agenor and Jaime Yzaga before and sat in the shade drinking water. Then, I did something for the only time in all the many hours I would watch tennis in the months to come, I fell asleep, albeit for a short period of time. When I woke up, I felt better. It dawned on me that I just might have got away with it. But I took note and stayed out of the direct view of the sun even more than I would have done normally for the rest of the week.

A range of talents
By the third round, the seeds who had survived the first round had all survived the second. But some would not reach the quarter-finals; Sergi Bruguera lost to the ever-advancing Jim Courier; Emilio Sanchez lost to fellow seed, Michael Chang; and Alberto Mancini lost to in-form Petr Korda.

Fabrice Santoro is a name known these days for his charming and professional television commentary and on-court player interviewing skills, especially at the French Open and when he was playing, for his amazing racket skills. He could play single and double-handed strokes off both sides, imparting vicious and wicked spin on the ball. The first winner of the Italian Championships in 1930, Bill Tilden, in his first book on the sport, *The Art of Tennis*, talked about how the main aim of the game was to disrupt the other man's way of playing. Fabrice was a master at doing this. Most other players would concentrate purely on their game and how they played, effectively disregarding their opponent's strengths and weaknesses. In contrast, Fabrice did the things that most of his opponents, including some of the very top names, dreaded. In fact, a few well-known names stated that whoever the draw threw up, they hoped it was not Fabrice. In Rome that week, a young Fabrice - he was just twenty – came through the first round against Michael Stich after the German retired in the second set.

In the second round, the Frenchman beat the Israeli player, Amos Mansdorf and only bowed out of the tournament when he came up against Spain's Carlos Costa. Fabrice went on to play for years, reaching a career high ranking of No. 17, winning six singles titles, and in doubles, won the Australian Open and earned serious prize money. Amos Mansdorf who I would watch in New York in a few months' time and also in Sydney, was also a player, well known to some and less well known to others. But Amos was another top player on the tour, reaching a similar top ranking high of No. 18, winning six titles.

As the number of singles matches on the courts reduced as the rounds progressed, the doubles competition took their place. I started to watch one particular team. Brad Pearce and Byron Talbot were two good examples of players who survived on the pro tour successfully, mainly in doubles. Pearce was from Provo, Utah in the US. He had some success in singles including a Wimbledon quarter-final in 1990, reaching a career high ranking of No. 71. He played a lot of doubles, winning four titles and reaching eight other finals, all with eleven different partners. His highest ranking in doubles was No. 24. One of his partners and his team-mate in Rome, was Byron Talbot. From South Africa, not as successful in singles as his doubles partner, Byron won more titles in doubles, eleven in total, most of them with Czech player, Libor Pimek and those wins would come further on into the mid-nineties.

While in Byron's case, more a doubles player than a singles specialist, players like these two were in another league entirely when compared to many pros and aspiring players below them on the tour's hierarchy but completely separate from club players like me and many others. There are, what writer John McPhee once called, 'levels of the game' and although they too had those above them in the rankings, Brad and Byron were super tennis players. They were not as well-known as top ten players, but this was as much an issue of exposure to the tennis public. As my good friend, journalist Steve McCormack explained to me one time, a point that even applies on internet news reporting today, the main media only have so much space to communicate what is going on. Unfortunately, they only have time for the top ten and sometimes, the top five players. The newspapers only have so many column inches. For me, though, ever since I was a teenager and watching professional sport with a better formed view than when it all began for me as a child, I have always been interested in the players at all levels. Players like Brad Pearce and Byron Talbot were just the type of team I was very happy to watch and then start to follow as they progressed through the tournament. I enjoyed watching them play as the light and heat went away in the early evenings and the floodlights took over. Brad and Byron didn't win the doubles but I would watch them play again in Paris, Wimbledon and in Melbourne as my Grand Slam trip unfolded. Just before Wimbledon, our paths would even cross, as we shall see.

All of these players I have mentioned above were what kept the tour going week to week in singles and doubles and every one of them was a marvellous tennis player. They could not have been there if they weren't.

Have my ticket
As the end of the week came into view, so did the latter stages of the tournament. On the Saturday, I actually took a break from the tennis. The reason for this absence was that, by now, all the matches in singles and doubles were scheduled for the main show court and I did not have a ticket. Also, I needed a rest. So, I took it easy. I still planned to go along the next day and see if, somehow, without paying the earth for a ticket, I could get into the stadium to watch. This, I managed to do but not before Jim Courier had beaten Spain's Carlos Costa, to take the singles title. As used to happen quite a lot at Wimbledon, before more structured re-sale procedures were implemented, it was someone coming out of the stadium that just gave me their ticket and in I went. At least I could watch the doubles final where the Swiss partnership of Marc Rosset and Jacob Hlasek beat South Africa's Wayne Ferreira and Australia's Mark Kratzmann. The tournament was over. It had been an amazing, if exhausting, week.

I spent a day walking some more and ticked off my list some of the major tourist sites but quite quickly decided to move on. For this visit, my job was done. With every train trip now, I would be edging closer to Paris and the French Open which started in just over a week's time. However, I still had two important cities that I had to visit, albeit briefly, before leaving Italy with quick stops in Vienna and Zurich to follow. So, after all the great tennis, many miles of walking around the city and many more cups of amazing coffee and plates of scrumptious pasta, I left Rome and headed north to Florence and Venice.

Chapter 4

Sun, Wind and Rain at Roland Garros

My dodgy passport
After Florence and Venice, both fascinating but as unique as Rome and cities worth a holiday in their own right, I was on the train again, this time to Vienna. From there, I would head for Paris making one more stop in Zurich, where I had worked for three months on a secondment off my Middle East assignment for American Express back at the end of 1989. I planned on visiting my old colleagues. However, as I left Venice, I nearly didn't make it across the border into Austria.

Looking out of the window, thinking about the trip so far, I was interrupted by two very large, uniformed border guards who were checking everyone's passport. I showed them mine and my stomach twisted as one of them said, "We can't let you into Austria with this." Dumbfounded, as they explained, I realised that a clerical error made in the British Consulate in Bahrain a couple of years before, might be coming back to haunt me. Whoever processed the document had made a small mistake, one which was corrected by using a black biro. Then, the pages were laminated but with the correction clearly visible beneath the shiny surface. I kept calm and told them what I thought had happened, as if I was some sort of passport protocol specialist. I pointed out that the correction was not made outside the laminate covering but underneath it, as if they'd react with relief and tell me that everything was acceptable after all. It didn't happen quite like that but my explanation did make them stop and look and after going backwards and forwards a few times, they agreed that I could enter Austria but that as soon as I arrived in Vienna, I had to go to the British Embassy and get a new passport. I agreed to this plan but seeing as these gentlemen could never check what

I was to do or not, I was safe for the time being. Then, they proceeded to take out everything from my large Prince tennis bag piece by piece and leave it all on the seats and the floor of the small compartment that I was sitting in. With everything everywhere, they nodded at me and walked out, leaving me with a nice re-packing job to complete as the miles went by.

When I arrived in Vienna, I did go to the British Embassy but they said a new passport would take a few days, time I didn't have. So, I declined the offer, taking the risk that a similar objection would not be raised as I crossed the border into Switzerland, France and then the UK. Indeed, the passport was not queried again throughout the rest of my trip over a period of nine months with numerous views of it by various immigration officials. After a couple of days, I moved on to Zurich where I saw my former American Express colleagues for a cup of coffee. I knew Zurich quite well, having spent three months there back in 1989, a time which was tennis-free other than going to watch the BMW European Indoor Tournament, one on the WTA Tour, which Steffi Graf won. Next, it was on to Paris.

Arriving in the French capital, I found my small hotel, another one found in my *Let's Go Europe 1992* guide, booked with a phone call ahead, made from Zurich. Having checked in, I went out again in search of Roland Garros. This trip was not difficult. My landlady had instructed me, in French, to walk down to a main road south of the hotel, get on any bus going west and after a short trip, once I had crossed over the River Seine, to get off in sight of the grounds. Indeed, it was as easy as that. Outside the site, I managed to buy a ground pass cheaply off someone standing nearby and this would be the last one I had to purchase as once inside, by chance, I bumped into the British player, Clare Wood, who I had known back in Sussex at the Southdown Club in Lewes a few years before when she was a promising junior. Clare had advanced through to the second round of qualifying for the singles before being knocked out. She was staying on to play doubles and mixed. Very kindly, she told me that she would leave a ground pass ticket for me each day for as long as she remained in the tournament. Effectively, this help from Clare set me up for the bulk of the remainder of the first week which had just started and into the second week as well. I could now settle down, take stock and familiarise myself with the courts and the layout of the site and decide who to watch.

Championat Internationaux De France
Even in the opening few minutes after arriving and sorting myself out with Clare, I got an immediate feel for the stature of the event. Looking back to 1968, although the British Hard-Court Championships had been the first open professional tournament in April, what had now become called the French Open was the very first of the Grand Slams to play as an open event a few weeks later in May. But going back to the start, the national championships actually began in 1891 when the Championat Internationaux de France began. However, at that time and into the 1920s, the competition was only open to members of French clubs.

1925 is often referred to as the start of what we know as the modern incarnation of the championships. That was the year that the event was opened up to all amateur players internationally. The winners that year were the top French players, Rene Lacoste and Suzanne Lenglen. Before tennis went open in 1968, it had been Lenglen who had won most singles titles with four and Henri Cochet, also with four, on the men's side. Since then, two modern-day greats, Rafa Nadal with thirteen and Chris Evert with seven, have won the most times. Michael Chang and Monica Seles were the youngest winners, both in their teens at the time of their victories. The players with the most match wins in the tournament's history up to and including 2020, were Rafa Nadal with one-hundred and Steffi Graf with eighty-four.

For many years, the French Open stood out amongst other reasons, because it was the only one of the four Grand Slams not played on grass. This situation changed when the US Open was played briefly on green Har-Tru in the late seventies and before both the US Open and the Australian Open changed surfaces to cement-based hardcourts. One view that I've heard a few times was that the challenge of a Slam played on clay over two weeks and in the men's event, in best-of-five sets, requiring seven wins to take the title, was the ultimate tennis test. While Wimbledon has arguably always been the most prestigious Slam to win and therefore, perhaps the biggest overall challenge, the French Open remains a gargantuan task to complete and win from every perspective.

The French Open has always been played in the spring as the culmination of the European clay court circuit, after which the players would cross the channel and get ready for the grass-court season and Wimbledon. However, in 1946 and 1947 and in 2020 (due to the Covid-19 pandemic), the tournament was played after Wimbledon. The usual short gap between the end of the French Open and the start of Wimbledon, for many years, just two weeks, was extended recently by an extra week, allowing the players a longer familiarisation period on grass, if only by a few days.

Great War aviator
The French Open is often called by the name of the location of the tournament, Roland Garros. The original 'French club member-only' championships, pre- and post-Great War were played in a number of venues and it was for the 1928 championships that a brand-new facility was built. The site, named after an aviator who lost his life in the Great War, had been constructed to provide a suitably prestigious venue for France's defence of the Davis Cup. The previous year, the famous group of French stars, 'the Four Musketeers', Jacques 'Toto' Brugnon, Jean Borotra ('the Bouncing Basque'), Henri

Cochet ('the Magician'), and René Lacoste ('the Crocodile') had beaten the United States.

The site, in South-West Paris, close to the Bois de Boulogne, was built around a huge Court Central, what became known in more recent times, as Court Philippe Chatrier, with a capacity of nearly fifteen thousand people. Nineteen others surrounded this court including a popular Court No. 1, which became known as the Bullring because of the almost circular shape of the stadium. This was a court that I would enjoy watching matches on, as we shall see. The courts were built with different orientations, unlike the other three Grand Slam sites. There were all the usual refreshment outlets and gift shops dotted around, especially after Chatrier, as head of the French Tennis Federation, made a number of changes to the site. Most of the outside courts had some form of seating while a few only had walkways beside them.

In the seventies and eighties, a number of top players missed the tournament for a variety of reasons. Chatrier's master stroke was to get one of the French television companies to broadcast the tennis all day and every day, like the BBC had been doing for years with Wimbledon. This exposure lit the fire in the French fans and with this increased interest, so the domestic prestige and importance of the tournament increased too. The players started coming back and the tendency to miss the two weeks on clay dissipated.

While Roland Garros was a major venue, certainly, back in 1992 when I spent my time there, it had a bit more of a relaxed feel about it compared to the Wimbledon I had become used to. However, the atmosphere on the show courts could be both incredibly quiet with few people either in attendance or interested, if they were, in contrast with explosive and tumultuous noise and excitement from a crowd packed to the rafters, especially if a French player was involved, as I was to discover.

The surface, as in Rome, was known as clay. The actual surface is various substances, including limestone, concrete and brick, laid at various levels, crushed and rolled. It is called European clay and is referred to as red in colour (although it might be called orange), as opposed to American clay, Har-Tru, which is a grey-green colour, made up of a different combination of substances, playing a bit quicker. The nature of European red clay creates a certain type of play which is quite different to grass or the types of hardcourts now used in New York and Melbourne. Compared to Wimbledon, where up to the early nineties, when I was travelling, matches were usually dominated by the serve-volley playing style, in Paris, as it had been in Rome, such a style could never work effectively other than in short bursts or for the odd point.

On clay, the ball bounces differently, the timing and rhythm of the ball going from racket to racket is different and because of this, on average, points take longer to complete both in terms of number of strokes and time taken. Opportunities have to be crafted, at times, a few shots ahead, painstakingly manufactured with much patience and perseverance. Grass-court tennis makes different requirements of players. On grass, in the times before the courts were deliberately slowed down, usually the server would deliver a quick knock-out blow, while on clay, the competitors would often resemble the type of boxing seen when Muhammed Ali was dancing around an opponent, seemingly for minutes at a time. The opponent would try to work out whether they should attack or dance too, biding their time in a weird sort of neutral mode. Both surfaces demanded different mind-sets.

While comebacks might always occur on any surface, the cliche and truism that the match was never over until it was over, applied to an even greater extent on clay than other surfaces. Comebacks from almost impossible positions were much more likely in Paris, especially for the men players over the best of five sets. In 1958, Robert Haillet was 0-5 and 0-40 down in the fifth set against the American, Budge Patty, yet came back to win. Grown adult players would have been more likely to end up after matches in Paris having lost from winning positions than in just about any other arena. Tears would often follow matches, shed by both women and men including from the great, Manolo Santana after the 1961 final where he completed his match against the Italian, Nicola Pietrangeli and that was after the Spaniard won!

Seeds, nationalities and early rounds
As the tournament got underway, looking at the men, the seeding list, led by Jim Courier again, was similar to Rome, although a few names had entered, including Stefan Edberg, Carlos Costa (a seeding no doubt influenced by his appearance in the final at the Foro Italico), Andre Agassi, Brad Gilbert and Jacob Hlasek. The departures from the Rome list were Alberto Mancini, Emilio Sanchez, Karel Novacek and Sergi Bruguera, all of whom would still play in the first round. Fifteenth seed, Brad Gilbert, much to the joy of the French crowd was beaten by Cedric Pioline in five sets and sixteenth seed, Jacob Hlasek, was knocked out in the first round. Other than Frenchman, Guy Forget, the rest of the seeds all made it through to the third round or better.

After Rome, I had a new batch of names to look out for on the courts. Of the Italian eight from the Foro Italico, five were here plus Massimo Cierro who had qualified. Nargiso, Pistolesi and Pozzi made it to the second round but all were knocked out there. Where in Rome, my focus had been on Italian players and their fans, here in Paris, I added the French players and theirs. On the men's side, there were fifteen players and I knew many of them. Of these fifteen players, eight had been awarded wild cards and six made it through to the second round, including Henri Leconte who would provide me with one of my most memorable moments from the tournament and one which gave me a perfect example about how passionate the French crowd felt about one of their own.

First round casualties included Fabrice Santoro as well as Jaime Yzaga and Ronald Agenor. Keeping an eye out for the British players was always a priority. But in the men's event, there was not a single British player in the draw, not even Jeremy Bates whose ranking at the time would have left him close to a direct entry.

On the women's side, the seeds were the top players in the world, headed by Monica Seles, Steffi Graf and Gabriela Sabatini, the winner in Rome. The remainder were the usual assorted mix of top performers on the tour including the young Jennifer Capriati and Jana Novotna, two French players, Natalie Tauziat and Mary Pierce, and Katerina Maleeva and one of her sisters, Manuela who was, by now, playing under the Swiss flag, having begun to represent the country in the Federation Cup in 1990. While they all made it through the first round, Sabine Appelmans from Belgium, and Katerina Maleeva, knocked out by Ukrainian player, Elena Brioukhovets, were defeated in the second round. Most of the rest would fulfil their seedings reaching the fourth round or later.

In addition to Tauziat and Pierce, the French contingent included another seventeen players, making nineteen in all. With a small number of exceptions, I was aware of most of them. As with the men, the eight wild cards for the tournament had all been awarded to French players. Six of the players, mainly the better-known names, reached the second round.

On the British front in the women's event, in qualifying, the two British players involved, my former Southdown Club member and now, ticket supplier, Clare Wood had drawn fellow Brit, Amanda Grunfeld. That meant a Brit got through to the second round but Clare was halted there by the Czech player, Radka Bobkova. In the main draw, Jo Durie and Monique Javer flew the flag with Jo advancing to the second round while Monique didn't, losing heavily, 6-1, 6-1 to the Italian, Sandra Cecchini.

Following the straight road
At the end of my first day, I headed back towards my hotel. After dinner in a Chinese restaurant nearby in which somehow, the waiter understood my poor French, it was back to bed. So began a daily routine for this tournament just as I had slid into one in Rome and would adopt for each tournament I watched as the months slipped by.

Breakfast was easy, as ever in France, with great coffee in large cups and wonderful French bread. The lovely texture and smell are something to do with the dough, apparently. However, this means that the bread goes stale quickly; eat by four in the afternoon, or dentists beware. A few fresh croissants were always on offer too, accompanied by loads of lovely jam. In the hotel I was staying in, within the breakfast room, there was one large table with all the coffee pots and food laid out in the middle. You helped yourself and made small talk with those around you who could have been from anywhere. It was simple and easy and all carried out without any fuss. If you didn't feel like chatting, that was fine too. It was all similar to a small bed and breakfast establishment I had stayed at in the Hague a few weeks before on the trip, where rather sweetly, if a little obsessively, the proprietors had placed little national flags at each place setting to correspond with the nationality of their guests. These flags were on square supports, a bit like paperweights. By the time I came down to breakfast, there was no-one else there. I sat behind my little British flag and enquired where the other guests were. Pointing at the other flags sitting there looking a bit forlorn, my host told me that they were Japanese and as was the way with their fellow countrymen, because they had such short holidays, made even shorter by the long flights getting to and from Europe, they tried to pack as much into each day as possible. Families would often get up really early, eat breakfast, sitting at the appropriate place behind their flag, of course, then get on with whatever they were going to do. However, this commitment did not just mean seeing everything the Hague had to offer but often would involve travels much further afield. He related how one family had covered parts of three countries in one day in their rental car and arrived back to tell the tale, get to bed at a reasonable hour and be up and at it the next morning again at the crack of dawn. Each to their own, of course. We all had our own agendas and restrictions to deal with. My mind wandered to a possible exchange between hotel owner and his guest. Had my hotel owner instructed his Japanese clients to turn right when they reached the Netherlands after a day covering various countries?

Once I had arrived at Roland Garros, I would go to the window at the gate where Clare had left me a ticket and after picking it up and entering, I'd check to see if Clare was scheduled to play a doubles or mixed doubles match. Then, I would start to wander around and watch whichever match took my fancy. Snacks and drinks, usually involving more coffee and baguettes, would be consumed as the day unfolded and when it was all over, once I was back in the vicinity of my hotel, I'd get off the bus and seek out another restaurant, often a Chinese or an Indian one, as these were always my preference. On arriving back at my hotel, I would often read the latest edition of whichever English newspaper I had managed to find at the various newsagents and supermarkets I passed on my way back. The hotels I had been staying in were the low budget type which probably had a television somewhere, probably in a lounge, if there was one, but not in the rooms. This meant that after a brief chat in very basic, clipped French with my landlady, a well-built woman with her hair in a bun and striking eyes, a modern-day version of Rene's wife, Edith in *'Allo, 'Allo!* the popular wartime television comedy, who was always in her little booth next to the kitchen,

I'd lie on my bed and read the paper from cover to cover; I'd never been so well informed. Then, I'd go to sleep, wake up and start it all over again. It was a simple and basic existence with a focus entirely on the tennis which would take up many hours through the bulk of the day. But that was where I wanted to be and this was what I wanted to be doing, so I was happy, very happy.

Experienced veterans
On the men's side, also competing alongside all the players who were aged mainly in their twenties either towards the top of the rankings, on the way to the top or hanging on so they didn't slide back down again, were two names, one from the eighties, Kevin Curren, and the other, going back to the early seventies, the great Jimmy Connors. Curren was edging towards the end of a really good career and as for Jimmy Connors, well, he had played his first professional tournament when the youngest of the male tour players were toddlers.

British tennis fans would remember Kevin Curren for his run to the Wimbledon final in 1985 when he was a casualty of the young Boris Becker's dynamic rise to fame. Achieving a career-high ranking of No. 5 in a fourteen-year career, he won five titles. In addition, he had a stellar doubles career, very much in the days when the top players still played both singles and doubles, winning twenty-six titles, mainly with Texan, Steve Denton, including a Grand Slam victory in New York, where he also won two of his three mixed doubles titles, Wimbledon being the third, all with Anne Smith.

Both Kevin and Steve had huge serves and one time at Wimbledon, when I was watching them as they played on Court No. 11 and Court No. 12, there were moments when they would serve within a split-second of each other from the same end of their respective courts. If you turned your head quickly enough, as their opponents floundered in their attempts to make a return, you could see and hear both serves hitting the green canvas at the back of the court, also, a split-second apart, thud, thud! Here in Paris, Kevin was going about his business as part of a schedule which saw him play in nineteen tournaments through the year. He won his first-round match but lost to Ukrainian, Andrei Medvedev, in the second round.

Jimmy Connors, 'Jimbo', was still going strong, a few years older than Curren, and now approaching forty-years-of age. Jimmy loved to play, loved to compete and seemed unable to stop. Although he hadn't won a title in a while, he would end up with a total of one-hundred and nine, a tour record, along with 1,557 matches played and 1,274 wins. He was still very much a huge name in the sport. Jimbo could compete with the best of them. However, by the look of it, not here in Paris, where he was knocked out by fourth seed, Michael Stich, 6-2 in the fifth set. Jimmy would still play in seventeen tournaments in 1992. As the years passed, his involvement reduced and his ranking dropped; it would be into 1996 before he retired.

On the women's side, since the sport went open, the average age of the players had gone about a gradual process of getting younger and younger, an issue with many ethical and moral implications, especially amongst the younger players and those who had just become teenagers. Indeed, one of the teenage prodigies of the time, Jennifer Capriati, was going through her own tennis meltdown throughout the bulk of the time I was on my travels in 1992. While not exactly babes-in-arms, the remainder of the women's draw included a slightly younger crowd of aspiring pros when compared to the men. Indeed, world No. 1, Monica Seles was just eighteen-years old as the tournament began and was already the winner of multiple singles Slams. She had played on the pro tour at an earlier age as had Capriati who bizarrely, had been younger than even the rule created to accommodate her in her first event back in 1990.

Therefore, any label of old, however loosely defined or applied, might be attached to women of a slightly younger age than on the men's side. Ros Fairbank-Nideffer had played her first Grand Slam back in 1979 and now approaching thirty-two years-of age, was still playing the tour. She had reached a career-high ranking of No. 15 and had won one singles title. Like Kevin Curren, she had experienced significant success in doubles, where she had won eighteen titles, including two Grand Slams, both here in Paris in the early eighties with Tanya Harford and Candy Reynolds. She had lost in New York in the doubles final and in the mixed, with Australian Mark Edmondson. After retirement, Eddo had played in one of the Sunday mixed doubles afternoon tournaments at White City that helped keep me sane in Sydney as mentioned above, although Eddo would play in the afternoon's tournament a few sections higher up than the one I was in. Ros also reached a mixed final here in Paris, although she lost. At Roland Garros this time, Ros would beat the American, Kimberley Po-Messerli but then was knocked out in the second round by French player, Julie Halard.

One day; two chance meetings
Towards the end of the week, I was in the main concourse near the entrance and I bumped into two people. One, I had an idea I might see but the other, one of the great personalities of the sport, was one I was delighted to have the opportunity to meet.

I became aware of someone calling my name. Turning around, I was pleased to see my drinking buddy from the Munich beer halls, Gary. He had told me that he would be in Paris and that he would try to get to Roland Garros, so this meeting was not a complete surprise. But as we talked, I became aware of bright colours. Just to the right of us, the American journalist, broadcaster and author, Bud Collins, was standing, looking around. Bud had made his name for a number of reasons including his propensity to wear bright coloured bow ties and trousers, or pants as the Americans call them. I had read his book, *My Life With the Pros* and just as I was about to nudge Gary, he saw Bud and exclaimed, "Mr Collins!" Some well-known people run for the hills when they are recognised. But not Bud. He shook our hands and seemed very happy to stand and chat with us. We talked about nothing in particular and at the appropriate moment, we all shook hands again and went in our separate directions.

Gary and I spent an enjoyable afternoon watching the tennis. Strangely, while I handed him one of the small cards I had had printed before the trip with my details on it, I didn't make a note of his in return. I still cannot remember why but maybe it was down to something as simple as a lack of pen and paper.

Battle in the Bullring
As the middle Saturday went by, the third round in both men's and women's singles was being completed. On the men's side, by the early evening, there was one more match involving a seed and it was being played in the Bullring. As the late afternoon turned into early evening, I found myself a seat on the upper levels of the court's seating watching the type of match which really brings tennis to life. Here in front of me was the tall Swede, Nicklas Kulti, playing the much shorter American, Michael Chang.

Kulti, twenty-two years old and ranked No. 94, had turned pro after winning junior Wimbledon three years before in 1989, in the same year that a seventeen-year-old Chang had won the French Open. Chang was the fifth seed this year in Paris and was playing well. As the match progressed, it always looked like Kulti would prevail but Chang, as gritty a fighter as you could seek to find, kept coming back at the Swede. The pair traded the first four sets and as the sun started to go down, the epic fifth set went to fourteen games before Chang, match point down, finally dumped a Kulti passing shot into the net.

The crowd loved this match and so did I. While there was a lot of baseline play, thankfully, unlike one French Open final back in 1982 between Guillermo Vilas and Mats Wilander, which I watched on television in my flat down in Hove, when the second point in the match extended to nearly sixty strokes as both players did their best imitation of two juniors trading moon balls at each other, both Kulti and Chang were always on the lookout to attack the net which made for exciting mid-court and net play. The match finished at just before nine o'clock in the evening with Kulti, at first waving his arms in excitement, then reverting to a more respectful stance as he shook the American's hand. From my seat, I could look down and survey the whole scene, battling players and enraptured crowd appreciating both players' efforts, especially Chang, as time after time, he ran down seemingly impossible balls, returning them with interest to win the point. What a sight it was and what a match it had been.

That Saturday had not been a good one for men's seeds as a number had fallen in addition to Chang: Second seed, Stefan Edberg had been beaten by Russian, Andrei Cherkasov; Michael Stich also lost – he could not get past Henri Leconte, much to the delight of the locals; Richard Krajicek of the Netherlands lost to Uruguayan qualifier, Diego Perez; and Aaron Krickstein was down a set to another Uruguayan, Marcelo Filippini, when the American retired because of a blister on his right foot.

In the women's matches, only two went to three sets. Amongst the straight sets victories, seeds Manuela Maleeva-Fragniere and Mary Joe Fernandez both lost. Jo Durie, the last British player in the draw, was beaten by Akiko Kijimuta while two other Japanese players competed against each other with Kimiko Date beating Mana Endo. At the top and bottom of the draw, Monica Seles and Steffi Graf powered onwards.

I made my way home feeling happy not realising that Nicklas Kulti and I would come together again a few days later.

Doubles and troubles

At that time, Wimbledon was the only Slam where historically, the tournament had taken a break with the middle Sunday being a rest day, a policy that will be changing soon in 2022. That meant that I was back at Roland Garros the next day for more matches. As the singles advanced into the fourth round, the schedule started to become more crowded with doubles and mixed doubles matches. I could now show some loyalty to my ticket provider, Clare Wood, watch her play and support her while I did.

In the doubles, the seeds in the men's event read like a who's who in top pairs of the time with eight of the sixteen coming from the US. Although many of these players were in the middle of their careers and would not retire until towards the end of the decade, these were top doubles players and top teams on tour at the time. By the end of their careers, the combined total of ATP Tour doubles titles which would be won by the thirty-two players just with the partners they were playing here at Roland Garros would be approaching two hundred. But if you added to that number the additional four-hundred and twenty-six titles that both players in each team had won or would win with other partners, you ended up with a staggering number of nearly six-hundred titles won by this pool of players playing here in 1992, across their careers.

The sixteen pairs also included a number of Grand Slam titles in their win lists (both as pairs and as individuals with other partners) and a few Grand Slam mixed doubles titles too. It was a quality list of pairings, that's for sure, although perhaps, only as you would expect. One other point, however, was that these doubles players didn't only play doubles back then but most of them were still active and continued to be so, in pursuing singles careers first and foremost. Richey Reneberg and his partner Jim Grabb both reached career high rankings in singles within the top thirty as well as winning nine doubles titles together, including two Grand Slams and twenty-four other doubles titles with different partners. Despite their pedigree, the seeds began to fall with the casualties rising as the rounds went by. My team from Rome, Brad Pearce and Byron won their first-round match but lost to Todd Woodbridge and Mark Woodforde, the 'Woodies', in round two.

In the women's doubles, there were also some outstanding doubles players and teams in the list of seeds. As with the men, although many of these players were in the middle of their careers and would not retire until the end of the decade, if not later in a few cases, there were some outstanding performers. Looking at the same analysis of title wins with the partners they were playing with in this tournament, the combined total of WTA Tour doubles titles which would be won by the thirty-two players just with the partners they were playing with amounted to seventy-one. But if you added to that number the additional six-hundred titles that the individual members of each team won with other partners, you end up with an even more staggering total than their male counterparts at this Roland Garros, won by this pool of players playing here in 1992, across their careers.

Seeds also fell regularly. Clare Wood's partner was Tracey Morton from Australia and they pulled off a stunning first round victory by beating the number three seeds, Americans, Mary Joe Fernandez and Zina Garrison, 8-6 in the deciding set. Clare and Tracey were successful again, in the second round where they beat German player, Eva Pfaf and the French player, Catherine Suire. Sadly, in round three, their progress came to a halt when they were beaten by the French team of Isabelle Demongeot and Natalie Tauziat in three sets.

While watching Clare and Tracey play, I met and spent some time with former British player, Andrew Jarrett, who was working for the LTA (Lawn Tennis Association, sometimes referred to as British Tennis) keeping an eye on the British players. Getting to know Andrew while watching Clare, I always felt that he had the ideal personality for keeping a watchful eye on younger pros and it was no surprise that he made such a success of being the tournament referee at Wimbledon for fourteen years.

It was while watching doubles on the outside courts that at one point, I heard a loud voice. Looking across towards the seating behind the umpire's chair, I realised that the voice belonged to Jim Pierce, the father of French player, Mary Pierce. Especially on the women's tour, there were a few tennis fathers who had developed reputations. At this time, in May 1992, quite early in Mary's career, Jim was on this list with a reputation for being a handful, to say the least. While his tennis relationship with his daughter helped take her into the world's top twenty, incidents on and off the court would lead to his expulsion from the circuit, with the enactment of an official anti-disruption regulation named after him. He would also be banned from Mary's life, although a reconciliation of sorts took place a few years later, after she had won her only Grand Slam, the 1995 Australian Open. On this occasion, on one of Roland Garros's outside courts, things seemed, from afar, to be satisfactory. Mary was playing a doubles match with her partner from Argentina, Patricia Tarabini; they advanced to a quarter-final exit.

Clare Wood was also playing in the mixed doubles, so I kept an eye out for her matches. She was playing with American, Charles Beckman, a former top college player from the University of Texas with a shock of blond hair which he kept under control with a Pat Cash-style headband. He reminded me of an American version of Swede, Joakim Nystrom. After college, Charles played on the tour, mainly in doubles for a few years including a continuous run of Grand Slam appearances from US Open to US Open between 1989 and 1992.

The mixed doubles had some strong players and partnerships participating. The number one seeds were Jana Novotna from the Czech Republic who would go from heartbreak to glory in two Wimbledon finals later in the nineties. Her partner was seasoned pro, John Fitzgerald, an Aussie who had a really solid career in singles, reaching No. 25 in the world with six title wins, and an even better record in doubles, where he won a career Grand Slam with seven wins at the four locations, spread across a decade, reaching No. 1 in the rankings. He had also won the mixed at Slams twice, including the 1991 Wimbledon title with Elizabeth Smylie. Byron Talbot was the sixteenth seed with French player, Isabelle Demongeot, although after a first-round bye, they lost their first match in three sets. Brad Pearce was also in the mixed, partnering American, Beverly Bowes. They did not get past the first round.

However, the pair which caught my eye was the unseeded American team of Bryan Shelton and Lori McNeil. I didn't know much about Bryan, but he was yet another player with a solid pedigree. He had been a top college player, an All-American, who won two titles on tour and reached No. 55 in the rankings. On the other hand, I was well aware of Lori McNeil, who had a lovely way of playing with fluid movement, reminding me of Evonne Goolagong, comfortable in all areas of the court and against the growing trend amongst the conveyor-belt academy produced players, hit a single-handed backhand. Lori played on the tour for two decades, reached a ranking high of No. 9 and won ten titles in singles and thirty-three titles in doubles. In Paris, back in 1988, Lori had won the mixed doubles title with Mexican player, Jose Lozano. She and Bryan had to play a first-round match and they won it, coming through to play a seeded pair. Clare and Charles also came through.

Ground level reporting
In the men's fourth round matches, there were no big surprises with top seed, Jim Courier, advancing in another three-set demolition, this time, of Andrei Medvedev. But the one that I watched was a really enjoyable exhibition of quality tennis on clay between Pete Sampras and Germany's Carl-Uwe Steeb, again, on the Bullring.

I have never had a preference for where in the stands I would want to sit. For the Kulti-Chang match, I was at the top of the stands and that position gave a particular view with its own perspective on what was in front of me. As Sampras and Steeb began their match, I found myself at the side of the court but right down at the front. However, on this court, I was not in the lowest position. Ground level on the Bullring took on a new meaning because at one end of the court, a press box had been built slightly below ground level. From this position, members of the press could watch the tennis in front of them through mesh windows which were located at about knee level of the players out there on the court.

For me, watching from the normal ground level and almost within touching distance of the players, provided the opportunity to really appreciate how they moved and how they hit their shots. You could also track the ball with its different trajectories depending on the spins imparted by the players. Both Pete and Charlie, as he was often referred to, hit mainly flat or with topspin on their forehand sides and with both slice and topspin off their backhand wings, although Steeb hit his topspin drive double-handed. Both players were also willing to attack the net and play all-court tennis when it was needed. Pete Sampras was still young and at the start of his career but as you would expect, his game was pretty much complete at this point and he was really exciting to watch. As might be imagined from a player of his calibre, he hit what is known as a 'heavy ball' (a combination of lots of both spin and speed).

Charlie Steeb was a left-hander and another really good pro, a player who those who followed the professional tours would have known about but those who only followed their home Grand Slam might not. Steeb was a pro for a decade and reached a career high ranking of No. 14, winning three titles from five appearances in finals. He also won three doubles titles and represented Germany in the Davis Cup. So far, in Paris, Charlie had beaten Grant Connell, Patrick McEnroe and Alexander Volkov. On this occasion, however, he could not get past Sampras and lost in straight sets. The fourth round was as far as he reached in Slams. The match may have been a bit one-sided but I really enjoyed watching both players.

In the women's event, again, there were no fourth-round surprises, although double disappointment for the French crowd as Mary Pierce (to Jennifer Capriati) and Natalie Tauziat (to Manon Bollegraf) both lost. At the opposite ends of the draw, Monica Seles and Steffi Graf made their almost inevitable advance towards a meeting in Saturday's final.

Leconte!
Now into the second week, the singles had reached quarter-finals stage. On the men's side, Jim Courier won, as did Andre Agassi, despatching Pete Sampras in three sets with relative ease, and Petr Korda did to Andrei Cherkasov what the Russian had done to Stefan Edberg in the round before and beat him, also in four sets. That left crowd favourite, Henri Leconte who had advanced a long way courtesy of his wild card and usual flamboyant play. His quarter-final opponent was none other than Nicklas Kulti and once again, the Swede would be part of an amazing match. This one was played on Court Chatrier and I managed to get on there for the last set

after a steward, seeing that I didn't have a ticket, waved me through to sit on a vacant seat nearby.

The stands were packed and the crowd were going mad every time Henri won a point. The excitement was because a comeback was underway. Kulti had won the first two sets but Leconte had won the third, 6-3. Then he won the fourth by the same score. Could he do it again? With one service break, yes, he could and the fifth set also finished 6-3 to the Frenchman. Once more, as with Kulti's match against Chang where I had found a seat on the rim of the Bullring, I was way up high here on Chatrier and could witness not just the fantastic tennis but the explosive crowd reaction too. This was another day when I went back to the hotel very happy. On arrival, landlady Edith asked me how my day had gone and unable to restrain myself, I gushed about Henri Leconte. "Ah, oui, Leconte!" she confirmed with a big smile. With an equally big smile on my face, I went back out in search of more Chinese food.

In the women's quarter-finals, the top four seeds, Monica Seles, Steffi Graf, Gabriela Sabatini and Arantxa Sanchez Vicario all justified their seedings by advancing to the semi-finals. Steffi had needed three sets to dispose of Natasha Zvereva. For Natasha, hopefully, this put to rest some of the ghosts she may have had about playing Steffi after their final back in 1988 when the German took just over half an hour to beat the Russian 6-0, 6-0. I would be seeing more of Natasha in the tournaments to come as she began to become a force in doubles with Gigi Fernandez.

Mac and Monique

The weather had become a bit variable. When I arrived in Paris, it had been hot and dry but as the days passed, wind, damp and all-out rain crept in and became the norm. Somehow, probably because unlike at Wimbledon, where even the slightest drop of water on the courts can make them lethal for the players, here on the clay, the courts could take a bit of damp before play was suspended. This meant taking my bulky, all-purpose coat, like a big, green Parka with its numerous pockets and zips, along to the courts just in case. Thankfully, the coat was one of these contraptions where if you could work out which way to pull and push the zips, miraculously, the inner padding could be removed and you would be left with a lightweight version, the outside part without the inside, one perfect for conditions which were warmer but still a bit wet. Really, I had two coats in one, a heavier, cold-weather version and the lighter, warmer-weather version I now wore.

It was on one of these damp and chilly afternoons as all the events progressed to their conclusion and the matches on the outside courts thinned out that walking past one of the courts without any seating, I realised I was close enough to one of the players practising that I felt I could start a conversation with him. If I had, I would have been chatting to the great John McEnroe who was hitting balls back and forth. Clay had never been McEnroe's best surface. He had won four of his seventy-seven singles titles in North America on Har-Tru. He had reached the final in Paris back in 1984 playing brilliantly in the first two sets against Ivan Lendl before things had started to go wrong, with Lendl winning his first Grand Slam title, in five sets. This year, John had lost in the first round of the singles to none other than Nicklas Kulti, in four sets but he was doing well in doubles where he and Andre Agassi had reached the quarter-finals. McEnroe was never one to play doubles as an after-thought and he had used the event as a substitute practice for singles. But he was such a great player that he won a further seventy-eight titles in addition to his singles victories, mainly with his friend from teenage times, Peter Fleming. In the early days of his career, he had also won the mixed doubles in Paris with Mary Carillo who went on to a successful career as a television commentator and presenter on the sport. But something felt a bit odd as I stood there and then I realised that no-one else was watching, except me, that is, and also, this interesting fellow fan.

Standing next to me was a petite woman, maybe in her sixties and very well-dressed with a beret-style hat and an umbrella. She reminded me a bit of my dear mum both in age and in dress sense. We started chatting and to my relief, she spoke English and introduced herself as Monique. She told me that she always came to watch the tennis and also that she loved to watch John McEnroe. The conversation was a pleasure as was watching such an amazing player so close up.

On that same afternoon, while queuing for yet another baguette, I met a couple of English tennis journalists who were also having a snack and we talked about things back home as I asked them how the tournament was going for them.

Finals weekend
Unfortunately, Clare Wood and Charles Beckman had been knocked out of the mixed doubles and my supply of tickets had stopped. Even if Clare had been able to carry on with the supply, she would not have been able to get me a ticket for either men's or women's final. I asked around and the only way I could get one was by purchasing one from a ticket tout and the price was prohibitive. So it was that I watched both finals on television in a bar a few doors down from my hotel.

However, I had managed to get onto Chatrier to see the semi-finals on the men's side where Jim Courier had made short work of Andre Agassi and Petr Korda had brought Henri Leconte's run to an end. In the final, it was all a bit straight forward again, as Courier pounded Korda into submission and beat him in straight sets too.

The women all worked much harder as both semi-finals went to three sets. The top four seeds had justified their seeding and come through to face each other. In the final, things went the distance as Seles finally won the trophy winning a fantastic match. Monica began all guns blazing and won the first set. Steffi fought back to take the second. Then, in a close third set, the games went on and on. Just as one player looked like they would get ahead, a mistake would surface and things would level up. Finally, Monica broke Steffi and served out the match for the title, 10-8 in the third set. It had been a final fitting for a Grand Slam.

In men's doubles, as in Rome, the team of Jacob Hlasek and Marc Rosset prevailed. In the women's doubles, Gigi Fernandez and Natasha Zvereva won the title beating the Spanish pair of Conchita Martinez and Arantxa Sanchez Vicario. In the mixed, my chosen team of Bryan Shelton and Lori McNeil had done really well advancing to the final. I had spent so much time watching them that I must have become a fixture at the side of the court. As Monica Seles would find out, there are all sorts of people including sadly, some bad ones, sitting in the stands, so most pros keep an understandable divide between their world and that of the fans. But at the start of one match, Lori McNeil saw me and gave me a nod of the head. I mirrored the greeting. It was all rather formal. After winning five matches, the sixth was a match too far as they lost in straight sets to, Todd Woodbridge and Arantxa Sanchez Vicario. The Spanish player had reached a semi-final in singles, lost in the final in the doubles but had now won the mixed. It had been quite a good two weeks' work for her.

Meeting Albert in Albert
Roland Garros was over and my first Slam had been ticked off the list. With Wimbledon only two weeks away, time was tight. I left Paris and boarded the train for a short visit to the site of the battle of Verdun, east of Paris (with its Douaumont Ossuary, a sobering place to visit) and then north, for the site of the battle of the Somme, both thought-provoking experiences, even though, by now, many years after the horrors of the Great War, the countryside had recovered and was back to its natural beauty. In Albert, I asked the hotel owner how I could get

around the large Somme battlefield and he organised a local man to drive me. So, one afternoon, I spent a delightful, few hours in the company of a man whose name matched that of the town he lived in, Albert. Originally from the UK, Albert Bridges was now in his seventies. After the Second World War was over, he didn't know what to do. Then, he saw an advertisement for jobs to help the Allied War Graves Commission in Northern France. He went over, enjoyed helping to create all the cemeteries that tourists then began flocking to see, loved the country, married a local girl and decided to stay, at one point, playing in goal for a local team in the French F.A. Cup. He knew the area really well and we got on well too. At the end of the afternoon, I asked him if I could pay him for his time. He refused my offer of payment point blank. Spontaneously, I suggested that at the very least, I wanted to contribute to his petrol costs. He was happy with this idea and I handed him some French Francs and he nodded his thanks with a smile. It had been a special afternoon.

Finally, I arrived in Calais and before long, was back in Dover on a train heading for London. As I arrived back in Wimbledon and dumped my bag in my flat, the first major leg of my trip and the experience of my first Grand Slam tournament was complete.

Chapter 5

Inter-City Epiphany

No time to rest

As I unpacked, I thought about the previous three months. I had completed everything I had planned to do; visited and stayed in twenty towns and cities in twelve countries; managed all the travelling; dealt with all the hotels and sight-seeing; and spent quality time at the Foro Italico and Roland Garros. Also, financially, I hadn't spent a fortune. Now, I could take stock and start my preparations for Wimbledon which was coming up very soon. But I had almost no time to rest. The tennis tour caravan had already arrived in the UK and although on the one hand, I could have taken off any time I wanted, on the other, I felt a commitment to keep going.

The time I'd spent travelling back through France had been spent at a small but necessary cost. Immediately after Roland Garros had finished, the very next day, build up tournaments for Wimbledon would be starting back in the UK in London and in Birmingham, ones I would have to miss. After my Great War battlefield visits to Verdun and the Somme, whistle-stop as they were, plus another day travelling across the Channel home, it was towards the end of the week and unless I had tickets for the show courts at both events for the final weekend, it was not worth me going. Also, although I was keen to keep moving with my tennis journey, I needed to prepare for the following week, the one before Wimbledon. This would be a busy one, where I had planned to go to the tournaments for the women in Eastbourne, the men in Manchester and then locally, over to Roehampton, where the Wimbledon qualifying events for men and women were taking place. As I travelled around the country on the train that week, I would arrive at an important decision.

Keeping tabs
On the men's side, in the week after Roland Garros, the Wimbledon build-up tournaments were the Stella Artois Championships in London and a grass-court event in Rosmalen. There was also an event in Florence on clay. The Dow Classic in Birmingham was the only tournament on the WTA Tour.

The men's tournament at Queen's had been around for a long time in one form or another going back to the late nineteenth century. It was originally called the London Athletic Club Tournament, changing its name to the Championship of London and in 1890, moving to Queen's which had been established in 1886. Originally, the club had been set up to offer multi-sports, including athletics, ice skating, tennis, rackets and real tennis. In 1895, it had even hosted a football international between England and Wales. Also, until 1922, it had been the home of Corinthian F.C. As the years had passed, the focus of the club, which catered for an upscale membership, oriented itself more towards racket sports, especially tennis. Dan Maskell had been a ball-boy and then one of the tennis coaches there in the early part of the twentieth century when he was a young man beginning his working life. Also, since the sixties, the club had been owned by the LTA whose headquarters were on the site, just inside the main entrance, until the decision was made to sell the club to new owners and move those headquarters to the National Tennis Centre at Roehampton in 2007. The tournament, in its current form, as a stop on the newly formed ATP Tour had been sponsored for a few years by a beer company. As many called the French Open, Roland Garros, many called this Wimbledon build-up event by the name of its sponsor, the Stella Artois.

The 1992 incarnation of the tournament was a World Series event, the lowest level of tournament on the ATP Tour in a system categorised by prize money and ranking point levels, a status which for Queen's would go up a level, years later in

2015. It may well be going up again soon, it has been reported in 2021. It was still a big tournament with a fifty-six man draw and although a third-tier event on the tour, it was still above Challenger and Satellite level events. Also, because of the tournament's proximity to Wimbledon in both geography and time, it had usually attracted a strong field. Back in 1982, Kyri and I had watched Jimmy Connors beat John McEnroe in the final. In fact, the most frequent winner has been Andy Murray and most of his appearances and wins had been during the time when he was at the top of the world rankings. In this 1992 version of the event, many of the top names, like Stefan Edberg, Pete Sampras, Boris Becker, Goran Ivanisevic and Ivan Lendl were all playing.

We were now in the grass court season and the seeds list reflected this with the likes of David Wheaton and one of my Italians from the Foro Italico, Gianluca Pozzi, making the list. Just as Italian players had been given wild cards in Rome and the French players had been awarded them in Paris, so the British players tended to be given wild cards for the Wimbledon build-up events, as well as the tournament itself. Here at Queen's, Jeremy Bates and Chris Wilkinson were given wild cards while Danny Sapsford had qualified.

As the tournament progressed, seeds fell with consistent regularity and only seventh seed, Brad Gilbert, surpassed his expected destination in the draw, reaching the semi-finals. Top seed, Stefan Edberg, lost to Japanese player, Shuzo Matsuoka, who had been the first player from Japan to win an ATP Tour event, in Auckland, 1991. But Shuzo ultimately lost to veteran performer, Wayne Ferreira, in the final. Wayne, who I would meet a few times in later years, had many highlights in a sixteen-year career as a pro, including fifteen titles in singles and eleven in doubles. He was Mr Consistency in Grand Slams, appearing in fifty-six consecutive Slams between the 1991 Australian Open and the 2004 US Open.

In the doubles, the winners were top doubles players, Swede, Anders Jarryd and our man from Down Under, John Fitzgerald. The players would now make their way to Manchester, to Halle in Germany, or to Roehampton for the Wimbledon qualifying event.

The first WTA tournament after Roland Garros was up in Birmingham at the Edgbaston Priory Club, a place I had played at once when visiting my friends from Vale de Lobo days, Michael and Rita Bunn, who lived up that way. Like Queen's in London, Edgbaston Priory had been an established venue for tennis in Birmingham. It was probably regarded as the premier club across the West Midlands. The club in its current incarnation was formed in 1964 with an amalgamation of two clubs. Before this, the Priory Lawn Tennis Club and the Edgbaston Cricket and Lawn Tennis Club operated separately, offering members various types of competitive play, often attracting players of international repute. After a fire at the Priory in 1963, the clubs merged. The tradition of quality play was upheld and after a refurbishment in 1992, developments have continued, like many other clubs, making the effort to offer more to members and guests alike as well as making the club even more attractive as a major tournament venue.

The club had always offered good grass courts and had a nice centre court named after Ann Jones, the former Wimbledon winner and member. The court had stands for major tour events like the Dow and a crowd of a few thousand could be accommodated. The women's event in 1992 had begun as the Edgbaston Classic a decade before and had always attracted a good set of players. Previous winners had included Billie Jean King, Pam Shriver, Claudia Kode-Kilsch and Martina Navratilova. According to the way the WTA Tour events were categorised, the Dow Classic was a Tier IV tournament which was one above the lowest level in the tour's structure and would be likely to attract a good draw. Like the Stella Artois, being so close to Wimbledon and offering good grass courts and facilities, the Dow would also attract higher-ranked players who might not usually sign up, based purely on the prize money and points on offer. Some would sign up because it was the only WTA event that week.

The tournament in 1992 was a fifty-six player draw with the top eight seeds receiving a bye into round two. The seeds included some well-known grass court players like Pam Shriver, Lori McNeil, Jo Durie, Brenda Schultz and Patty Fendick, although the American would fall in the first round, as would her compatriot, sixteenth seed, Katrina Adams. Of the British players, Jo Durie, Shirli-Ann Siddall and Amanda Grunfeld would advance to round two but Valda Lake, Sarah Loosemore and Clare Wood fell at the first hurdle. Jo Durie and Shirli-Ann Siddall then won their second-round matches, while Amanda Grunfeld lost to Gigi Fernandez. In the third round, it was the end for Shirli-Ann, beaten by top seed, Zina Garrison, who as a child back in Houston, was so keen to play that she had been the first at the courts as early as seven thirty in the morning when her coach, John Wilkerson opened up. The other seeds advanced to the quarter-finals other than Indonesian, Yayuk Basuki and Russian, Natasha Zvereva.

The seeds continued through to the semi-finals except for Lori McNeil, beaten by Australian, Jenny Byrne who went on to beat Jo Durie. Jenny had done really well to reach the final but the powerful Brenda Schulz, who had survived a tough second round match against another Australian, Kristine Radford, winning 11-9 in the third set, won in straight sets to take the title. In the doubles, the three British teams all lost in the first round, including Clare Wood, who was partnered by Belinda Borneo. The title was won by Lori McNeil and Rennae Stubbs. As well as reaching a singles ranking of No. 64 with two ITF titles, Rennae was outstanding in doubles, reaching No. 1 in the doubles rankings, winning seventy doubles titles in WTA and ITF events, a huge haul. She also won five Grand Slam titles in doubles and mixed as well.

The Dow Classic was over and the women would make their way to Eastbourne or to the Wimbledon qualifying event at Roehampton. As this first week of pre-Wimbledon tournament ended, I prepared for a busy following week where I'd be off travelling again, albeit this time, on day trips.

Thanks to the 8th Duke
I began my last week before Wimbledon with a trip down to the seaside. I did not have a car and in order to make a one-day trip worthwhile, I had to leave my flat really early on Monday morning. It was a lovely day. I walked to Wimbledon station, got a train into Clapham Junction, picked up a Brighton train going the other way and just under an hour later, pulled into the station that I knew so well, from living there in the mid-eighties. Then, I boarded another train which would take me eastwards, station by station, through the lovely East Sussex countryside along the coast to Eastbourne. I still arrived early enough to see the players practise before the matches began. I spent the day rotating between the centre court, the other main match courts and the numerous practice courts.

These were the famous grass courts which were not only used by the pros at tournaments like this but by the club members, by veterans, as part of major tournaments and also the county teams who played their five days of round-robin matches in their division at county week, another long-established part of British tennis, more formally known as the Inter-County Cup. The top six men's and women's teams in the country containing ex-professionals, those who aspired to be pros and a few who had given up hope and had settled for the top end of the amateur game, played their Group One fixtures against each other, a tie per day consisting of three, best of three set matches. Exhausting as that must have been, there was always time for fun in the evenings, taking part in regular antics, much of it alcohol induced. Steve Matthews, in younger days, was an aspiring young pro at the lower end of the hierarchy winning the mixed doubles with Amanda Brown at Beckenham one year in exalted company before a highly successful career in tennis coaching and club management. Steve was someone of much significance to my career path after this year of travel finished and he told me about one such ritual. In the swimming pool of the Grand Hotel where the teams stayed, there were some large mushroom-shaped structures fixed in the water at one end of the pool. Each year, on the Thursday evening before the final day's play, the men's teams had to nominate one player to dress up in women's clothing and walk across the pool using the mushrooms as stepping-stones but without falling off, a task made all the more difficult by the combination of growing fatigue after all those matches and all that booze in the evenings. Hence, Eastbourne became known, certainly within the upper echelons of the British tennis player community for one more thing other than quality tennis on carpet-like grass courts; 'walking the mushrooms' at County Week.

As with Queen's and Edgbaston Priory, Eastbourne was one of the original major club venues for tennis in the UK. Devonshire Park Lawn Tennis Club began life at around the same time as the All-England Lawn Tennis and Croquet Club, developed as a combined park and multi-sports ground, as part of bigger plans to develop Eastbourne itself. This expansion of the town took place through the second half of the nineteenth century, driven by one of the bastions of Victorian aristocracy, the Cavendish family, and specifically, the 8th Duke of Devonshire. Tennis gradually took over from both cricket and then football on the main field within the park where Devonshire Park F.C played before moving to the nearby Saffrons grounds. They became Eastbourne Town F.C. and I played there against them for Burgess Hill Town on Easter Monday in 1983 against the home team's reserve side during my last season playing football.

Also, a few years later, I would make a one-off trip back down to the cricket ground at the Saffrons to watch Sussex against Middlesex in a one-day game at a time when my dear friend, Bob Mitchell, was over from the US. Mitch was a tennis nut and one who had attended many US Championships at the West Side Tennis Club in his younger days (including the final between Tappy Larsen and Herbie Flam in 1950) and then US Opens at Flushing Meadows, later on. Mitch knew an awful lot about, surprise, surprise, US tennis, baseball (think about the campfire scene in the film *City Slickers* and the participants' knowledge, then increase it and keep going), but literally nothing about cricket. However, as a sports lover, he was keen to learn. He could not accompany me to Eastbourne that Sunday, so I went alone and it was when I was wandering around the boundary in the tea interval, I came across a book stall filled with a veritable library of assorted cricket books. After a minute or two of browsing, one title stood out, *How to Teach Americans Cricket*. Needless to say, a purchase was made for my tennis-nut, baseball-mad, sports-loving, new-to-cricket friend. At the end of his stay, after attending a Lord's one-day final where the terrifying Allan Donald bowled at a frightening pace, years later, not only would he inquire about the fortunes of the South African fast bowler but courtesy of the book I had bought him, the subject of the googly would also occasionally rear up during our trans-Atlantic conversations.

Anyway, back to this lovely park, located a few yards back from the Eastbourne seafront, tournament tennis had been played throughout Devonshire Park's history, initially as the South of England Championships, an event which attracted the best men and women from the UK and then became a tournament which players from abroad would attend. The origins of the 1992 tournament that I was now watching, were back in 1974, when the Eastbourne International began as the now open and increasingly professional sport started to organise itself. For most of the time, up to and after 1992, the professional pre-Wimbledon event was on the women's tour, although into the twenty-first century, a men's event has been held as the pre-Wimbledon programme of tournaments continued to be shuffled around as part of the ongoing evolution of the competitive structure of British tennis, especially in the pre-Wimbledon weeks. Previous winners at Eastbourne had included Virginia Wade, Chris Evert, Martina Navratilova, Tracey Austin and Helena Sukova. There had also been Davis Cup ties and Federation Cup matches played on the courts as well as tournaments for the professionals who back in the early days were mainly the coaches, Dan Maskell included, in the days before tennis went open.

In 1992, the Pilkington Glass Championships was a Tier II event which meant it sat below the Grand Slams and then tournaments like the Liptons on Key Biscayne in Florida, as it was then called, but two levels above the Dow Classic from the week before. In other words, it offered more ranking points for matches won and a bigger prize money purse to reward those winners. It was a sixty-four player draw and this week, the top seed was Martina Navratilova, still in the world's top five at this point in her long career. She would be searching for her eleventh title at Eastbourne, yes, her eleventh! Looking at the other seeds, there were a few who had played in Birmingham the week before, including winner, Brenda Schultz, although now, we had the additions of Mary Joe Fernandez, Jana Novotna, Helena Sukova, Kimiko Date, Natalie Medvedeva, Amy Frazier and Manon Bollegraf. Looking at the British players in the draw, again, there were some repeat appearances from Birmingham in Amanda Grunfeld, Shirli-Ann Siddall and Jo Durie. These three were supplemented by Monique Javer, and my former Southdown club mates, from just down the coast in Lewes, Sara Gomer and my Grand Slam buddy from Paris over the previous month, Clare Wood.

The first round saw five seeds depart, namely Manon Bollegraf, Zina Garrison, Amy Frazier, Brenda Schultz and Gigi

Fernandez. Two of the Brits, Shirli-Ann Siddall and Monique Javer drew each other, ensuring a British player would reach the second round but of course, at the expense of another. But it was in the second round that the biggest shock occurred when Martina Navratilova was knocked out by American, Linda Harvey Wild. At this point in her career, Harvey Wild was still developing and had been hovering just inside the top fifty. She had beaten top players before so this result was not a complete surprise but beating Martina at Eastbourne? It just wasn't done, was it? Well, it was, this time.

In the third round, the seeds held strong, although Natalie Medvedeva lost to Elena Brioukhovets. Of the Brits, Jo Durie also lost at this stage to Rennae Stubbs. Rennae kept going to face Ros Fairbank-Nideffer in the quarter-final and it was the South African who won the battle of the doubles specialists to come through to meet Navratilova's conqueror, Linda Harvey Wild, in one of the semi-finals. The young woman from Hartington Heights, Illinois, kept her good form going to reach one of her nine tour finals. In the other semi-final, Lori McNeil had come through to meet Mary Joe Fernandez who she beat in straight sets to reach another final.

In the doubles event, there was no Martina Navratilova-Pam Shriver team even though both were playing in the singles. They had broken up their partnership officially in 1989 after winning the Australian Open. However, after that, they did still play together occasionally, winning five more tour titles. The eight seeded pairs in a thirty-two pair event were strong with Jana Novotna and Larissa Savchenko-Neiland as top seeds. A pairing as experienced as Nicole Provis and Elizabeth Smylie were the eighth seeds, although they were knocked out in the second round by the Japanese pair of Kimiko Date and Maya Kidowaki. British interest was represented by Monique Javer and Valda Lake, Amanda Grunfeld and the third of my early eighties Southdown connections, Julie Salmon. Clare Wood played with Belinda

Borneo again. None of these home-country pairings reached the second round. Perhaps surprisingly, considering the number of seeded pairs I would watch get knocked out before reaching their predicted stage of the event in the months to come, the top four seeds advanced to the semi-finals.

The tournament at Eastbourne had always finished on a Saturday not a Sunday, probably to help the players, especially the top ones, who might appreciate a rest day should they reach the final, before the opening day at Wimbledon, where they might be required to play. For a few years now, both the men and women played on the first Monday, unlike in my childhood when the opening day was solely for men's matches and the first Tuesday saw the women's event begin.

However, through the week, there had been enough rain to disrupt the schedule sufficiently to mean that the final Saturday at Eastbourne began with the completion of the Linda Harvey Wild against Ros Fairbank-Nideffer semi-final before the winner faced Lori McNeil. In the doubles, the completion of one semi-final, Jana Novotna and Larissa Savchenko-Neiland against Arantxa Sanchez Vicario and Helena Sukova, was required and then, the whole of the second one, between Mary Joe Fernandez and Zina Garrison, and Gigi Fernandez and Natasha Zvereva before the final of that event. By the close of play, Lori McNeil had won the singles in straight sets, bringing Linda Harvey Wild's good week to an end, while Jana Novotna and Larissa Savchenko-Neiland had won the doubles, beating Mary Joe Fernandez and Zina Garrison, also in straight sets. With the tournament complete, the players and their entourages could move the WTA caravan up to Wimbledon which would start on the coming Monday, two days away.

On my day out at the coast back at the very start of the week, I began the return journey in the glow of an early evening summer's day coming to an end. But it would be straight to bed as another early start beckoned with another long day of inter-city train travel on the cards.

Wimbledon of the North
Taking in the Manchester tournament in one day in a way that would make it worthwhile, meant that I had to get up even earlier than the day before when I went to Eastbourne. So, a few hours after returning back from the coast, I was up early again. Another walk to the underground, a black coffee bought from one of the new coffee shops that were opening up more and more everywhere, another train into London, this time, all the way in and across to Euston and then an inter-city service, this time, to Manchester. I couldn't take an inter-city train without singing a little ditty to myself. This was the tag line of a major advertising campaign of television commercials for British Rail back in the late seventies, *This is the Age of the Train*, produced and broadcast when I was in the messenger job in the film production company in London's Soho. As well as any odd jobs that needed doing, all I did was ferry versions of television commercials in various stages of development either in film cans or video boxes to and from the advertising agencies who were commissioning the company I worked for to either shoot the commercials or complete the post-production editing of them.

One of those commercials was the new British Rail campaign to promote its inter-city services. Usually, all that was required of me was to leave the film can or videotape box with the receptionist and check to see if there was anything to return to my colleagues back at the studios. But on one occasion, arriving at Allen, Brady and Marsh, one of the industry's top agencies, I was instructed to go through to the offices where I handed the video directly to the television producer working on the campaign. Turning to go, the man asked me to hang on while he played the commercial. I did so but became a bit perplexed and even lost for words when he asked me what I thought of the powerful engine pulling its carriages on the Inter-City 125 service across the screen as the advertisement finished with the tag line that years later, I could not get out of my head. I replied with some sort of inane comment. At that point, unlike a few years later, when I had progressed up the marketing ladder for American Express and become more switched on in evaluating communications developed by advertising agencies, I had no idea how to appraise, even half intelligently, the advert he had just played.

Over a decade later, as the countryside sped by, memories of my exchange in the offices of ABM, as the agency was known, receded. ABM had won the business from British Rail by keeping the chairman and his team waiting in a dirty waiting room in a clever, if risky ruse to show the executives the type of experience that they were giving their passengers. Hopefully, this demonstration would prove that the agency understood the problem and were well-placed to produce an advertising-based solution. After just over two hours, I was on a bus that dropped me in West Didsbury, South Manchester, a short walk from the Northern Lawn Tennis Club. This was where the Direct Line Insurance Manchester Open, one of the stops that week on the ATP Tour, was taking place, the other being in Genoa for the clay-courters.

It was around midday on a beautiful sunny day and I reckoned I could stay for about six hours before starting the return journey. As I paid for my ticket and entered the club, again, just like the day before down in Eastbourne, I was walking into British tennis history. The Northern Lawn Tennis Club had been founded back in 1881, although not on this site but a few miles further west, at Old Trafford. In 1909, the club re-located to its current site and began to expand.

From those early days, a tournament had been established with the thought that it could become the Wimbledon of the North. The Northern Lawn Tennis Championships had been successful and lasted many decades into the twentieth century. In fact, in the early part of that century before the ITLF became established, the tournament was seen as being one of the top tournaments in the sport along with the Irish Championships, Wimbledon and the US National Championships, the four events effectively making up an early incarnation of a Grand Slam, although that concept and term was yet to be born. In 1990, the tournament had become an ATP World Series event and this was the third time it had been held. Later, in 1995, after the ATP had switched its event to Nottingham, a tournament remained at the club and was renamed the Manchester Challenger, at the next tier down just below the ATP Tour main circuit. It was held through to 2009 and then again, in 2015 and 2016. In 2017, the event changed to a women's tournament on the ITF circuit.

The 1992 version was a thirty-two player singles draw and a sixteen team doubles draw. Looking at the seeds for the singles, number one was Alexander Volkov, followed by two Americans, the Brad Gilbert and David Wheaton, two players who, in 1990 and 1991 respectively, reached the final of an event called the Grand Slam Cup. Since the game had gone open in 1968, the running of it had never been straight forward and this competition had been created by the Grand Slam Committee, under the auspices of the ITF, who retained overall control of the Grand Slams after the ATP took over the running of the men's tour in 1990, thereby creating the ATP Tour. The Grand Slam Cup was for the players who had won the most points for doing well in that year's Grand Slam tournaments. The prize money was enormous and although Gilbert lost to Pete Sampras, his earnings for the week were substantial. For David Wheaton, who beat Michael Chang, the prize awaiting him was two million dollars. The money for each round was significant too. The fourth seed in Manchester was Amos Mansdorf, the fifth was American, Malivai Washington and then came the two Russians, Andrei Cherkasov and Andrei Chesnakov with one of my Italians from Rome, Omar Camporese, completing the list.

Only Gilbert, Wheaton and Washington survived the first round. The British representatives were Jeremy Bates and Chris

Wilkinson. The second round or last sixteen actually included six Americans with Jeff Tarango, Paul Annacone and Todd Witsken joining their countrymen seeds. There were also two Australians, Wally Masur and Simon Youl, almost taking things back to years gone by on the tour when players from the US and Australia dominated the game.

Official, agent, or coach?
It was as I was watching Jeremy Bates play his match that my thoughts turned to other things, specifically what job I would do when all these travels were over. The reason my mind shifted onto this subject was the umpire, who looked about my age and even, a bit like me. Suddenly, I thought about becoming a tour official. I knew that the days of John McEnroe screaming at line judges, umpires and referees, as he had done at Wimbledon, were a rarity now, due mainly to the authorities responding to the pleas for better performance from its officials. Gone were the days where the tournaments relied only on volunteers to complete the on-court officiating. The ATP and WTA Tours needed a more professional delivery of such an important aspect of the sport. Now, officiating was a job, full time for some at the top levels, with training and tests helping the men and women who chose this path to progress. The only problem with this idea for me was that I just couldn't see myself as an official, for all sorts of reasons. Then, my thoughts drifted to other jobs in tennis as I sat in the sunshine.

The question of what job to do when this trip was over had been on my mind. I wasn't worried about it. But once I'd started the thought process, although I concentrated on making the most of where I was at any given moment, the topic never went away, only retreating into the back of my thoughts until I was ready to bring it back out again. While travelling around Europe, there were many hours to pass between the cities and on more than one occasion, I had written a list of options to pursue. These had included a wide range of possibilities like working in the environment or maybe, even a UK distributor for some fantastic plant-based food products I had consumed when living down in Sydney, ones I knew were not available in the UK. How that would work, I had no idea. I even thought of getting involved in politics, the subject of my degree, not necessarily for any political party but in some generic role for one of the organisations and companies doing all sorts of things with regard to the political process. Perhaps I could get a job working on a major issue like human rights with an organisation like Amnesty International. At this point, corporate jobs like I had just held were not on any of the lists I produced. However, the problem with all these ideas was that none of them really motivated me. They all interested me to varying degrees but in practical terms, where were the actual jobs I could search for and what work would I actually do?

Thinking again about my mum's encouragement to get involved in things you loved, a new penny dropped as Bates won the first set and I debated and then rejected the option of officiating. A new thought came to mind: I should start looking at tennis. Here I was, getting up at all hours of the morning to travel around the country, let alone the continent, to be involved with a sport I loved. Why not get involved in the thing I was passionate about but in a working role?

Later on, as I sped back down to London on another Inter-City 125, I started writing a new job list which only included jobs from the world of tennis with such titles as agent, manager, tournament organiser, administrator, journalist, commentator, equipment or clothing representative and finally, coach. The more I looked at the list, some of the jobs looked interesting, but I faced the same problem as with the other non-tennis options which was that I didn't really have any idea about what you actually did in any of them other than a very general one-line summary. I did have an idea what the marketing jobs, where relevant, might be, but my thinking was taking me away from a direct repeat of what I had been doing at American Express.

The only option where that wasn't the case was in being a coach. Not only had I spent a lot of time around coaches, usually paying them to teach me the game, but my work with American Express over the previous decade had involved people development, especially as I became a manager and then a director. The company even structured the appraisal and bonus systems on how well your staff had performed, not just you personally, requiring you to work on what is now called performance coaching of your staff. I had also been seconded to the European training department to help run business presentation courses, on one occasion, at very short notice, actually filling in for one of the course presenters who couldn't make it (the first trip to Rome mentioned earlier above). This meant that I helped to run the three-day course with a co-presenter as opposed to just chipping in here and there. Finally, in a very loose, unqualified way, as my interest in playing tennis had developed, I had often helped friends giving them tips and I had always really enjoyed that process. I still didn't know much about the day-to-day job role of a coach but I knew that there were all sorts of different jobs in clubs, parks, schools and then up to and onto the pro tours. But at this point, my ignorance on all of this didn't matter. The idea of becoming a coach sounded a really good one and I felt charged up enough to act on it. By the time I stepped onto the platform at Euston, my decision had been made. The following year, after my Grand Slam travels were over, my mind was set - I would become a tennis coach. Then, an incident shifted my thoughts away from future jobs.

Another huge bag
As I walked down the platform at Euston, I took a quick look behind me. I must have had some sort of sixth sense because about twenty yards back was a blond guy in tennis shirt, track

suit top and jeans with a huge, branded tennis bag bursting at the seams. In fact, he looked a bit like I must have looked as I walked down the platforms of all those European railway stations. Who was it? None other than Byron Talbot, the player I had watched in Rome and Paris with his doubles partner, Brad Pearce. I did a double take and when I had confirmed to myself that yes, this was Byron, I waited for him, began walking in step with him down the platform and explained who I was and how I'd become his number one fan. He laughed and took it all in without missing a beat and I asked him how the tournament had gone. He had just been knocked out of the doubles in which he had partnered the British player, Neil Broad, who was originally from Byron's home country, South Africa. They had lost to a partnership of British player Andrew Castle and the Italian, who I pointed out to Byron I had watched in Rome, Gianluca Pozzi.

Byron seemed happy to walk and talk and it transpired that he too was heading back towards Wimbledon to the place that he was staying at through the tournament in which he was playing doubles, again with Brad Pearce. So it was that we spent an enjoyable time on the underground, working our way back across town towards SW19. Byron got out just before Wimbledon and I wished him the best of luck for the upcoming tournament and the rest of the year ahead. What a coincidence and a pleasant one at that.

As the week in West Didsbury unfolded, by the time of Saturday's semi-finals, only Mal Washington of the American contingent remained. He beat Mexican, Luis-Enrique Hererra, to advance to the final where he would meet Dutchman, Jacco Eltingh, who beat Wally Masur in his semi-final. The title went to the man from the Netherlands who won in straight sets.

Looking back later, I wondered if Jacco had been feeling good that week. After calling a halt to his fine career, in which he won four singles titles and fifty doubles titles including a Career Grand Slam with six trophies, when he appeared in a charity event run by my good friend, Howard Rogg, when Howard asked him what the best thing was about being retired, Jacco thought for a moment and then replied, "Getting up in the morning without anything hurting!" a story, I think which says much about life as a pro and the demands it makes just on the body. In the doubles, the team of Patrick Galbraith, a future president of the USTA (United States Tennis Association) and Australian, David Macpherson, beat Jeremy Bates and another Aussie, Laurie Warder, who would also figure significantly in a future Slam, later in my trip.

Three matches away
Giving in to travel fatigue, I rested for a day and then I was off again, this time just down the road to Roehampton in South-West London. Grand Slam tournaments are similar to every other tour event in that prior to the official start date, a qualifying competition takes place to allow a few players whose rankings are lower than the cut-off for direct entry, a chance to play their way into the tournament. Wimbledon is no different from the other Slams in that the organisers, in this case, the AELTC, want to begin the first-round matches on pristine surfaces. The problem with Wimbledon is that its surface is grass. Grass courts will not look pristine if a qualifying event has been played on them beforehand. So, that event has to take place elsewhere, thereby protecting the grass courts that will be used for the main draw. In 2020, plans were released to expand the current site next door onto the golf course that the AELTC has purchased and part of that extension would be to create many more courts enabling the qualifying matches to take place on site but not on the actual courts used for the tournament. Until that extension has taken place, the qualifying event will continue to take place where it has been staged since 1925 and where I was headed back in 1992; namely, the grass courts at the Bank of England Sports

Ground, Roehampton, the location of my London Schools football summer camp week back in 1971.

While the facility has always been a good one for its members, one where various different sports had been played, as a venue for a Grand Slam tournament qualifying event, it has always been seen by many as leaving a bit to be desired. This is because, other than the courts themselves, which have rarely been thought to be a problem, the other facilities for players, officials and spectators, were a bit limited. The players have marquees housing them as they wait for their matches and there are very limited changing facilities. There are very few seats for spectators who, until recent times, could enter and watch for free. Even on the courts, there were umpires but skeletal crews of line judges and never quite enough ball boys and girls, which meant that like many lower-level events on the bottom tiers of the tour, players could find themselves picking up their own balls. The whole experience seemed to be in direct contrast to the opulent, upscale facilities and services on offer should they get through the competition and actually qualify for the main draw. Back in 1992, the prize money was very small too, although that has been increased quite significantly since.

For the men, in singles, the way it worked was that if you could win three matches, the first two rounds best of three sets, the third round, best of five sets, you would be allocated one of the sixteen places in the main draw of the tournament reserved for you. In addition, if you reached the third round of qualifying which was called, the qualifying round, but lost, if players already in the main draw withdrew for any reason, you had a chance of entering the draw as a lucky loser, based on your ranking, with the highest ranked going in first. For the women, the same system applied although in 1992, while the main draw was one-hundred and twenty-eight players, the qualifying event was sixty-four players (half the size of the men's) and there were only eight main draw qualifying places.

The lucky loser system was the same too. Today, all the numbers match between men and women, as does prize money. Wild cards would be added to the main draw in the same way for men and women. In some ways, these qualifying events summed up the brutal nature of tennis competition and Grand Slam prestige. Was it worse to lose easily in the first round of qualifying or get through to the third, qualifying round and possibly, in a very long, tiebreak-free set, lose at the last gasp, just as the main draw beckoned? It was still probably, the latter as at least, you might get into the main draw as aa lucky loser. When it began, you were three wins away from that main draw and a significant pay out, even if you lost in the first round of the tournament proper.

To get to Roehampton by train from Wimbledon, I went back in towards London to Clapham Junction and picked up another train heading west, getting off at Barnes. Then, there was a walk along Priory Lane to the grounds as I had done back in 1971. I spent a few hours wandering around, although watching was a bit difficult due to lack of space and seats. It was still a nice experience to be able to wander amongst all the players in an informal way, the likes of which was impossible once Wimbledon began. But my relaxed state was the complete opposite to most of these players as they had to endure the challenges of the short tournament where to get through the three matches would mean so much.

Tennis heartbreak time
In the men's event, which was now on the qualifying round stage, there had been thirty-two seeds including names like John Fitzgerald and a young Greg Rusedski, playing under the Canadian flag. Only thirteen of these seeds made it through to the final day. Ten British players were involved, including some wild cards and a young man called Mark Schofield who I would meet in a few weeks' time, a bit further north. Tim Henman was involved in the days when he was low in the

rankings and just another aspiring, young British player. He was drawn against another Brit, the more experienced Colin Beecher who won their match in straight sets. Along with Beecher, David Ison, Paul Hand and Miles Maclagan all reached the second round, although none of them advanced any further. Of the sixteen players who qualified, top seed, John Fitzgerald was one, as were six Americans and Greg Rusedski. Possibly, the worst heartache was felt by another American, Mike Bauer, who lost 11-13 in a fifth set to Slovakian, Branislav Stankovic.

On the women's side, there had been sixteen seeds from a mix of countries including four Australians and two each from Japan, including top seed, Akiko Kijimuta, Germany and the US with the interestingly named Peanut Harper. Seven seeds would ultimately go through to the main draw including two, Tami Whitlinger and Jo-Anne Faul, as lucky losers. There were six British players in the draw, including Julie Salmon from my Southdown days, who lost in a third set to Elizabeth Smylie, a wild card and number five seed. Two of the Brits, Julie Pullin and Caroline Billingham, both won a match and made it to the second round but advanced no further. Including the two lucky losers amongst the ten women who went through, there were two Americans, two from the Netherlands, two from Germany, two from Australian, an Argentinian and a Japanese player, although Rika Hiraki not Akiko Kijimuta. It looked like Hiraki inflicted the biggest heartbreak by beating Swedish player, Maria Strandlund, 9-7 in the third set of their qualifying round match.

Arriving home, I was able to take a few days off over the weekend preparing for Monday when Wimbledon would begin. My excitement really began to build as the hours ticked by.

Chapter 6

Joining the Queue in SW19

The view from the Church
It was Monday morning. I was up early again, although this time, not to catch a train, but to walk to the All-England Club, just under two miles away from my flat. Once there, I would take my place in the queue for a ticket to start my two weeks of spectating at the oldest and most prized of the Grand Slams, Wimbledon. Different people called the tournament different names. On a more formal basis, these have included both the club itself and the media using the club's name in the title, calling the tournament, the All-England Lawn Tennis Championships and also, simply, 'The Championships'. Most people would know what you mean if you just said, Wimbledon. On a more casual, unofficial basis, I had heard it referred to as 'Wimbers' and 'Wimby'. There were also different names for the tournament with different pronunciations dependent on where in the world people came from. Different strokes, for different folks applied off, as well as on the court, it seemed.

One of my favourite views of the large site on which this tournament was played was where I would start my wait in the queue on this first morning. Many people who watch the tennis on television may be aware of the church which is at the top of one of the panoramic views across the courts often shown as broadcasts are wrapped up. Just around from that church, St Mary's, in which tennis great, Lew Hoad, married his wife, Jenny, is where the queue sneaked down on the right side of Church Road tracking one side of the site towards Southfields. It was just there that I joined the back of all the other fans with their bags and coats, in case of rain, their newspapers and some with an occasional garden chair to make the wait more comfortable (such furniture could be deposited in lockers once inside). From this elevated position, you could look back at the site the other way from that television view, across the area where tents and marquees used for corporate entertaining were set up, covering the clay courts. Next, came the majority of the outside courts in three lines working their way towards the huge Centre Court where I had been captivated back in 1968. The old Court No. 1 was to the left. On the far side of the two big show courts, but out of sight from the queue, were more outside courts and Aorangi Park which consisted of the practice courts.

As I stood in the queue on a lovely day, I knew that the anticipation and excitement that I was experiencing was being felt by thousands of others both here at the All-England Club but also at home, like my mum used to experience. Many other fans, whether all-year-round ones or just two-week Wimbledon ones, were getting ready to begin their fortnight of watching the tennis on the television. The biggest and most prestigious tournament in the sport was about to begin.

By all accounts, this type of interest and excitement had been felt almost from the first time the tournament was held at Worple Road in 1877. For years, ticket availability had been split between those allocated to the All-England Club's small, elite membership; debenture holders whose investment in their tickets allowed them show court seats and certain privileges; those who entered the ballot either through their tennis clubs or through the post; and finally, on a first-come-first-served basis for those willing to stand in the queue as I was that morning. You would be assured the minimum of a ground pass for access to the outside courts, as long as you were within the daily capacity limits. If you weren't, you could continue to wait until people came back out when the gates would be open again, although that could be hours away. Disappointed no doubt, you could also turn around and go home. For a small number of fans right at the front of the queue, they would be able to buy a ticket to Centre Court, or, if there was one still available, for Court No. 1 or Court No. 2 from a small quota that was retained each day. There was also a part of the queue where the really hard-core fans were situated, the ones you would usually see on the television, who would effectively camp out for the duration of the tournament in order that they could be the first into the ground on finals day, assured a ticket for either the women's final on the second Saturday, or the men's final, on the last day of the tournament.

From croquet to Sphairistike
Since the early days, back in the late 1870s, the development of the All-England Club and its major tournament had gone hand in hand. The first incarnation of the club was one which played croquet. Its first name was the All-England Croquet Club. But then, the new game of lawn tennis, originally called Sphairistike, packaged and sold in a large box, became popular and the club was renamed the All-England Croquet and Lawn Tennis Club and after that, after another switch of words, the All-England Lawn Tennis and Croquet Club. In fact, the word croquet was then dropped although restored in 1899. The current incarnation of the club has a slightly different structure with a separate entity, the AELTC which is a wholly owned subsidiary that runs the tournament, different for various operational, financial and legal reasons. This means that the running of the club itself is kept distinct from the running of 'The Championships'.

The first tournament had twenty-two men and a few hundred spectators watching the tennis at the courts officially located at Nursery Road but known to most as Worple Road, off which Nursery Road sits. This was the site at the end of the garden of my flat. As the years passed, the other events were added so that by the start of the Great War, there were singles and doubles for men and women as well as mixed doubles.

After the First World War, interest in the tournament grew and it became clear that the Worple Road site was too small. Not only were there more events but the demand for larger draw sizes had to be met. In 1920, the draw in the men's singles was increased to today's size of one hundred and twenty-eight for the first time. The club purchased land on Church Road, a short distance away on the other side of Wimbledon, where the tournament is played today. The Championships moved there in 1922. Through the twentieth century, the site remained pretty consistent in size and layout, although in 1967, just before my first visit, Aorangi Park was purchased to enable more spectator facilities and practice courts to be constructed. Nothing stays still and currently, around a century after the move from Worple Road, more land has been bought on the other side of Church Road and the grounds will be extended again over the next decade, allowing the qualifying events to be played on site and more spectators allowed in.

Initially, the tournament catered for the best players of the new sport in the UK. Bit by bit, as the game spread internationally, so did the nationalities of the players. With a range of clubs like the ones I've talked about in the previous chapter, along with many others, offering quality tournament tennis across the summer and especially in the build up to Wimbledon, there was good reason for players from the US, Europe and as far away as Australasia, in the days before air travel, to make the trip to England by boat and stay a while, taking in the European clay court tournaments and then the grass court events both before and after Wimbledon.

After the Second World War, the tournament increased in popularity, established not only as the top tournament in the tennis world but also in London's programme of social, sporting events where everyone who was anyone sought to be seen. At the time of my 1992 trip, although Wimbledon was changing gradually, it was still steeped in tradition and it was the club's mission to maintain that tradition while modernising things along the way. Back in 1967, it had been Herman David, the chairman of the club, who had led his fellow club members and others in the British tennis establishment to move the game towards becoming open to both professionals and amateurs, something unheard of beforehand. Wimbledon was not the first open tournament – the British Hard-Court Championships down at Bournemouth in April 1968 had fulfilled that role – but it was the driving force behind the change.

The Championships survived controversy including the 1972 absence of WCT professionals and a players' strike in 1973 by the newly formed ATP. But most change happened slowly in response to a sort of unsaid competition between the Grand Slam venues as they all developed. You always felt change only arrived after extremely careful consideration that new approaches would not spoil what had made the tournament so special in the first place. So, as you walked through the gates for a day at Wimbledon, you were walking into a fascinating mix of tradition and gradual modernisation. In fact, quite dramatic change will take place over the next decade. But in 1992, almost reassuringly, the feel of things was comfortably predictable as I began my two weeks of spectating.

There are a huge number of statistics relating to the tournament's history. Books have been written focusing on all of these achievements by numerous players from way back in 1877 to the present day. In the pre-open days, William Renshaw and Helen Wills won the most singles titles. In the post open era, Roger Federer and Martina Navratilova hold the most. Boris Becker and Lottie Dodd were the youngest winners and Roger Federer (with one-hundred and one) and Martina Navratilova (with one-hundred and twenty), had won most singles matches.

A combination of characteristics

As I would discover on my travels, each Grand Slam had developed its own characteristics, almost like its own personality or, dare I use my old marketing-speak, its brand; the combination of rational and emotional features and benefits which everyone involved would experience to one degree or another. As far as Wimbledon's characteristics were concerned, there seemed to be a combination of these, certainly for all the time I have been going to the tournament and probably for much longer than that. Although these memories are about the tournament as it was in 1992, while there have been some changes since then, the overall experience is very similar nearly thirty years later.

One thing you could always expect on a day at Wimbledon was a positive atmosphere. Everyone always appeared to be having a pleasant time. The tournament was a bastion of what might be called middle-class conventions, behaviour and decorum. Everyone was polite. Despite the size of the event, there was an air of the weekend afternoon garden party atmosphere which must have prevailed at many of the early Victorian tennis clubs where club afternoons were set up as a way for young men and women to meet while playing a bit of tennis. Indeed, a recent development plan for the grounds used the expression, 'Tennis in an English garden' to summarise the aims of the re-development proposals. In addition, the daily experience was imbued with the acceptance and practice of various comfortable traditions, especially with regard to food and drink. In mid-summer, if you said to someone in the UK, that we were about to begin two weeks of strawberries and cream, they would probably know to what you were referring.

As part of this nice, pleasant atmosphere, was a feeling of organisation. Despite the huge crowds, or in some weird way because of them, everyone followed the instructions from signs and stewards. People always seemed to know where to go and what to do. If they didn't, they were totally accepting of instructions they were given. This feeling of certainty was a function of the superb organisation of the tournament both on and off the courts. Willingly, people did as they were told because if nothing else, one way or another, just about everyone got what they wanted out of a day at Wimbledon, whether it was a bowl of strawberries and cream, a glass of Pimm's or a sight of top players performing their craft on beautifully manicured grass courts, or even a close look at their favourite star as they were accompanied through the grounds on their way to a match or maybe to the practice courts.

Acknowledgement of the status quo was always the case at Wimbledon. People seemed to accept their place and what behaviour was required of them both before and after they stepped through the entrance gates. Whatever may have been going on politically, economically, socially or culturally outside the tournament, there never seemed to be an ounce of conflict during the fortnight and even with the huge crowds, the heat and the consumption of Pimm's and other alcohol, I doubt that there have ever been any fights or scuffles at Wimbledon, the likes of which have been seen at just about every other major sport at one time or another. People behaved themselves.

Pleasant imagery could always be expected at the All-England Club. From a visual perspective, what hit you when inside the gates, was a mass of green beauty, tinged with purple, a combination reflecting the club's colours, creating a massive self-branding of the site with an interesting mixture of the lovely grass courts and their satisfying look, especially in the early days of the first week combined with old and new buildings but all with that Wimbledon look which since my first visit in 1968, had been maintained despite, bit by bit, what was there in the late sixties gradually morphing into something much newer in terms of form and function. This colour imagery had increasingly been re-enforced by the stewards all wearing the green and purple club ties and many of the thirty-thousand-plus people inside the grounds each day, either carrying something in the club's colours or wearing a piece of clothing purchased from the large club shop or outside the grounds from numerous people touting various products in the colours of the All-England Club. In this way, people became willing advocates of the Wimbledon brand and its promotion, for the day.

Massive interest was another integral aspect of the Wimbledon fortnight. From its early days, the public interest in the tournament started to build. By the time the tournament moved to its current site, large crowds were the norm. Even when the number of big matches reduced as the singles events came down to their last few rounds, with the show courts usually still being full to capacity, there would always be over twenty-five thousand people in the grounds. It was true that not everyone was a hardcore tennis fan. But regardless of the number of official corporate guests, a segment of the attending crowd that some had complained about but which was always less, as a share of the total, than people perceived, you would always be amongst a broad continuum of fans ranging from tennis nuts and afficionados at one end to those who might not even like sport, let alone tennis but go because it was a social event and a thing, if not *the* thing to do, in mid-summer. These enormous crowds on-site were part of a massive wider interest created and catered for by the BBC's coverage at home and numerous other television channels from all over the world, pumping the matches on the grass courts to homes literally worldwide, either live or in packaged highlight programmes. This massive publicity was fuelled by the BBC's long-established commitment to broadcast the tournament, something which had been done initially on the radio, then when it developed, on television and then, more recently in the digital age, through every available medium.

Perhaps the final part of the Wimbledon brand was the court surface. From 1988 when the Australian Open changed to hard courts, the tournament remained as the only Slam to be played on grass. Certainly, until just after my 1992 trip, the serve-volley nature of grass-court tennis had been an integral part of the sights and sounds of Wimbledon. From just after the start of the new millennium onwards, this factor changed as a combination of court construction and racket and string technology began to equalise the balance of power between server and returner, thereby sounding the death-knell to serve-volley tennis and turning matches into grass court versions of matches played on hard courts or on clay. A different kind of grass, if not slowing the courts down, certainly made the bounce more consistent, and the ever-increasing power of modern rackets and strings, enabled players to attack, especially on return of serve and when hitting passing shots, where previously, playing with wooden rackets, they could rarely attack from these situations, and if they did, they did so not very robustly. Quite simply, players stopped serving and volleying, including Roger Federer.

These changes began to homogenise the type of tennis played, making it closer to what was on offer at the other Slams which had their own hard or clay surfaces. Certainly, on the men's side, prior to these developments, grass-court tennis both to play and watch seemed fundamentally different, with points and match lengths much shorter than other surfaces with the tennis often lacking the craft or nuance needed to create victories on hard and especially clay courts. Unless, of course, the match was being played by a few select players who knew how to do things differently, moving their opponents around with a variety of slices, dinks and lobs, like Fabrice Santoro did, as opposed to a relentless offering of hard serve followed by a crunching volley to win the point.

A final point on the grass is that with Wimbledon, there seemed to be an unsaid acceptance that the tournament would just not be the same if the court surface was anything other than grass. This feeling may have been voiced about the

Australian Open and the US Open both of which historically, had been played on grass but with those two Slams, the change to hard courts was seen as the way to go and if anything, although other factors have been involved, the popularity and success of those two championships has, if anything, increased since the change was made.

Down from Halifax
At just after eleven o'clock on day one, I was inside the grounds. As a result of being high enough up in the queue, by the time I was paying my money, there were still some Court No. 2 tickets available and I bought one without hesitation. After entering the grounds, I had a quick walk about. Everything looked clean, new and freshly painted. The courts, some of which had players practising on them, looked a sharp green colour contrasting with the clean white lines marking them out. After this, I decided to get a cup of coffee in the refreshment area underneath the east side of the Centre Court. I had bought a programme. Produced daily, these were now much thicker than the ones mum used to bring back for me. With those old ones, the only colour was on the front cover, framing a black and white photograph of one of the top players of the day with possibly some more colour in the product advertisements inside. From 1977, a fresh approach had been unleashed. Now, over a decade later, the programme was a thick tome and nearly all in colour. There was all the basic information you would expect from such a publication but now, there were many more features and articles on the top players, aspects of Wimbledon's development as well as the lists of winners from previous years, competing players and the day's order of play.

I sat relaxing at a table and I took some time to review the matches I could expect to see from my seat on Court No. 2. There was a men's singles between Alexander Volkov and Spain's Emilio Sanchez, Arantxa and Javier's brother; another men's match between Stefan Edberg and American, Steve Bryan; a women's match between the female Sanchez, Arantxa, against Georgia's Leila Meskhi; and finally, the almost ubiquitous Aussie, John Fitzgerald against the ubiquitous Grand Slam attendee, Wayne Ferreira.

As I took my seat high up on the side of Court No. 2, what better example of British people's love of an outing could be found than the two women sitting next to me. They had always wanted to come to the tennis and were fulfilling this long-held dream. They too, like me, had got up early, really early, but although they could stay for all the afternoon, they had a cut-off point after which they had to leave. The reason was that they had to get back up to King's Cross station to get their train back to Halifax in West Yorkshire. This was some commitment but their excitement at having made it down, even for a few hours, was infectious. What they had done was like my trip up to Manchester a few days before but in reverse.

I spent most of the day enjoying the view from my seat, the matches and Edberg's first volley. How did he get from the baseline almost up to the net to play the shot when most of the other players barely made it to the 'T' junction? His athleticism was amazing. I did, however, take time out to wander over to Court No. 4, where Clare Wood was playing her first-round match against Ukrainian, Natalie Medvedeva,

Seeds, nationalities and early rounds
As the second Grand Slam of my year began, the singles seedings were very similar to how they looked in Paris for the French Open just a few weeks before.

In the men's list, there were three changes with Aaron Krickstein, Jacob Hlasek and Carlos Costa dropping out and Boris Becker, Wayne Ferreira and David Wheaton coming in. Jim Courier was the first seed and Andre Agassi was down at number twelve.

By now, after watching a few tournaments, I felt a bit more knowledgeable about some players who before my trip, I'd read about in *Tennis* magazine but never seen play. Now, I had seen them in action, so I decided to use my growing knowledge to help decide which matches to watch as the hours and days went by. Of course, on the other hand, there was nothing wrong with watching without a plan and just moving freely from court to court but I found that I enjoyed adding that extra bit of significance to what I was watching. In simple terms, with these new associations with players, I not only watched them; I began routing for them.

There were six of my Italian players from Rome but not one of them made the second round. As in Paris, there was a large French contingent although Fabrice Santoro was absent. Half of them won through to the second round. As it was Wimbledon, the committee always awarded most of the available wild cards to British players and of the seven players here, six were wild cards with only Jeremy Bates gaining entry automatically as a result of his ranking. Like the days of my childhood, there were quite a few Australians and Americans. Of the nine Australians, six made it into the second round, including Pat Cash who had been awarded a wild card. Of the twenty-five players from the US, twelve made it through to round two. Already, this number of Americans in the draw was reducing as other countries around the world in Asia and Eastern Europe, were becoming stronger from a tennis perspective. A decade before, there had been over forty Americans in the first round of the singles. Two early casualties were my veteran picks from Paris. Jimmy Connors was beaten by Mexican, Louis-Enrique Herrera and Kevin Curren, lost to Lori McNeil's mixed doubles partner, Bryan Shelton, 9-7 in a fifth set. Ronald Agenor was not in the draw. Jaime Yzaga got through to round two, as did Amos Mansdorf and also, Nicklas Kulti, although all would lose there. Like the

Americans, the number of Swedish players in the draw was gradually reducing from the highs of the eighties.

Other second round highlights to note were some of the longer matches. In fifth sets, Jacob Hlasek beat Petr Korda 16-14; John McEnroe brought Pat Cash's tournament to an end, 6-2; Guy Forget beat Anders Jarryd 10-8; Boris Becker beat Martin Damm 6-3, and qualifier, Christian Saceanu beat Cedric Pioline 7-5. Jeremy Bates beat Emilio Sanchez and with Sandon Stolle's win over Chris Wilkinson and Marc Rosset's defeat of Mark Petchey, Bates was left as the sole British interest in the men's singles.

In the women's list of seeds, there were also three changes from Roland Garros. In came Martina Navratilova, Zina Garrison and Austria's Judith Wiesner. Out went Mary Pierce (and her dad), Leila Meskhi and Sabine Appelmans. The top three seeds of Monica Seles, Steffi Graf and Gabriela Sabatini were the same.

As in the men's draw, a number of British players always received wild cards. Monique Javer was the only player not to require one; eight others were issued. However, it was another underwhelming round as only two players, Shirli-Ann Siddall and Amanda Grunfeld reached the next stage. Clare Wood was one of the seven Brits who lost, in her case, 6-3, 6-3. Also, as in the men's draw, there were large numbers of Americans led by Martina Navratilova, the fourth seed. Of the twenty-seven who started, nineteen reached the second round, although that did not include Marianne Werdel, the sole survivor of the players featured in *Courting Fame*, the book I mentioned earlier. The successful ones did include Lori McNeil. In the second round, Kimiko Date, Arantxa Sanchez Vicario and Conchita Martinez were three seeds who bowed out. Amanda Grunfeld and Shirli-Ann Siddall also lost. All the Brits were now out.

A walk there and back

The first day is actually when play can wrap-up a bit earlier than on the other days, so I was home in the evening early too but was satisfied that a start had been made.

As the days passed by, I stuck to the routine that would take me through most of the tournament. I had been told by one of the All-England Club stewards that the queue on the first day was actually not so long as the other days. The numbers swelled as the days went by and more people became aware of the tournament or even inspired by matches that they had watched on television leading to the decision to attend. Good performances by British players could also help increase enthusiasm above the normal high levels and people would come and queue despite the fact that often, when players did really well, like surprising a seed, their next match or matches might well be put on the bigger courts, even the show courts. So, people coming to the tennis would be less likely to see the actual source of their motivation. However, no-one really minded. Just to be there and part of the atmosphere was always special and what was important.

Different people would enjoy the experience and the atmosphere in different ways too. With all that tennis going on around them, some people were quite happy not to watch it, although they would still follow the tennis, but in a different way. Often, crowds would gather in front of the scoreboards that were up on the side of the Centre Court wall that overlooked the three banks of outside courts, relating the scores of the matches on Centre Court and Court No. 1 where usually, the top seeds were playing. In days gone by, the scoreboards would change after each point and in some cases, if the set or even the match overall became close, or there was an upset in the offing, crowds got really large, blocking the wide walkway from which the very top players, celebrities and members of the royal family would be discharged from their cars to enter the Centre Court complex. Therefore, a policy was made to continue showing the scores but without the point-by-point changes, with the aim of reducing the logjams that could often be created. As the years passed, roped-off one-way walking lanes were created with stewards posted at the ends of the lanes to keep people moving. This was another example of the operating efficiency identified and implemented by the Wimbledon committee, although the change did take a bit of the fun and excitement out of one part of the experience, not only for those watching the scoreboards but those people watching the people who were watching the scores change. I had done this once with one of my American colleagues at American Express who I accompanied on a day at the tennis back in 1986, taking on the role of an unofficial tour guide as this was the first and probably the only time that she would visit the tournament. Mary Lively, on assignment from New York, was fascinated with the scoreboard watchers.

Of course, if you were happy not to watch live tennis, one up from watching the scores change on a wall-posted scoreboard was watching matches that were going on inside the show courts but were shown outside on a big screen. Later in the nineties, what became known as Henman Hill, located outside the new Court No. 1, would develop as a place in the grounds where hundreds would congregate with some refreshment to watch the show court matches on such a screen with the match often going on just a few metres away. I did watch the scoreboards occasionally and in later years, when passing Henman Hill, I'd cast my eyes onto the screen but that way of enjoying the tennis was never a favourite of mine. I would always walk past and would be happier to see a live juniors first round match on the nearest outside court than watch the board or effectively, watch a large television.

So, back to my routine, the first task on the second day was to get established in the queue. As I had done on the first day, I would try to get up and walk up to the site and join the end of the line, usually with a take-away coffee and pastry in hand, as early as I could and certainly no later than eight o'clock. If possible, I'd try to get there a bit earlier. Once inside, after another brief sit down, as there would be many hours on your feet on a day on the outside courts, I'd wander around to see which players were practising. If I had only got in after eleven o'clock when the matches on the outside courts began, I'd see who was playing. Then, I would create my own very loose order of play. As in Rome, Paris and the other tournaments, food and drink were consumed when required.

When it came to food, the grub on offer used to be quite limited but as the years went by, the range became a bit more varied. It was all what might be called convenience or buffet food and it was consumed in staggering quantities over the two weeks by the fans. A little guidebook, produced each year, called *This is Wimbledon,* had a small section which talked about the nearly three-hundred-thousand cups of tea and coffee that were served over the fortnight and vast numbers of strawberries, pizza slices, portions of fish and chips, ice cream, mountains of sandwiches and pastries, let alone thirty-thousand meals just for the young men and women, usually teenagers, who worked for the catering company on a temporary basis during the tournament providing all this fuel for the spectators.

I would usually stay at the tennis until the last ball on the outside courts was hit, moving from court to court, as each match finished with the clock ticking around approaching nine o'clock when usually, it would become too dark. Then, I'd make my way home and although I would walk through the organised chaos of Wimbledon village and all its restaurants, bars and pubs, all packed, I rarely stopped. I would carry on the mile to my flat. By that time of evening, it was still interesting to spot the pros out with each other or their coach or a family member having their dinner. I would later learn that there would be favourite restaurants each year and rather like a herd, when the word went around the player community, some new restaurant would find itself mobbed by the pros and their entourages. Once home, I'd have something to eat, watch *Match of the Day* on the BBC if it was on that late and then get to bed as it would be an early start the next morning to do it all again.

Aiming for the second week
Towards the end of the first week, two rounds of singles had been played by the end of Thursday. The third round, the last thirty-two, started on Friday and would be completed by the end of Saturday. For many players, this was a benchmark moment in a Slam. Getting into the fourth round, the second week, was always deemed to be an achievement, especially by the slightly lower ranked and unseeded players. Not only was it a mark of achievement but there was also a considerable prize money increase too, even if a player ended up as a fourth-round loser.

In the men's third round matches, there were some interesting battles. Of the seeds who had come through, the biggest shock was the defeat of top seed, Jim Courier, beaten by the Russian qualifier, Andrei Olhovskiy. The Grand Slam Cup boys mentioned before, David Wheaton and Brad Gilbert, were despatched by John McEnroe and the good grass-court player, Australian, Wally Masur, respectively. Dutchman, Richard Krajicek was beaten by Frenchman, Arnaud Boetsch and finally, Alexander Volkov was beaten by the solid Swedish player, Henrik Holm, who had qualified and now won through three more matches making six wins in all, so far. Holm would face another Swede, Stefan Edberg, in the fourth round. Ivan Lendl beat Fred Stolle's son, Sandon and there was a bit of joy for British fans as Jeremy Bates beat Thierry Champion, although French numbers were depleted by one more, as Guy Forget beat fellow countryman, Henri Leconte. Back in my Paris hotel, Edith would not be pleased. The Germans were doing well as Boris Becker came through against Bryan

Shelton, Christian Saceanu beat Jacob Hlasek and 1991 tournament winner, Michael Stich beat the other Swede in the round, Magnus Larsson. Goran Ivanisevic beat Hlasek's doubles partner, Marc Rosset and there were two all-American contests in which Andre Agassi beat Derek Rostagno and Pete Sampras beat Scott Davis.

In the women's matches, as with the men, five seeds were beaten: Mary Joe Fernandez, Manuela Maleeva-Fragniere, Anke Huber, Jana Novotna and Judith Wiesner. In the other matches, Lori McNeil, perhaps surprisingly, lost to Natasha Zvereva, while other Americans; Gigi Fernandez, Martina Navratilova (beating the previous year's junior Wimbledon champion, Barbara Rittner), Jennifer Capriati and Zina Garrison, all made it through to the fourth round. At top and bottom of the draw, number one and two seeds, Monica Seles and Steffi Graf, also moved on to the fourth round. Completing the list was Natalie Tauziat, Katerina Maleeva, Julie Halard and Gabriela Sabatini.

All of these winners would have Sunday off and would be in action again on Monday. The losers either licked their wounds, picked up their prize money and went home or took stock and focused on doubles or mixed doubles as the second week began.

Do you speak English?
Monday arrived at the start of the second week and it was another warm day, although I still felt the need to wear my dark green sweatshirt which proudly stated on the front the word's 'Italian Open'. After my week at the Foro Italico, I wore this garment with pride. I was wondering around when someone walked in front of me and asked, "Do You speak English?" When I confirmed that I did, the man explained why he had stopped me. His name was John Kosta; he was from the US and he ran a travel business based in Michigan. He took groups of clients to special events and these included trips to

the US Open in New York and also to Wimbledon where he was, right now, with some clients. He told me that it was in his plans to go to Rome with a group and take in all the wonderful sights the city had to offer but to make the Italian Open the focus of the trip, just like it had been on my visit a few weeks before. He asked me various questions about the city and the tournament. I suggested that the best thing might be for me to write up a report for him in which I would put down everything I knew about the tournament in the hope that the information might help. I would also send him copies of all the photos I had taken while there. He was delighted with this idea and we exchanged details. It was when I told him that I was coming to New York in August, he told me to stay in touch as he was taking a group there and we could meet up. Later, when I examined John's address, I realised that he lived with his family in Ann Arbor, the home of the University of Michigan. This was significant as if there was one college football stadium I had to visit while on my US leg of the trip, it was the one in Ann Arbor. The stadium had a capacity then, of over one-hundred thousand fans and after seeing a photograph of it many years before, I had vowed that one day, I would sit in the stands watching a match and take in, what I imagined, was an amazing atmosphere. Now, I could do just that when I went over to the US and hopefully, meet up with John and his family in addition to seeing the Wolverines, in their huge stadium.

Still four more matches
The start of the second week was sometimes referred to as 'Manic Monday' because all eight fourth round matches in both men's and women's singles were completed. It's about the last time that top names could be seen in singles on the outside courts, albeit usually the slightly larger ones with more spectator capacity. Although it was an achievement to have reached the fourth round, for all the participants, to win the

title you would still have to win four more matches from this point onwards.

On the men's side, playing like he did in days of old, John McEnroe won while Guy Forget brought British fans' hopes to an end for another year by beating Jeremy Bates, although he needed five sets to do it. Boris Becker, Andre Agassi, Pete Sampras and Michael Stich all advanced, as did Ivan Lendl. Stefan Edberg beat countryman, Henrik Holm bringing his long run of matches to an end.

On the women's side, most of the matches were relatively straightforward with three going to a final set, including Steffi Graf's win over Patty Fendick, Natasha Zvereva's win against Zina Garrison and Jennifer Capriati's defeat of Naoko Sawamatsu. Monica Seles, Natalie Tauziat, Martina Navratilova, Katerina Maleeva, the last of the Maleeva sisters still in the draw, and Gabriela Sabatini, all reached the quarter-finals.

The men would have a day off, while the women would only have the rest of the day to recover. To be ready for a Saturday final, their quarter-finals would be played the following day.

Els's meals and Richey's shoes
By the afternoon of the second Tuesday, the outside courts were filled with doubles, mixed doubles and matches in the junior and over-age events. I was wandering around slowly enough to take in a point or two as I meandered through the crowds between courts or stopping to watch, if there was a player that I was interested in. I would often do this in the second week and on at least one occasion, bumped into my long-time friend from my Liverpool University days back in the mid-seventies, Steve McCormack. Steve and I had first met when we were both playing football for the university. It was when I was captain that I picked Steve to play in the first team, a moment, he reminds me, he still remembers in the same way,

it seems, that I remembered being picked that first time too. After our time in Liverpool, we had always kept in touch.

To see Steve here at Wimbledon was not a complete surprise with the social nature of Wimbledon and also, he was another tennis nut, played regularly and was just the type of fan you would expect to see. But additionally, in a professional capacity, Steve was working for the BBC as a sports news reporter. Recently, he told me about how, one year around this time, he had come up with the idea of producing a radio feature for use by the various programmes at the BBC who might be interested. He planned to find out about how the players would live during the fortnight as much off the court as on it. After some research, Steve had found a woman who was one of a number of people who made the most of the opportunity to house the considerable pool of players and coaches, which ran into hundreds, who needed a place to stay during the tournament. This landlady was looking after the Belgian player, Els Callens, not just renting her a room but cooking meals for her too, almost like a surrogate tournament mother. Els needed a home away from home with some human contact and this landlady provided just that.

At the time, Els was in the early days of her career. She would go on to play on the tour with a break in 2005, for around two decades. Although she had more success in doubles, she reached a career-high in singles of No. 43 and was a runner-up in one WTA tour event. She had more singles success in ITF circuit events reaching the finals of fourteen of them, winning eleven. Els reached the second or third round in all four Slams. In doubles, she reached twenty-two WTA Tour finals, winning ten of them. On the ITF circuit, she reached a further seventeen finals, also winning ten of them. She reached four Slam doubles quarter-finals, including two at Wimbledon and a semi-final in New York. Her highest doubles ranking was No. 12. In addition, she was a Federation Cup winner and a bronze medal winner at the Sydney Olympics. Not a bad record, I'd say.

The landlady also put Steve in touch with the American player, Richey Reneberg, whose needs were a bit different. Reneberg was older and at that time, more experienced than the young Belgian. Richey was also travelling with a female partner. They were staying in a nice flat not too far from the courts. He was relaxed about meeting Steve and made him feel welcome. When Steve asked him for any highlights or interesting aspects of playing at Wimbledon, Richey immediately took Steve over to a cupboard and opened the door. The shelves were full to the brim with about forty pairs of the special grass-court shoes the players used at SW19. These tennis shoes have small, rubber pimples on them but they don't last long. Even one match could sometimes wear the pimples down making them useless for the next practice session, let alone a competitive match. Steve departed with the image of a shoe store within a flat firmly in his mind.

Richey Reneberg was a fine pro but another player those who followed the sport would know about, but those who only followed the Grand Slams, or maybe their own country's Slam, might not. Richey had a long career, spending thirteen years on the tour. In singles, he spent the best part of a decade in the top one hundred with a career-high ranking of No. 20. His record at Slams was consistent, often reaching the third or fourth round. He reached seven ATP Tour finals, winning three titles. In doubles, often partnered by fellow American, Jim Grabb, as was the case at this 1992 Wimbledon, he spent a year in the doubles top ten including a month at No. 1 in February 1993 after a really good run. He reached thirty-five finals, winning nineteen titles, including two Grand Slams. Richey and Jim would figure a few more times in my story as we shall see.

Steve and I coined our own catchphrase, "See you by Court No. 6," in recognition of our chance meetings when we were both meandering.

Doubles teams and trophies

As the singles thinned down in numbers, so the doubles events became more visible on the outside courts or finishing off the order of play on the show courts.

In the men's doubles, there were two changes in seeds. Sergio Casal and Emilio Sanchez dropped out as did Patrick Galbraith and Patrick McEnroe, although both returned to play unseeded with Jared Palmer and Jonathan Stark, respectively. Guy Forget and Jacob Hlasek, and Omar Camporese and Goran Ivanisevic were now in the seeding list. In the first three rounds, despite their undoubted pedigree, a number of the seeded pairs fell by the wayside. In the second round, Fitzgerald and Jarryd were beaten by the strong pair of John McEnroe and Michael Stich, who in the third round, would also dispose of fifteenth seeds, Kent Kinnear and Sven Salumaa. Wayne Ferreira and Piet Norval lost at the first hurdle to Diego Nargiso and Marc Rosset, although this Italian-Swiss team too would be dumped out in the next round by Paul Harhuis and Mark Koevermans. The Dutch pair would then go on to beat the eighth seeds, Ken Flach and Todd Witsken. Kelly Jones and Rick Leach were next to go, knocked out in the third round by Guy Forget and Jacob Hlasek. At least, meeting their seeding expectation, Steve Devries and David Macpherson were knocked out by fellow seeds Scott Davis and David Pate in the third round. Grant Connell and Glenn Michibata lost in the second round to Patrick McEnroe and Jonathan Stark and the American pair went on to beat Luke Jenson and Laurie Warder who had beaten my team from Rome, Brad Pearce and Byron Talbot in the first round. Tom Nijssen and Cyril Suk also lost in the first round, as did Omar Camporese and Goran Ivanisevic. Five British pairs started out but only Nick Brown and Andrew Richardson, made it to the second round where they lost. Jeremy Bates, playing with Christo Van Rensburg and Neil Broad, playing with Bryan Shelton, both got through a round before departing.

Looking at the women's list of seeds, as with the men, it was very similar to the one in Paris. In came Martina Navratilova with Pam Shriver, playing together again, and Gretchen Magers with Robin White. There were three new pairings involving players who had been at Roland Garros but were now with new partners: Arantxa Sanchez Vicario, now with Helena Sukova; Lori McNeil, now with Rennae Stubbs; and Nicole Provis, now with Elizabeth Smylie. Out went Mary Pierce and Patricia Tarabini, and Ros Fairbank-Nideffer and Rafaella Reggi. With the addition of Martina Navratilova and Pam Shriver, they added a massive total of two-hundred and eleven career doubles titles between them, including seventy-eight together, to the group's list of tournament wins. It has always stuck with me how Martina Navratilova not only won her one-hundred and seventy-seven doubles titles but this superb achievement was in addition to one-hundred and sixty-seven singles titles.

In the early stages, most of the seeds fulfilled their seeding expectation and reached the third round. Casualties were twelfth seeds, Rachel McQuillan and Claudia Porwick and eighth seeds, Jill Hetherington and Kathy Rinaldi. Clare Wood, playing with Belinda Borneo again, and Julie Salmon, playing with Amanda Grunfeld, were amongst the five pairs involving British players. Of these, only Jo Durie, partnering Yayuk Basuki, went through to the second round where they lost to the sixteenth seeds, Americans, Gretchen Magers and Robin White.

In the mixed doubles too, the seeding list was a strong group of teams where every player was in a seeded pair in the men's and women's doubles. Top seeds were Todd Woodbridge and Jana Novotna who beat Byron Talbot and Isabelle Demongeot in the first round. Across the draw, nineteen of the teams involved one player from the US and some were all-American. In the first three rounds, despite the quality of the teams, nine of the sixteen seeds would fall. Of the four British teams, former winners in 1987, Jeremy Bates and Jo Durie reached the third round but were beaten there by Tom Nijssen and Manon Bollegraf. Clare Wood and Neil Broad had a heartbreak first round match losing 12-10 in the final set to Argentinian pair, Javier Frana and Gabriela Sabatini. Mark Petchey and Sarah Loosemore, and Chris Wilkinson and Sara Gomer both lost in the first round. My Paris favourites, Bryan Shelton and Lori McNeil, kept winning and were through to the quarter-finals which now came next for all the pairs in all three doubles events who had survived the first three rounds.

Kimiko's camera snappers
A theatrical moment took place on one of the outside courts during the women's doubles first round. The match was being played at the end of the afternoon and into the early evening. For once, the light was poor. The Japanese pair of Kimiko Date and Maya Kidowaki were up against the team of American, Jennifer Fuchs and her partner, Karina Habsudova, from Slovakia.

There were still many fans all over the grounds and the court was surrounded. In fact, it was packed and other than the one row of seats along each side, people were standing three-deep. The fans were mainly Japanese, not a surprise considering that one of the pairs on the court was a Japanese team and also, one of the players was Kimiko Date who was much loved. It is true that when outside Japan, as tourists, the Japanese do like to take photos and it seemed as if just about everyone around the court was doing so as the points were played. This would not usually be a problem. But in such poor light, the flashlights of all of these cameras seemed to have been activated.

After a game or two of this, the chair umpire paused between points and made an announcement. As he spoke, a hush descended if only because on many of the outside courts, this one included, there were no microphones on the umpire's chair. This was not a problem as the players could usually hear the umpire calling the score. But for the spectators, things could get a bit more difficult. To even just stand a chance of picking up the message, everyone had to be quiet. Indeed, people seemed to be craning their necks to try and hear what the umpire was saying. It was of little surprise to hear him make the request that not only could spectators refrain from taking photographs when the point was in play but could they also ensure that when they did, the flashlight was not used. The Japanese spectators all looked at each other and seemed to nod their understanding of the message. Problem solved then, or so I thought.

The players came out for the next game and as the first point began, just as the server made contact with the ball, again, there was an explosion of camera clicking and flashlights going off. It was as if the umpire hadn't said a word. I found myself laughing at the farcical and comedic nature of the situation.

On reflection, it would be easy to conclude that the misunderstanding was down to language. However, I don't think this was the case. Quite simply, other than those spectators next to the umpire's chair or directly opposite from him, it was really difficult to hear what he was saying in the absence of a microphone. I knew what he was saying because I'd seen the situation many times before. Nontheless, there were a few smiles around the courtside as the bulbs flashed as if a major celebrity had just arrived on a catwalk somewhere. Anyway, somehow the match was completed without too much distraction to the players or damage to everyone's eyesight on or off the court. The Japanese pair lost in straight sets; I imagine much to the disappointment of their photography-mad fans.

Kimiko Date was an amazing player. Despite a large population, Japan had rarely produced top players. The likes of Kosei Kamo in the fifties was an exception to the rule. But they were beginning to do so as the expansion of tennis interest and national association-led programmes to get people playing in Japan was happening, as it was in many erstwhile non-traditional tennis countries. She began her career in 1989 and retired in 1996. But having produced a family, she returned to the tour in 2008 at the age of thirty-seven. She played on, finally retiring for good in 2017 at the age of forty-seven after achieving respectable wins against top players and the addition of some ITF circuit titles to her career record. At her peak, she reached No. 4 in the rankings and she won eight singles and seven doubles WTA Tour titles in addition to more in ITF events. In Grand Slams, in singles, she reached three semi-finals and one quarter-final. She was the fifteenth seed in the singles at this Wimbledon. Her success was achieved with an interesting style of play. She had short backswings on her flat groundstrokes and reminded me of a cross between Francoise Durr, before her and Agnieszka Radwanska, after her. It seemed like her home fans loved her and it was no surprise that the courtside for her doubles match was packed with them, all armed with their cameras.

Top seeds rise up
The tournament had arrived at its final stages. By now, the crowds were easing on the outside courts and with all the events coming to a conclusion, often not all the courts would be occupied with matches. As I had discovered at the French Open, by this time in the second week, my interest in seeing who would win was still there but my physical energy was on the wane after all the early starts and long days in the sun circumnavigating the crowds to get to the matches I wanted to see. While again, I was pleased that I'd done what I'd planned originally, I was looking forward to a rest once the tournament was finished.

The men's singles quarter finals were contested by seeded players except for John McEnroe who, nontheless, went through to the semi-finals with a victory in straight sets over Guy Forget. The other straight sets win was by Pete Sampras over defending champion, Michael Stich. The other two matches were five-setters with Andre Agassi putting out Boris Becker and Goran Ivanisevic defeating Stefan Edberg.

In the women's singles, the last eight also had seven seeds and one unseeded player, Natasha Zvereva, who faced Steffi Graf again. The German star repeated her French Open final victories from 1988 and her recent victory from a few weeks before. Monica Seles beat Natalie Tauziat in straight sets; Martina Navratilova beat Katerina Maleeva, also in straight sets but close ones; and Gabriela Sabatini beat Jennifer Capriati but needed three sets.

In the men's doubles, after some tough four-set battles in the quarter-finals, John McEnroe and Michael Stich came through to the final after beating Guy Forget and Jacob Hlasek. Richey Reneberg, probably wearing a brand-new pair of pimpled tennis shoes, came through with Jim Grabb after beating the Woodies.

In the women's doubles, the top four seeds came through to meet each other in the semi-finals where the Jana Novotna and Larissa Savchenko-Neiland and Gigi Fernandez and Natasha Zvereva partnerships prevailed.

In the mixed doubles, Larissa reached another final with Cyril Suk after beating my Paris favourites, Bryan Shelton and Lori McNeil. In the other all-Dutch semi-final, Jacco Eltingh and Miriam Oremans beat Tom Nijssen and Manon Bollegraf.

Rain, rain, go away

The last weekend began with the women's final on Saturday. In the semi-finals, played two days before, Martina Navratilova was knocked out by Monica Seles sporting her new brown hair. Martina had complained about Monica's grunting, something that would become ubiquitous in female players on the tour just about from that point onwards. Steffi

Graf powered past Gabriela Sabatini in straight sets, setting up a much-anticipated final between the top two seeds.

As in Paris, I could not get hold of tickets for the finals. In fact, I didn't even try as although I had the money, I just didn't feel like parting with the amounts required to see the matches live. I decided to watch them at home on the television. In the women's final, Graf won the title surprisingly easily, 6-1, 6-2, to win her fourth Wimbledon title in five years and her eleventh singles Grand Slam to date; she would go on to win twenty-two in singles plus the 1988 Wimbledon doubles as well. Interestingly, the Seles grunt was no-where to be heard. The match lasted just fifty-eight minutes but took much longer because in these pre-roof days on Centre Court, there were three rain delays which seemed to benefit Graf more than Seles, although such interruptions can sometimes favour the player who is behind at the point that the match is interrupted, not the one who is in front, as Graf was.

The men's final on Sunday was between Andre Agassi and Goran Ivanisevic. Andre had come through after a brutal semi-final against John McEnroe with their contrasting styles, let alone their haircuts, providing the Centre Court crowd with the spectacle of McEnroe trying to get to the net at every opportunity and Agassi firing his passing shots past the fellow-American cross court or down-the-line with ruthless efficiency. That was his trademark, after years of hitting thousands of balls from a very young age, many of them struck on Nick's court at Bollettieri's academy in Bradenton, Florida. The pair had been practising together and had played doubles together in Paris. McEnroe had suggested that Agassi shorten his takebacks on grass and this tip worked, although against the man who had given the tip. In the final, Agassi would play Goran Ivanisevic and beating him in five sets, Andre won the first of what would become a career Grand Slam and eight Slam titles in all. Agassi, who had been going through another new fitness regime around the time of the summer tournaments, had not been confident of success at any time during the tournament. It was a huge relief to win; Goran's time at Wimbledon would come later.

The rain delays on the Saturday led to a decision to play the men's doubles on Sunday as well as to put the women's doubles onto Court No. 1 on that day too. The men's doubles final, between John McEnroe and Michael Stich, and Jim Grabb and Richey Reneberg, was stopped on the Sunday evening at 13-13 in the fifth set. The match was resumed the next day, still on Court No. 1 and the John McEnroe and Michael Stich team went on to win the title 19-17. Seven thousand five-hundred fans were allowed in for free to watch and looking back, I didn't take advantage of this opportunity. I was tired out, and fancied a lie-in, rather than get up one more time at the crack of dawn to stand in another queue. In the women's doubles, Gigi Fernandez and Natasha Zvereva beat Jana Novotna and Larissa Savchenko-Neiland to win their second consecutive title. The mixed doubles final was also played on the Monday in which Cyril Suk and Larissa Savchenko-Neiland again, beat Jacco Eltingh and Miriam Oremans.

With Wimbledon now over. It was time to think about the next stage of my master plan, the one I had come up with first on that flight from Sydney to Perth a few months before.

Chapter 7

Ickringilled in Ilkley

A new British Tour
I had about six weeks before the US Open began in late August over in New York City. In my original plan, I had imagined cycling around some of the more interesting and beautiful parts of the UK where I had never been. With these thoughts still in mind, I did go ahead and purchase a superb bike suitable for touring in the way I had envisioned. I spent the same amount of money again on all sorts of items that would go along with it, including clothing, shoes, panniers, lights and water bottles. I found myself enjoying a few local rides where I did my best to look like I was on a training ride for the Tour of Britain. However, these short trips made me realise my lack of experience in this potential new hobby and that the idea of actually riding across the country or even just around one area of it, like the Lake District, might be a recipe for disaster. I now realised that although my idea had sounded simple, the achievement of the plan would require much more organising, know-how and experience than I had ever envisaged or possessed, especially if I was doing everything on my own.

After my three months in Europe, the build-up to Wimbledon and another two weeks of day-to-day attendance, I felt like a bit of a rest before setting off on the next leg of my trip which would take me away for just under six months. But one part of my plan did still appeal to me and that was spending a week away from London at a tennis tournament in which I could compete alongside all sorts of players, both ones of my standard as well as those who were significantly better. I selected the tournament at Ilkley to meet these needs.

I had heard about the new British Tour. This was a tier of tournaments, created by the LTA for aspiring players as the next level up from club tournaments whether the normal knock-out ones or the two-week ratings events which had begun a decade before with the first one held at my club back in Sussex. In the men's tour hierarchy, above these British Tour events came the Satellites, then Challenger tournaments and then the full ATP Tour. On the women's side, the hierarchy was similar but the name of Futures was applied to Satellite and Challenger levels in events organised by the ITF, below the full WTA Tour. A number of the British Tour events had previously been ratings tournaments where, depending on where you started in the draw based on your own rating, you would play matches against players of your ratings level. Assuming you kept winning, you would then come up against better players with higher ratings and then finally, the top players with the best ratings. But these new British Tour events would now be run like traditional non-ratings tournaments, taking a week to complete from start to finish like most junior events and full tour events too, other than the two-week Grand Slams, of course. You could be drawn against the top seed in round one on day one. Ilkley was one such event.

Prize money for British Tour events was also higher than for ratings tournaments and using the 1992 Ilkley tournament as an example, if you reached the second round and then lost, you would receive some money, albeit a small amount, but for reaching each additional round, the prize money rose until the final, where the winner would receive a couple of thousand pounds, a reasonable prize for young touring pros for a weeks' work at the time. Providing young British players with an additional level of financial support like this was an important part of the thinking behind these tournaments, as well as establishing another tier of official competition in the domestic competitive pathway on the way towards the top of the sport.

Although it wasn't packaged and promoted officially as part of a tour with a name augmented by sponsors' branding, in the days before tennis went open in 1968, for some time, there had been a loosely organised British circuit. As well as regular annual tournaments like the ones already mentioned in previous chapters at places like Queen's, Eastbourne, West Didsbury and Edgbaston Priory, in England, there were tournaments at long-established clubs in Bristol, Lee-on-Solent, Chichester, Bournemouth, West Worthing, Beckenham, Surbiton, Paddington, the Cumberland, Felixstowe, Frinton, Nottingham, Hoylake and others.

Elsewhere in the British Isles, in Ireland the Irish Championships were played in Dublin and back at the start of the twentieth century, as noted above, this tournament formed part of an early top four of the sport with the Northern Tournament held at West Didsbury, the US National Championships and Wimbledon. In Wales, the Welsh Championships was held at four venues across its duration. In Scotland, the Scottish Championships was held, also at various clubs throughout its life.

The honour rolls of all of these tournaments include many recognisable names most tennis fans who know the history of the sport would recognise. A name less immediately recognisable might be Judie Erskine, who won the Scottish Championships in 1981 in her playing days before she concentrated on coaching. Using her married name of Murray, most fans would immediately spot the mother of two pretty good male British tennis players of recent years, Andy and Jamie.

The timings of all of these tournaments throughout the year were fixed loosely to match the likes of the European clay-court tournaments followed by a switch to grass but the courts used in clubs were usually one or the other in the days before all manner of hard court and synthetic grass surfaces were developed. Ilkley was one tournament which had been played slightly later in the summer around the August Bank Holiday weekend.

A piece of British tennis history

Although I didn't realise it then, in entering the tournament at Ilkley, I was taking part in a really established piece of British tennis history and one which had shaped the culture of the sport in this country, as it still does today.

The Ilkley club was established in 1880 around the time that the new game of Lawn Tennis was expanding rapidly through the nation, exemplified by the establishment of many of the clubs across the country already mentioned in previous chapters and above. I've heard of a few clubs providing tennis balls for various club activities but at the new Ilkley club, the committee bought rackets for the club members as well as balls for them to use when they played. The tournament was first held in 1885 with five events and sixty-one entrants and it would continue to grow and grow. The 1992 version I was about to compete in had twenty-eight events and four-hundred and forty competitors. Previous versions had experienced even higher numbers of participants.

The Ilkley tournament became known as being one that catered for just about every level of competitive club player up to those of international repute. Into the twentieth century, especially in the hey-days of amateur tennis, Ilkley was always on the unofficial circuit of UK events which the top players, including those from overseas who planned to play after Wimbledon, used to enter. This was before the days of open tennis, way before the pro tours we are used to today got organised and way before things like ratings tournaments or the British Tour were introduced for younger, aspiring domestic players to help bridge the gap between juniors and adult competitive tennis.

The reputation of the tournament had been made by its core player audiences of county players, club players including the Ilkley members and juniors. Peter Johns, an LTA secretary from the seventies, once made a similar point, stating that the tournament was in the middle ground between the top, sponsored events and local club tournaments. While there would be many of the young players in the main men's and women's events that I was about to spend the week amongst in 1992 who probably did have loftier aims fixed in their heads and hearts, many, if not most of those competitors, myself included, would have fitted into Peter's description.

However, after the Second World War, the tournament did become an attraction for young British players with higher aspirations, including the likes of Roger Taylor, my mum's favourite. There were others. Mark Cox became a top player, winning twenty-one singles titles and reached No. 13 in the world rankings. Mike Davies was a Davis Cup player, winner of twenty-four singles titles, a finalist in the 1960 Wimbledon men's doubles, an early defector into the old-style pro ranks run by Jack Kramer and after his playing days were over, a respected tennis administrator, all of which he was recognised for by his induction into the International Tennis Hall of Fame. David Lloyd was a future owner of the chain of tennis and leisure clubs which bore his name. Graham Stilwell came into the limelight during Wimbledon with doubles partner, Peter Curtis, after they beat Newcombe and Roche at Wimbledon. Curtis would marry the American player, Mary Ann Eisel and win the US mixed doubles title in 1968 with her. John Feaver broke the top one hundred in the rankings and reached the fourth round at both Wimbledon and in New York. He once held the record for the largest number of aces in a match in 1976 at Wimbledon although unfortunately for him, he was up against the great John Newcombe who still won the match. Gerald Battrick was a Davis Cup player who won six titles and reached No. 53 in the rankings. John Paish was a Davis Cup player and Wimbledon doubles semi-finalist in 1973. John Clifton was another Davis Cup player who played the very first match in the open era against Owen Davidson at Bournemouth. Stanley Matthews was a winner of Junior Wimbledon and son of the great footballer, Sir Stanley. Paul

Hutchins would become Davis Cup captain, father of pro, Ross Hutchins and in his later years, a tennis consultant working hard with the LTA to boost the spread of the game across the UK.

On the women's side, Elizabeth Starkie was a Federation Cup and Wightman Cup player, and Australian Open semi-finalist in 1963. Rita Bentley reached the third round at Wimbledon, also in 1963. Nell Truman, Christine's sister and a Wightman Cup player, reached the fourth round at Wimbledon. Winnie Shaw, another Federation and Wightman Cup player, a semi-finalist at the Australian Open in 1970 and 1971, was a player who I would watch at Wimbledon on one of my early visits with mum in the late sixties.

Other known names who graced the Ilkley courts included Wimbledon champion, Jaroslav Drobny; the Dane, Torben Ulrich; and another of my mum's British favourites, Davis Cup player, Bobby Wilson, a former winner of Junior Wimbledon, who partnered Mike Davies in the 1960 Wimbledon men's doubles final. In 1963, Wilson reached the quarter-finals of the Grand Slams in Paris, Wimbledon and New York.

As well as all the players involved in shaping the personality of the Ilkley tournament, a key role was played by the referees who had run the event over the years, including, in his post playing days, the former top British player who reached two Wimbledon finals, Bunny Austin, the first man to wear shorts there as opposed to long white flannels. Austin was a strict disciplinarian in delivering his mission and players of all ages had to beware of incurring his wrath.

It's a small world
Peter Johns, the LTA secretary mentioned above had a lifelong association with tennis. Johns's father helped to start the Coolhurst Tennis Club in the Crouch End area of North London. Then, in 1949, Peter married Katie Whitefield, a good

British tennis player. The couple had a son, Richard and on various occasions, the family made the trip to Devonshire Park, Eastbourne, where Peter helped run the tournament described in some detail above, for the LTA. After a stint as assistant secretary, Johns became secretary of the LTA at Baron's Court, where the Queen's Club and the LTA headquarters were located. He held the position in the seventies and early eighties prior to his death in 1983.

Meanwhile, son Richard became interested in cricket. In the late seventies, he joined Finchley Cricket Club in North London. By the early nineties, he had become the captain of what was one of the strongest club teams not only in London but in the country. He later became the club manager, a position he held for many years. Richard will be remembered for his wide-ranging contribution to the club, including leading the first team to three Middlesex County League titles in the five years he was skipper.

Amongst many fine performances, club members who remember it have talked about one innings he played in a 1979 National Cup match when he was picked for the first team while serving his dues in the club's league second eleven, at the time his father was in charge at the LTA. Close to reaching a final of the competition, which was to be played at Lord's cricket ground, almost unbelievably, Finchley's strong batting line-up had been swept away in a shock early-overs collapse against a strong team from Bishop's Stortford. Richard came into bat and put on sixty-nine runs in a seventh wicket stand which gave the team a chance at making the game competitive. When Richard was out for forty-two, his partner in the stand, who had gone in before him, carried on. Batting for most of the innings over a two-hour period, that player scored fifty-eight runs and everybody watching stood and applauded as he came off when he was out in the penultimate over. While these efforts did not secure victory, they stood out as both batsmen were junior members of a player hierarchy which included a number of players with First-Class experience. In the local paper the following Friday, Richard was shown standing hot and sweaty looking a bit embarrassed at this little piece of local notoriety. The other batsman in the partnership stood next to him looking equally frazzled and awkward. I understood those feelings because that other batsman was me.

Certainly, from my perspective, after that stand together, I always felt bonded to Richard, a bit like being brothers-in-cricket. Sometimes, it's a small world and all sorts of connections exist which you don't know about or expect, including a link between an old friend made in one sport and that friend's father in another.

The other John McEnroe

In order to play in the tournament, I had to complete a number of tasks back in Wimbledon beforehand. These were pre-internet days, so I had phoned up the Ilkley club and requested the entry forms. These had been sent through the post. I had entered the men's singles and also the men's doubles and handicapped mixed doubles, requesting a partner in both doubles events. Hindsight is a marvellous thing and looking back now, I would have been better off playing in various other events which were more tailored to my standard in addition to the main singles and doubles events. But in a way, it was because I might be drawn to play a top player that was the attraction of entering the main events and I did, as we shall see, find myself drawn against interesting opponents, that's for sure. Back then, I regarded playing in the events more suited to my standard, as being more of what I had been doing already. The chance of being in the draw with top players was new and not something I had taken part in previously. It fitted the bill more in terms of what I wanted to experience in my year of activities. If I were to repeat the exercise, I would enter the men's evening singles and all the handicap events. I would have been better suited to the standard and I would have played more tennis that way. But at the time, I was happy to take my chances with the main events in singles and doubles and if I came up against players much better than me, then so be it.

Next, I had to organise somewhere to stay and found details of a small hotel not far from the club which offered bed and breakfast and evening meal if you wanted it. I booked that and then turned to the issue of how to get there. I did not have a car throughout this year out. I could have gone by train but I now wanted the freedom a car would give me. I found a rental company in Wimbledon and booked a small car for the week.

I owned plenty of tennis kit but after my tennis watching so far, I'd really liked the Adidas kit that many of the male players had been wearing on the ATP Tour. Going to Lillywhites in central London (not Hamley's this time), I found the kit and bought myself the outfit with a couple of spare shirts and pairs of socks. I knew I was going down a path that another club player I had once seen had clearly decided he would follow, regardless of what anyone else thought. In wearing this clothing, I might have looked like some of the pros but I certainly didn't aim to become a tennis playing double of Stefan Edberg, a player at the very top of the world game, then wearing Adidas or the Rome finalist, Carlos Costa, who wore this particular design of clothing that I had just bought. The gentleman who came to mind as I checked the racks at Lillywhites clearly had another player in mind.

It was back in 1982 when I had moved down to Brighton with American Express. One of my colleagues there had found out that I played tennis and she had invited me to a club night at West Worthing. If I liked it there, I could apply to join. As usual, at club nights, there were all sorts of players, dressed in all sorts of tennis clothing. Then, a latecomer arrived and I had to do a double take. He was a tall man, with a shock of brown hair kept under control by a wide headband. He was dressed in the Tacchini brand of tennis clothes. The design was exactly the same one that John McEnroe often wore, the white shirt with the royal blue stripe across the chest. He also wore the same Nike shoes worn by Mac. In fact, from afar, the man looked exactly like the American star, if a little bit taller. Then, when he started playing, although he was a right-handed player, the man tried to play like Mac as well. His execution of ground strokes was similar, and when he served, he adopted the same position Mac then used, standing almost along the baseline, as opposed to being at right angles to it. Then, he contorted himself and his racket into the ball as he launched upwards to make contact. Did he actually play like Mac? No, he didn't, otherwise he would not have been spending his time in a club night at West Worthing. But he seemed happy enough and enjoying his tennis just like the rest of us were enjoying ours. However, from that moment on, whenever I wore branded clothes that top players were wearing, as I was about to do at Ilkley, I always remembered that club night and almost wanted to assure those I might be playing with that I really wasn't a wannabe, well not really or maybe, on second thoughts, just a bit.

Of course, the reality is that at various conscious and subconscious levels, there is wannabee-ism going on all the time with recreational sports players and the purchasing of their equipment and clothing. You see your favourite player and you make some sort of association with him or her and then maybe, you think you'll try the racket the player uses, or in my case, you like the designs on the clothing. Who knows, as well as feeling as if you look good, you might just play a bit better with your favourite athlete's gear on you. It's what the clothing and equipment companies are relying on as they make their products available in the mass market.

The final piece of my pre-tournament plan was to ensure that at least, before stepping onto the courts at Ilkley, I had hit some tennis balls recently, so I played a couple of times locally in Wimbledon. Then, armed with appropriate maps, on the

Sunday before the Monday start to the tournament, I set off in my rental car from Wimbledon, bound for Ilkley and the British Tour.

Signing in
After a relatively straight-forward drive up the M1, Ilkley was reasonably easy to find north of Leeds. I was pleasantly surprised by my hotel which looked as if it had once been someone's house. My room was spacious and light. The owner was friendly and relaxed. Having checked in, I drove the short distance to the tennis club and as I made my way through the entrance, got a good feeling about the week ahead. In front of me was a wonderful sight for any tennis players and fans alike. Stretching out across a large area were many lines of grass courts. Parking was easy and I went in search of the office.

There were various people checking paperwork, taking and making calls and looking suitably busy for the day before the start of this mammoth festival of tennis about to be unleashed on the green courts outside. I was given a competitor card and had a look at the draw for the men's singles which had already been made. On paper, as per the draw sheet included in the programme, it looked like I was supposed to play the fifteenth seed but that's not how things worked out. Due to a slight re-jigging of the draw, in my first match, I ended up having to play the man who coached everyone and ran the club shop, the ex-Yorkshire champion, Simon Ickringill, who had also just started to play for the Great Britain Over-35 team. Well, I'd accepted the risk of being drawn against someone of an excellent pedigree and that eventuality had come about. At some point during the following day, I'd have to pit my wits and my new Adidas kit against this local hero. Despite my general feeling of well-being with the world at how my trip was going so far and my usual positive attitude to new challenges, in this case, I really didn't hold out too much hope.

Making someone else's day

The club produced a thick programme which in its own way, was a mark of the importance of the tournament and was a page-by-page demonstration of the club's commitment to its annual event. The front cover design immediately told the reader that this was the ninety-sixth version of the tournament; that it was part of the LTA's British Tour; that it had a major sponsor, in this case Allied Textile Companies PLC; and finally, that this was 'The North's Premier Tournament'.

The programme was full of advertisements taken out by local companies, many of them with somewhat cliched but understandably coined tennis-related messages, assuring 'Ace Service' in one and encouraging the reader to 'Take Advantage of our Service' in another. After a few of these, there was a message from club president, Andrew Wade. He talked about how the tournament was a milestone for the club as a result, switching the date from its traditional August Bank Holiday timing, the involvement with the British Tour and a new sponsorship. But he emphasised how he didn't want the tournament to change fundamentally; how the junior events which he saw as a seed bed of the game's future, were really important; and that the club had big ambitions for the future with plans for improvements. Andrew Wade then thanked Mike Boyle for all of his work in the role of referee over the previous thirteen tournaments. Mr Wade ended with a positioning of winning and losing that I have never read before. He said, while emphasising how the club could not control the weather, for everyone to remember that 'if you lose your match, you have made someone else's day'. I was about to make a few peoples' day.

The programme went on to give details of the club's officers and a one-page message from the tournament referee, Peter Greatorex, the LTA's Regional Tournament Co-ordinator who ran many of these British Tour events as part of his job. As well as talking about the British Tour, he finished with a warning to players in which he reminded them that point seven in the Lawn Tennis Association Code of Conduct, shown on the following page, 'forbids swearing, racket throwing and ball abuse'. In the following pages were details of the tournament trophies and cups, its business patrons, and a left luggage tent that everyone could use, although a small donation to charity was requested. Then there was a list of sponsors and a page on the entertainment organised in the evenings.

In the middle of the programme was a separate section on all the events, draws and competitors. In a different coloured paper, these pages were stapled into the middle of the programme. I didn't know then, but have spotted now, that the 1991 winner of the junior U18 event was Tim Henman. There were pages advertising the club shop, run by my first-round opponent, Simon Ickringill. There was also a page advertising the club as the location for Group Six of the Inter-County Cup, otherwise known as County Week, which would follow the tournament. While the Group One men would be walking their mushrooms down at Eastbourne, I'm now wondering what the Group Six women got up to at Ilkley.

Seeds
From the programme's central section, it showed that the men's event was a sixty-four player draw with sixteen seeds while the women's event was a thirty-two player draw with eight seeds.

In the men's singles, the seeds were all from the group of young British players aspiring to get as high up in the world game as they could. Top seed was Danny Sapsford and others who had been good enough to play in Wimbledon qualifying or be awarded a wild card to play in the main draw, included Darren Kirk, Paul Robinson, Nick Fulwood, Mark Schofield, Nick Gould, Paul Hand, Gary Henderson and Lawrence

Matthews. My opponent, Simon Ickringill, although a top player in national terms, was not even seeded.

Danny Sapsford had turned pro in 1989 when he was twenty-years-of-age. As with many other young, aspiring British players of his type, he had risen through the junior tournament ranks and until the age of twenty-one, benefited from financial support from the LTA, an arrangement a bit like a partial loan, in that any prize money won in singles events had to be paid back to the governing body, while anything won in doubles could be kept by the player. Once a player was twenty-one, the funding stopped but so did the paying back. All prize money could be retained but the player would now have to fund all the expenses, often considerable, for staying on the tour both domestically as well as internationally, in the hunt for wins, prize money and the computer points that would help with elevation up the world rankings.

Danny did well into the mid-nineties and then experienced some stagnation. But he adopted an interesting strategy to boost his career which came to him as a bit of a surprise, he has since told me. Eligible for Challenger events just below the main ATP Tour, Danny struggled but when he entered the qualifying events of main ATP Tour tournaments, he found that not only did he do well but when he made the main draw, he won matches too. At this higher level, that would mean more points and prize money. In one year, he qualified for eleven main ATP Tour events using this approach. He played on until the end of the nineties when he had hit thirty-years-of age, and by now, had a young family to support. Then, he was offered a team management coaching role by the LTA, a job opportunity too good to turn down at that stage in his career. His final tournament proved to be his swansong. He played Wimbledon in 1999 and reached the third round where he came up against none other than Pete Sampras. Playing on a show court, Danny played well but lost in straight sets. His highest ranking in singles was No. 170 and in doubles, was No. 83. In 1996, one of his best years, he won an ATP Tour doubles title at Nottingham, partnered by Mark Petchey.

At the time of the Ilkley tournament, such events were important to Danny as he could use them to fill gaps in his international schedule and due to his higher ranking in this group of players, feel reasonably certain of doing well and earning some decent prize money. The two thousand pounds received by the winner of the men's singles at Ilkley would be worth just over three thousand five hundred pounds today.

In the women's singles, the players were of the same type as the men, all quite young and aspiring to bigger and better things in the game. Top seed was Amanda Grunfeld and like a number of the other seeds, including Virginia Humphrey-Davies, Julie Salmon, Caroline Billingham, Lucie Ahl and Valda Lake, had played in either Wimbledon qualifying or in the main draw itself, often through the award of wild cards. Many of these players had played, or would go on to play, for Great Britain in the Federation Cup.

Amanda Grunfeld had been an outstanding junior and was twenty-four years-of-age at the time of the tournament. She won three ITF circuit titles in singles and two more in doubles, reaching a career high world ranking of No. 138 a couple of months after this Ilkley event. She played Federation Cup in 1993 but a shoulder injury brought her career to an end around that time, after which she went to study at Manchester University.

Two tough draws
My match against Simon was scheduled for the afternoon, so I spent the morning watching other people play in the men's and women's singles.

While I watched, I contemplated the match ahead. I was in a fortunate position. I was doing all of this entirely for recreation, for fun. But for pros, the considerations were different. Those who played for a living saw the game in another way. They had to. If the result of your upcoming match determined if you could pay the next month's rent or mortgage payment as opposed to shift your perceptions of exactly how good you were, these were two very different places to be at, mentally.

I felt that in many ways, being drawn against a player like Simon Ickringill could be defined as a tough draw, a very tough draw. But seeing as I was not a pro, nor an aspiring one with payments on the line depending on the result, in many ways, I could be quite accepting of the impending drubbing that in all probability, I could expect to receive. I was in the privileged position that I could accept whatever was going to happen without any real jeopardy other than bruising to my ego. I could experience and learn.

When the match was called, we were allocated a court just to the side of the clubhouse. I noticed that unlike many of the other matches, there was a small crowd which formed on one side of the court. Maybe, they were wondering who this southern upstart was, challenging their local, star man? After the knock up, when the match began, I thought of Peter Burwash and his concept of being 'in emergency' from ball one. Certainly, I felt as if I was in Burwash mode as Simon's serves started to zip past me and thud into the back of the court. Memories of Kevin Curren and Steve Denton's serves at Wimbledon came to mind. His service games seemed to be over so quickly that in no time, it was my turn to serve again. As often happens when playing a better player, you feel you must do more than usual and so, overhitting my first serves, I had to rely on my weaker, spun second serve, a stroke it would take me another decade to reach a level of proficiency that I would be happy with. Simon attacked my serve ruthlessly and before I knew it, I had lost the first set, 6-0. The crowd started to disperse – 'No problem for our Simon here', I imagined them thinking. In the next set, I got my racket on more balls but the result went the same way as the first. I had been bagelled, double-bagelled again, 6-0, 6-0 to a fine player. In fact, in this case, I reckon I could re-name the experience: I had been Ickringilled. I had hit a few good shots and my game didn't fall apart completely, despite what the score might suggest. But my new Adidas clothing was barely bothered by sweat as it had all happened so fast.

Ultimately, I wasn't too disappointed at what had happened. I certainly hadn't made a fool of myself. I had hardly served any double faults and managed to get enough balls back, including a couple which forced errors in Simon's play. Very quickly, I accepted a re-enforced appraisal of my level and a new realisation of those levels above me and what they represented. I was way too old to have any expectations in relation to this level of tennis but I had always had an attitude which said I could get just a bit better than I was now, at any given time. This thrashing, in many ways, helped me to set out in my mind the need to keep going and to keep improving, even though it would never again involve playing someone as good as Simon, or so I thought, until I would face a similar experience in Texas later in the year. I had my new quest. Simon was an absolute gentleman afterwards and over a drink which he insisted on buying, we had a chat about what I was doing in my year off. He went off back to the club shop while I decided what match to watch next.

My doubles first-round match was the following day and again, the sun shone. I had been allocated a doubles partner; a young man called Richard Hewitt who was in the U18 boys' singles event and like me, he did not have a partner in the doubles. We had been drawn against a top team from Lancashire, Mark Schofield and Paul Robinson, both players who played for Lancashire at County Week and were of the quality that saw them play in the qualifying event at Wimbledon; Mark had played there a few weeks before. My partner, Richard, was a decent player for his age and stage but the Lancashire lads were, again, just too good for us and the match was over quickly. Although it may sound odd, both in the singles match against Simon and this doubles match, I found it fascinating to be so close and able to watch, let alone react, to a level of player and play that I had never experienced before. There are many factors involved in separating levels of players but the two Lancastrians had an efficiency about their techniques combined with what seemed like perfect decision making as to tactically, what shot to hit in each situation, something that again, would take me a few years to really appreciate and execute to an acceptable standard.

Evenings off the court
The third event I had entered was the handicap mixed doubles and although the match would be my third loss, my opponents were so pleasant that they invited me over to their home, the following evening. Although I was quite happy looking after myself once the tennis was over, I sensed that they felt a bit sorry for me. However, I didn't mind and was happy to accept their offer. After dinner, they took me on a walk around the Bolton Priory on the Bolton Abbey estate, six miles and a short drive away. The Priory had been a target of Thomas Cromwell's dissolution of the monasteries in the reign of Henry VIII. The place oozed history.

On another evening, I ended up in a curry house next to four young men who were talking in an animated way. After a while, I realised that they were cricketers playing for Leicestershire second eleven in a match against Yorkshire. For some reason, despite my background in that sport, I left them to their own devices and refrained from striking up a conversation with them. Perhaps, this was because they seemed so serious about the topic they were discussing. In a way, these young men were cricket's version of many of the young men and women I was spending the week with at the tennis tournament, in that while they were performing at a high level by the standards of mere civilian mortals like me, they aspired to something better and a chance to earn their livelihood from their sport. The place they were at currently (in the case of the cricketers, the match as well as the curry house) was a stop on the way up, hopefully, to much higher levels of performance, reward, satisfaction and job security if they could make it that far.

Meanwhile, back at the club, when the tennis was over for the day, there was an impressive programme of entertainment activities on offer each evening. On Sunday, there was a treasure hunt; on Monday, an all-comers disco; on Tuesday there was a bar quiz; on Wednesday, there was a junior rave where the added instruction was 'No Wrinklies Allowed'; on Thursday, it was karaoke night; and finally, on Friday was a 'Final fling' disco.

Countdown to trophies
On Saturday, Danny Sapsford and Amanda Grunfeld won their events and the cups were presented by Richard Whiteley, of the popular television programme, *Countdown*. After the singles finals, I decided to head for home and said my thanks and goodbyes to Ilkley. It had been a really good week, one where, if nothing else, I had been able to witness a snapshot of the life of the young men and women who aspired to follow their dream and one day, maybe, walk out on the centre court of one of the Grand Slams to compete for and perhaps win a prized trophy.

My appearance on the new British Tour had been extremely short. At least, I suppose, I could say that for one tournament, two matches, lasting about ninety minutes in total, I'd played on tour, just. But not really. The need to earn money for paying my bills was not dependent on how well I did. For me, this week had been purely recreational and although I took it seriously, it was always for fun. I'd had no aspiration other than to experience whatever came my way, have a good time and learn whatever lessons might present themselves.

After a really enjoyable week, I went from the British Tour to the non-Tour of Britain. I progressed, or maybe regressed might be a better way of saying it, into the one bigger part of the original master plan which didn't happen. Although I enjoyed a few rides around Wimbledon on my new touring bike, I decided to leave the Tour of Britain to the professional cyclists. I stayed in Wimbledon for the few weeks I had left before I needed to leave for the US Open in New York City towards the end of August.

Chapter 8

Heat and Noise in Flushing Meadows

America-bound

My down time through the rest of early August was up. It was time to head off to the US for the next phase of my trip, beginning with Grand Slam tournament number three in New York City.

The ticket I had bought for this next phase of my travels was an around-the-world one which had a number of stops built into it for its specified price. These locations started in London and then included New York, Los Angeles, Hawaii, Cairns, Sydney, Hong Kong and back to London. The dates had been left open and I would choose these as I went. Any trips and flights outside this itinerary would have to be booked and paid for on the way, like my intended trips to Brisbane and then Melbourne to and from Sydney. When inside the US, I planned to use Amtrack wherever possible and had managed to buy a rail pass which worked in a similar way to the one I had used in Europe. For any domestic flights, I would have to buy tickets for those legs on the trip. I intended to cross the country to the west coast and then come back east in order to reach Florida for the tennis fantasy camp I had booked while in Amsterdam back in April. After this, I would head back west again, the way I had just come and I had decided to complete that part of the trip by air. I had a good supply of travellers' cheques, my credit cards and enough dollars for the first few days in New York, all kept secure, along with my passport, in a sort of wallet made of synthetic material. By chance, this fitted perfectly inside a pouch pocket of a tracksuit-style top which I could wear in most weathers. Other than making me look as if I was developing a slight beer-belly, it was perfect for the job and had worked well in the first leg of the trip in Europe. My valuables felt secure. For additional funds, I could always use the emergency cheque cashing service in American Express Travel Offices where an American Express card could be used to endorse a bank cheque. Thirty years on, chip and pin cards and global connections make such a way of obtaining money seem a bit archaic but it was a really good service at the time.

I'd booked the first leg of the trip, a flight across to New York, on the Thursday prior to the start of the US Open which began on the following Monday. Having closed everything down in my flat, which I wouldn't see for the best part of six months, I shut and locked the door. I made my way up to Wimbledon station bound for Heathrow Airport. My neighbours, the freeholders of the building in which my flat was located, had keys should anything serious go wrong. I had known John and Marisa since purchasing the flat back in 1986. I liked and trusted them. They were happy to keep an eye on the flat while I was away. Although living in Cheltenham, my mum, who also had keys, could always help, as would Ben and Zoe who both lived in North London.

This was the first time I had flown to the US since my trips to Florida back in 1984 and 1985 and I'd read up my guide, this time, *Let's Go USA 1992*. It had given the usual comprehensive information on the travel basics of arriving at New York, although I would actually be flying into Newark Airport in New Jersey which would entail a slightly longer journey into the city than if I'd flown into JFK in Queens.

On arrival, once outside the terminal, I could have taken a taxi into the city but the bus service was much cheaper and easy to use, so I looked around for where to buy a ticket. That done, I walked to the stop where the bus would pull up and when my luggage was stowed and I was in my seat in a bus that was not that crowded, I sat back to enjoy the ride.

Once in the city, the bus station was huge and located in midtown on 8th Avenue, where my hotel was situated too, although a few blocks further uptown towards Central Park.

As I stood on the sidewalk working out if I could walk to the hotel or if I should take a cab, I felt really excited. As I looked up 8th Avenue towards my Days Inn Hotel which I could see in the distance, I had one of those classic views of the city that most of us have probably seen in one film or other. Before me were lines of traffic full of yellow cabs stopping, starting and changing lanes; people everywhere, all walking quickly, some heading uptown, others heading downtown and many crossing the street in both directions every time the signs allowed them. There were shop signs of all shapes and sizes everywhere including large neon ones. There was constant noise from everywhere with car horns blaring. If the traffic was even slightly slower than drivers wanted it to be, or if they saw something they didn't like, everyone seemed to use the horn. In nearly twenty years of driving in the UK, I could remember using the horn probably twice and once, as a car slowly crashed into me as the driver was looking the other way!

I decided that although I could see the hotel in the distance, it was quite some way and although I could walk short distances with my large bag, packed as lightly as possible this time, unlike when I set off around Europe, it was easier and wiser to pick up a cab. I made the mistake of doing the communication with the driver London-style, where you lean through the passenger window and agree that he or she will take you to where you want to go. In New York, your first job is to get into the cab. Then, you tell the driver where you want to go. He had sprung open the boot or trunk as it's called in the US and after a short drive, I was unloading everything, including myself, paying the fare and entering the lobby of the hotel where I stood in line waiting to check in.

I waited and waited, then waited some more. I stayed in this hotel for the duration of my stay which was just over three weeks. Throughout, it was the one slightly challenging aspect of the hotel's operation that the receptionists seemed to have been beamed in from a parallel universe in which time had slowed down. There was no hustle and bustle, the likes of which was going on just outside the hotel's front doors on 8th Avenue. Guests would wait and had no choice but to wait. If all you wanted to do was collect your room key and get on upstairs, you still had to wait in line along with everyone else, even if those other people were all checking in with extremely complex reservation requirements. It was a bit like being back in the queue at Wimbledon; you were in for the long haul.

Finally, once I had been checked in, I reached my room and got on the phone to two people. Firstly, I called Peter, who I had met in Amsterdam and he told me that he had a cocktail party reception to go to at the famous Plaza Hotel, organised through his work. I would be able to go with him. Next, I phoned the man who had started everything off, Simon Rogers, who had also suggested I stay in this particular hotel. He agreed to come down for breakfast the following morning in the diner attached to the hotel which you entered through the hotel reception. Plans made, I ordered a club sandwich from room service and when it arrived, I thought the kitchen staff had made me a replica of the stadium court at Flushing Meadows where I was about to spend many hours over the next two weeks. The sandwich was huge and in the short time I had to get ready before leaving for the Plaza Hotel, even though I had taken a few large bites, it looked like I hadn't eaten any of it. Such were many food portions in New York.

After a fun evening with Peter which involved the party, a cab ride downtown, some bar hopping and a trip back uptown to my hotel, I fell asleep, although despite my exhaustion and double-glazed windows, as I lay in bed, I could hear the relentless sounds of the city going on outside on 8th Avenue and beyond.

In search of Flushing
Up early, although not too early, I met Simon on a beautiful, sunny morning and we had breakfast with plenty of coffee re-

fills and a long catch-up in the hotel diner. Simon then had to get home for some family matters and off he went uptown to his apartment on the Upper West Side. I set out for Flushing Meadows where the US Open had been held since 1978. This trip involved walking a few blocks down to catch the 7 Train out to Queens. It was easy to know you were about to arrive because not only would you see the tennis site on your right-hand side but on your left-hand side, was the massive Shea Stadium, the home of the New York Mets baseball team.

Stepping out of the station, I walked onto a sloping boardwalk which took me down towards the entrance to the National Tennis Centre. At the ticket office, I enquired about availability across the fortnight and especially for the finals weekend. To my delight, not only were tickets available for the days up to the last two but there was availability on both those days as well. Therefore, I was able to buy a ticket for every day and would be in the stadium for those moments when the sun went down and the Manhattan skyline would light up and become a silhouette against the darkening sky. Having bought the tickets, I walked inside the grounds. There was no-one on the gates and only a few people walking around inside. I wandered around to orient myself and on one of the courts at the far side of the Louis Armstrong Stadium, there was none other than Clare Wood, who was practising. What a pleasant surprise that was. She shouted hello and after she had finished, we had a brief chat before she had to go. She had won through the qualifying event and was drawn against the top British player, once No. 4 in the world, Jo Durie. I told Clare I would look out for her.

I enjoyed the weekend doing a bit of sightseeing and in the evenings, experiencing the seemingly endless nightlife of the city that never sleeps with my friend Peter, who knew all the good places to go to ensure that if the night would end, it would begin well into the early morning of the next day.

Nationals to Open

The tournament that was about to begin here in August 1992, had its origins way back in the late nineteenth century. The history had involved a fragmented development of the events, one where they were all played at different locations for the singles and the doubles.

The tournament started in 1881 when a men's event had begun at the Newport Casino site in Newport, Rhode Island. From 1884 until 1911, the challenge system that had been used by Wimbledon was in place where the defending champion would only play one final match against the winner of all the rest who had worked his way through a knockout event involving all the other participants. The event was known as the US National Singles Championships for Men.

In 1887, the women's event began but was held at the Philadelphia Cricket Club. The men's doubles began but was also held somewhere else, the Orange Lawn Tennis Club in South Orange, New Jersey. When the women's doubles event was established, it operated a different type of challenge system from the one used in the singles events with pairs qualifying through to a final from different regions. In 1915, the men's singles moved to the West Side Tennis Club in Queens while the women's singles stayed in Philadelphia.

By the mid-twenties, both men and women were playing at West Side. Seeds were introduced in 1927. As the event continued, it was known as the US Nationals. However, that just dealt with the singles events. From 1917, with a break in the Second World War, the doubles events, including the mixed, were held at the Longwood Club in Boston and would be followed by the singles events at West Side the following week.

Hester's Place

Following the start of open tennis in 1968, the tournament became known as the US Open and all the events were held at

West Side. Historically, like Wimbledon and the Australian Championships, the tournament had been held on grass. But as the years passed, there were question marks over the quality of the courts. In 1975, the surface was changed to green Har-Tru, an American version of European red clay. Floodlights were introduced too. But by this time, the USTA felt that the tournament had outgrown West Side. The driving force behind a move was William 'Slew' Hester who had risen up the ranks of the USTA to become president in 1977 and 1978. Slew convinced New York City officials to turn what was known as the Singer Bowl in Flushing Meadows, a few miles away from the West Side Tennis Club, into what became known as the USTA National Tennis Centre. In the early days, one of the restaurants was called Hester's Place in recognition of the former president.

The site was built close to where the World Fair had been held in the sixties, and in 1978, the Open moved. As when I arrived in 1992, the main show courts were the Louis Armstrong Stadium with the Grandstand Court attached to it on one side. There was bleacher seating on a number of the outside courts but unlike Wimbledon, other than a small number of people who were given complimentary passes and ground tickets, the only fans allowed in for each session were the ones who held a show court ticket. This meant that the outside courts were a bit less crowded, something that I liked.

When looking at former winners, Richard Sears, William Larned and Bill Tilden for the men and Molla Mallory for the women, won most singles titles in the pre-open era. Since 1968, Jimmy Connors, Pete Sampras and Roger Federer along with Chris Evert and Serena Williams have won most titles. Youngest male winners were William Larned and Pete Sampras and youngest female winners were Molla Mallory and Tracey Austin. Most singles match wins have been achieved by Jimmy Connors, with ninety-eight and Serena Williams, with one hundred and six.

New York, New York
Although the comfort levels have improved since 1992, back then, the US Open at Flushing Meadows was a different proposition from the other Slams. I've talked about a loose definition of what might be called the brand for Wimbledon back over in SW19 but if I did the same for the Open in New York, that definition would be very different. If Wimbledon could be described as genteel, the US Open was more demanding and unforgiving. Although a lot of this was down to the fact that at the time of year the tournament is held, it was really hot, a test for just about everyone involved. It was a concrete jungle with few areas where you could find any shade except underneath the Louis Armstrong Stadium Court with its mass of steel and girders. Mind you, at Wimbledon, when the heat levels rose, things could get uncomfortable too. But where Wimbledon and to a degree, Roland Garros, had lots of green everywhere, at Flushing Meadows, that colour was more likely to be grey, although today, it is a more pleasant shade of blue, certainly on all the courts themselves.

The day-night system of matches, allowing for prime-time television coverage in the evenings, was always a concern to the players involved, perhaps not so much the women, whose singles match would usually go on first, but certainly the men, who would start at an unconfirmed later time. If the match was a long one, they could be playing way past midnight. Of course, this sort of scheduling happened at other tournaments, on the indoor winter circuit and at the Australian Open too, after that tournament switched to Flinders Park in the late eighties. But it didn't mean that the players liked it. They endured it. Some, like Jimmy Connors, seemed to revel in it using an often alcohol-influenced and rowdy crowd to his advantage. What came to be known as Super Saturday where, for television purposes, both men's semi-finals were played the day before the final and split in timing by the women's final stuck in between, was almost universally hated by the players.

This day has now been abandoned with the men's semi-finals being played two days before the final, as in the other Slams.

As a fan, you had to get your mind right, get prepared, make sure you had your water, your sunscreen and your hat and put your best foot forward. As I would experience on my trip a few months later, the Australian Open in Melbourne was hot, very hot, but in New York, you had noise too, especially from the crowd in the night sessions, if they got behind an American player like Jimmy Connors or John McEnroe. In the past, there had been even more noise from the planes overhead. Earplugs helped when the planes were taking off from runway thirteen at nearby La Guardia Airport. In addition, planes in and out of JFK Airport, which was not far away from La Guardia, added and still adds to the noise pollution. Everyone breathed a sigh of relief, when in 1990, Mayor David Dinkins, a big supporter of the Open and frequent fan, who sat in a special box, negotiated a change in routes out of the airport with the management of La Guardia.

In contrast to some aspects of the event which had to be endured or handled with some degree of fortitude and resilience, just as the tournament represented characteristics of the city it was held in, so the food, superb in New York, was also the best compared to the other Grand Slams. There was a quality selection on offer from around the world, just as you could find them in the city in various locations renowned for a particular type of cuisine. The food on offer was also more expensive than at the other Slam locations but it was worth it. You really did get what you paid for.

Having said all of the above, I didn't enjoy the US Open any less than the other Slams. In fact, I enjoyed it as much, if not more. I just accepted what was on offer and made the most of things. For me, the beauty of the Slams was their differences as much as their similarities. The things that made Flushing Meadows different were what made it interesting. Writing about it now, I only have fond memories.

Seeds, nationalities and early rounds
Looking at the men's seeds in comparison to the list at Wimbledon, there were three changes, with Carlos Costa, Malivai Washington and John McEnroe coming in. Jim Courier and Stefan Edberg were the top two. As the tournament began, there were few early-round surprises although Petr Korda was knocked-out by Emilio Sanchez in a fifth set tiebreaker. In the second round, Michael Stich lost to Brad Gilbert with an interesting score in the deciding tiebreaker of 7-0 to the American.

Looking at clusters of players by nationality, as I had found myself doing in Rome, Paris and Wimbledon, in the men's singles, there were the usual compliment of Italians and French including names that I had come to know well by now. Unfortunately, there wasn't a single British player in the first round, although four, Chris Bailey, Danny Sapsford, Andrew Castle and Mark Petchey had tried to qualify. As might have been expected here in their home Slam, there were thirty-one Americans. There were also ten Swedes and five Australians, a dwindling group these days when compared with the pre-open days of Harry Hopman and his conveyor belt production of top players.

In the early rounds of the men's singles, perhaps one of the most significant things to happen was that Jimmy Connors would play his last match at the Open. His first-round match, a win against Brazilian, Jaime Oncins, was played in the night session on Jimmy's fortieth birthday. He received a huge welcome when he arrived on court. In the second round, Ivan Lendl proved too strong and beat Jimbo in four. Connors lost his final set 6-0, in an event he had won five times. I couldn't relate much to one of the greatest players the game has ever seen but after my experiences being double-bagelled in Bahrain by Frank Sabaratnam and Ickringilled in Ilkley by club coach, Simon, on this occasion, maybe just a teeny-weeny bit, I could.

Obviously, for every round that is completed in a knockout draw, the number of players is cut in half. Looking at things from a nationality perspective, other than the Swedes, who lost six of their ten players who started in the first round, the Italians, the French and the Americans all did a little better and retained just over half of their group. For the Australians, things were even better as all five of their players won. However, in round two, the draw brought together the Woodies, as we have seen, the top doubles team of this era and possibly of all time to that point, based purely on number of title wins, before the ascendancy of the Bryan brothers. Mark Woodforde beat his mate, Todd Woodbridge and went through to the third round in straight sets along with countrymen Richard Fromberg and Wally Masur. The second round delivered further cuts. Only two Swedes made it through. Nicklas Kulti fought out another five-setter, this time losing to fellow Swede, Jonas Svensson who would himself, play against fellow countryman, Stefan Edberg, in the third round. Of the Italians, only Omar Camporese made it through. Guy Forget and Cedric Pioline would fly the French flag. Twelve Americans took their place in the thirty-two slots in the third-round draw.

One first-round match I did watch brought together two of my players from Rome with the Italian, Gianluca Pozzi playing Israel's Amos Mansdorf. This became a hard-fought contest in which Mansdorf needed an energy boost at one point. As he sat in his chair at the changeover, he stared straight ahead and called out something, possibly "Bananas." I looked around and then, very slowly but surely, an older man in a suit, sitting behind the players, started to move, muttering as he did so. Amos has told me since that this man was a family friend, Ira, who Amos stayed with when playing in New York. Anyway, Ira proceeded to disappear for about ten minutes, returning with a handful of the energy-giving fruit. He dropped them over the fence where Amos picked them up and started working his way through them. They didn't help as Pozzi won, 6-1 in a fifth set.

In the women's list of seeds, there were only two changes from the list at Wimbledon with Helena Sukova and Mary Pierce coming in and Kimiko Date and Judith Wiesner dropping out. As far as early surprises went, the Belgian, Sabine Appelmans, played well to beat seed, Jana Novotna in the first round. Also, the American, Ann Grossman beat the eighth seed, Conchita Martinez. But perhaps the biggest shock and loss to the tournament although an exciting win for the victor, was Maggie Maleeva's second round straight sets defeat of fourth seed, Martina Navratilova, playing in her twentieth Open. In a post-match press interview, Martina alluded to the mental approach to the match asking a journalist to understand the different situations both players found themselves in. Martina emphasised how she had everything to lose while her young opponent had everything to gain. Nerves did appear to restrict Martina's performance, especially considering that she won the second set by 6-0. Her upset after the defeat was clear.

As at Wimbledon, there was a very large contingent of Americans; thirty-eight in total, including Linda Harvey Wild who had done so well at Eastbourne. This number included seven of the eight wild cards handed out by the USTA and also, four qualifiers, including Camille Benjamin, another of the players featured in the book *Courting Fame*. Camille had reached a career high of No. 27 back in 1984 and had won an ITF singles title at Schenectady in 1987. Both her finals appearances in WTA singles events had ended up in defeats to fellow *Courting Fame* participant and winner from the Florida Federal Open that I had watched at Hopman's back in 1985, Stephanie Rehe. The other *Courting Fame* participant here in New York, Marianne Werdel, lost to Brenda Schultz, the winner in Birmingham earlier in the summer. After beating Marianne, Brenda advanced another round, beating the French player, Pascale Paradis-Magnon. There were four British players in the draw. In addition to Clare Wood and Jo Durie, there was Monique Javer and my Southdown Club connection, Sara Gomer. Steffi Graf led a group of seven players from Germany including Meike Babel who was drawn against an unseeded Kimiko Date, no doubt with plenty of camera-wielding fans to support her. As in Paris, there was a strong French contingent. There were also smaller groups of players from the Czech Republic, Argentina, Italy, Spain and the rest were spread across the nations of the ITF.

Seventeen of the American contingent were knocked out in the first round leaving twenty-one players remaining, although these were predominantly the bigger names. Four Germans had come through, including Steffi Graff and six of the French had also won, including Mary Pierce, although twelfth seed, Natalie Tauziat, was beaten by the young South African, Amanda Coetzer. With the British players, both Monique Javer and Sara Gomer lost. But after a good win, beating Jo Durie, Clare Wood would be flying the flag in the third round where she would play Sabine Appelmans. In other second round matches, all the seeds who had survived the first round, progressed to the third.

From one tennis fantasy to another
One morning in the first week when the early rounds were still in progress, just before leaving my room at the hotel, the phone rang. It was the organiser of the tennis fantasy camp that I had signed up for in October down in Florida. He said that he had bad news but some good news too. On the bad side, due to the effects of Hurricane Andrew which had swept up the Eastern Seaboard in the weeks before the Open had begun, the camp would have to be cancelled. However, he knew of another guy who was running a similar camp around the same time down in Texas. His name was Steve Contardi and not only did Steve now have my details but he had my deposit too which my original contact had transferred. It all seemed to be okay as

instead of travelling all the way back east to Florida, I would just stop in Texas instead. On the other hand, when something sounds too good to be true, especially when money is concerned, it usually is. But in this case, after bidding the organiser goodbye, I called Steve, the owner-organiser of the other camp, who was based in Cincinnati, to discover that everything was as had just been explained to me.

Steve was service personified and he said he would send details to my hotel and when I told him I would be arriving in San Antonio by rail, he told me that this wasn't a problem and when the time came, if I kept in touch with arrival times, he would ensure I was collected. He also confirmed that as well as some of the top American players from the sixties and seventies, the core of the group of legend professionals who would be team captains for the week, were the Australian stars from that time, like John Newcombe, whose tennis ranch the event was held at. This sounded even better for me than the original camp I had signed up for. So began a friendship with Steve, his family and the staff at The Club at Harper's Point in Cincinnati, which lasts to this day. Also, on arrival, as we shall see, I found out that instead of ending up at an alternative version of the fantasy camp, I was actually at the original one. I could not have been happier. With an added skip to my Adidas shoe-clad step, I headed out and started my trip to Flushing Meadows.

The collapsing man

The fact that I had secured tickets for the tennis each day made the whole experience a bit more civilised. I didn't have to be up at the crack of dawn to stand in any queue. If you had a ticket for the day session, this meant that you had to leave the grounds by about seven o'clock, so that the fans for the night session could be allowed in.

This meant that I could get up and into the diner for some breakfast at around nine o'clock and then repeat the trip I had made on the Friday before the start of the tournament. The weather was good for most of the two weeks which meant I could walk down to the 7 Train and find a seat quite easily and then relax as the train headed east across the Hudson River and into Queens. There was only one rather strange incident that I witnessed in the fortnight and it involved a tall man who was standing near to me as the train went along. At one point, he began a gradual collapse as if he was feeling ill. It all happened very slowly and I'm not sure how many people actually saw the man's demise. Maybe, this was New York and people just didn't get involved. I wasn't sure if I should do something or not. But as he reached the floor, people had to move. Recently, I have seen British comedian, Terry Alderton, doing a brilliant routine where he pretends that his body is a balloon gradually losing air. The more air that seeps out of him, the lower he drops towards the floor. When I saw Terry's act for the first time, immediately, I thought back to this tall man on the train out to Flushing. Then, a strange thing happened. As the train arrived in a station a couple of stops before the tennis, the doors opened, a second went by and then the man just got up and walked out onto the platform and off to the stairs down to the street. Hardly anyone left on the train said anything, the doors closed, the train headed off and people went back to doing what they had been up to before the incident. Welcome to New York.

On arrival at the tennis, I'd do what had now become my established routine. I'd get a coffee, look at the order of play and decide who I wanted to watch that day. I had the choice of watching matches on the main centre court, the Louis Armstrong Stadium, or I could wander and watch a growing number of players who were now on my watch list after all the tournaments I'd attended so far that summer, starting in Rome. I would usually have one snack in the middle of the afternoon and when the day-session crowd started to leave, I too, would make the return journey into the city, usually back on the train, the way I had come.

However, there was one day when I spotted a bus at the back entrance to the site which was taking players and members of their entourages back to mid-town. No-one seemed to be checking passes or badges, so spontaneously and in a way very unlike me, I stepped up onto the bus, took my seat next to a photographer and travelled back into the city in a different way than usual. The bus deposited everyone at the Marriott Hotel in mid-town and no-one seemed the slightest bit bothered that I was there. Perhaps it was the Adidas clothing I had bought for Ilkley that I was wearing that day? Maybe I really was turning into something like the other John McEnroe from West Worthing, somehow convincing watching eyes that I was a legitimate part of the two tours. That wasn't my aim but, in this case, I experienced a comfortable ride back to the city and was spared any further risks of being collapsed upon by 7 Train passengers.

On my return to the hotel, after a shower and a rest, I'd be off to meet Peter to have some dinner and then a few beers in various bars. Of course, as someone who knew the city like the back of his hand, Peter took all the sights and sounds in his stride. But I was a new tourist and walking around, I found myself staring at anything and everything from the buildings to the traffic to the people. After all those years watching all those films and documentaries about the city, here I was, experiencing it for real. Peter was working full time, so we didn't stay out too late every night except at the weekends.

Finally, it would be back to the Days Inn, into the reception queue with the hope that there wouldn't be too many people in front of me making me wait ages for my key.

Leaving Arthur in peace
There was one small area on the far side of the outside courts where there were some park benches, actually quite close to

where I'd watched the Mansdorf-Pozzi match. If I needed a short rest, I used these seats as a place of refuge. As I sat looking back across towards the huge show courts in the distance, a tall, lithe figure appeared coming towards me, on the pathway that ran past the seats. It was Arthur Ashe. He was on his own, looking pensive and staring down towards the ground. Up to that point in the trip, despite travelling on my own, in fact probably because I was on my own, I'd spoken to literally hundreds of people whether I had to, in the case of hotel owners for example, or if I didn't but wanted to say something to someone. This latter case applied to just about anyone but especially, to top tennis players who I might have wanted to chat to, even though I would have understood, if they had not wanted to talk. Most had not been like that, including Byron Talbot, as we chatted on the way across London after the Manchester tournament back in June. Bud Collins had been charm personified in Paris and there were other positive examples too. Although we weren't strangers, I did not know Clare Wood well but she had been so friendly and helpful in Paris. Maybe, in this case, because of the stature of the man in question or maybe because it felt as if I would be invading his privacy if I spoke to him, bearing in mind how engrossed he looked in his own thoughts, I did not say anything but left the great man alone.

I knew no more about Arthur than any other tennis fan might have picked up along the way. I had read his autobiography and his diary of life on tour in 1973. I knew a fair amount about the issues he had faced. On the court, I had seen him play, although not live, but had followed his career as I had followed that of many others through the scrutiny of the sport that looking through the prism of Wimbledon provided. I had been playing cricket on the day he beat Jimmy Connors in the 1975 Wimbledon final, a performance heralded as one of the tactical masterclasses in the sport's history. I had seen the highlights which showed him sitting at the changeovers with his eyes closed as he focused on slowing his breathing or maybe, visualising what he intended to do in the next game. He played a wonderful attacking style of tennis and was a serve-volley player with a lovely service action. His volleys were a thing of efficient simplicity. What a handful he must have been, as Peter Burwash had testified.

I knew that he had grown up in the racially divided, pre-civil rights South and had succeeded in the sport the hard way. Also, I knew that he had won the US Open in 1968 in the first summer of open tennis. He had also won the Australian Open in 1970. I knew that he had decided to play in apartheid South Africa for reasons he saw as positive but his justification for going had not been seen that way by everyone else in the anti-apartheid movement. I knew too that the man had HIV, a disease contracted from a blood transfusion when he had been operated on for a bad heart. In short, I felt like I knew him. But I was almost overawed by his close proximity.

Often, in these situations, I would do what my friend Simon Rogers once suggested and say the first thing that came into my head, about the weather or anything. That moment passed and Arthur walked by. He was not a well man. He would be gone by the time of the US Open the following year. In 1997, the new centre court at Flushing Meadows would be named after him, a man who had won three Grand Slams, seventy-six tour titles and had been placed at the top of the rankings in the days when respected people in the sport produced their lists based purely on their opinions prior to the computer-generated ones. Althea Gibson had been the first black woman to win a Grand Slam and Arthur Ashe had been the first black man. Even though I was trying to be respectful, as he walked on, in the time that has gone by since, I couldn't help feeling that this was a lost opportunity, if not for him, then certainly for me. After thinking about the situation for a few moments, I stood up to get on with my spectating. What was done was done. It was time for another match.

Goodbye to the Aussies and to Jen

In the third round, half of the men's matches were completed in straight sets. The only seed to fall was Goran Ivanisevic. In the battle of the Sanchez brothers, Emilio came out on top in five sets. There were various nationality clashes: Boris Becker beat Charlie Steeb; Stefan Edberg beat Jonas Svensson; Pete Sampras beat qualifier, Todd Martin, in five sets; Brad Gilbert beat another qualifier, Tommy Ho, also in five sets showing a proficiency for final set tiebreakers again, winning this one 7-0; and Ivan Lendl beat Chuck Adams. But it was goodbye to the Aussie mates, as Mark Woodforde, Richard Fromberg and Wally Masur all lost. Jim Courier, Andre Agassi, Wayne Ferreira and Michael Chang all won.

In the women's singles, two seeds were beaten: Jennifer Capriati lost to Canada's Patricia Hy, who played one of the matches of her career; Katerina Maleeva also departed, beaten by Chanda Rubin Of the remaining matches, eleven were over in straight sets, including wins for Steffi Graf and Monica Seles. Gigi Fernandez, Helena Sukova, Gabriela Sabatini, Sabine Appelmans, Mary Pierce, Mary Joe Fernandez, Carrie Cunningham, Manuela and Maggie Maleeva, Arantxa Sanchez Vicario, Zina Garrison and Florencia Labat were also winners.

Those successful would make the second week and increase their prize money winnings substantially, even if they advanced no further than the fourth-round matches which began over the middle weekend of the tournament as the Labor Day holiday approached.

Three contrasting dinners

On three of the evenings during the tournament, I went for dinner with friends. Each one was a quite different experience.

The first was after Simon contacted me and asked me if I would like to meet that evening. It would have been a fun evening just with Simon but on this occasion, there was the added bonus of meeting former British tennis player, Anne

Hobbs, who was a friend of Simon's through his neighbour. Anne had been a pro for twelve years from the end of the seventies to the end of the eighties. She had been the British No. 1 and had won two singles titles and eight doubles titles, reaching two Grand Slam doubles finals with Wendy Turnbull and Kathy Jordan as well as one mixed final with Andrew Castle. Her career high rankings were No. 33 in singles and as high as No. 6 in doubles.

The three of us met in a restaurant on the Upper East Side. Simon was always great company but Anne stole the show that night with her bubbly personality, her stories and musings about a variety of topics. I felt as if I had hardly said a word, which is very unlike me!

The second dinner was one with Peter, who recommended we go to a place he knew well, downtown in Little Italy. Off we went to a restaurant called *The Luna*. It was basic but Peter assured me that the food was amazing which it was. But the memorable highlight was the service provided by a woman who might have been the inspiration for Dale Carnegie's book, *How to Win Friends and Influence People*, in that she was the epitome of how not to establish rapport and get on with your customers, on the face of it, at least. She was efficient but to the point of being brusque and officious. She took our orders and then dumped some bread on the table. Drinks came next but there hadn't been the hint of any warmth. I took this to be down to life in New York where everything seemed to be going on at a ridiculous pace with just no time for the usual civilities you might expect elsewhere.

Then, out of the blue, once we had finished our meals, when she started to clear away the plates, she picked up a spoon and contorted her hand into a strange shape. With a nod of her head and an encouraging facial expression, she made me look into the surface of the spoon. All I will say is that the image before my eyes was a bit near the knuckle, something a bit like an Avant Garde interpretation of the female form.

Immediately, I recoiled a bit as if I'd seen something shocking, which, in a way, I had. On seeing my recognition of the image, the faintest of smiles showed on her face and as she picked up the plates, turned and strode off towards the kitchen, she barked out, "Welcome to *The Luna.*" Peter exploded in laughter. I reckon he might well have seen this little routine before. I left the restaurant with a smirk on my face. It was impossible not to see the irreverent and funny side of the waitress's act, even if it was a party piece that may have been enacted hundreds of times for unsuspecting tourists visiting the restaurant. If there was a *Little Italy's Got Talent* programme, our waitress would have had to enter.

The third dinner was when, as he promised, John Kosta got in touch and arranged for me and a friend to go to one of the night sessions at Flushing. Afterwards, he would take us to dinner along with the group of clients he was looking after. I asked Peter if he'd like to come. The only problem was that it was the worst evening of the fortnight as far as the weather was concerned with torrential rain. Not a ball was hit and after returning to the city, at least we had dinner in a big group in a mid-town Italian restaurant although this time, there was no added entertainment from the staff.

I confirmed to John that in a few weeks' time, I would be coming to his hometown in Ann Arbor, Michigan where I had a weekend of American football planned. He told me to get in touch with him when I was there and we would meet up.

Doubles ins and outs
Back at Flushing Meadows, as was the way in these two-week Slams, as the singles draws shrank, the doubles events kicked in. In both the men's and women's events, the core of the seeded teams remained as it had been both in Paris and Wimbledon.

In the men's, four pairs dropped out of the list and Wimbledon champions, John McEnroe and Michael Stich came in, along with Patrick Galbraith and Danie Visser, David Adams and Andrei Olhovskiy, and Sergio Casal and Emilio Sanchez who had played in Paris but not at Wimbledon. Jacob Hlasek was reunited with Marc Rosset. By the end of the third round, nine of the pairs were out. Brad Pearce and Byron Talbot had lost in straight sets to the fourteenth seeds, Ken Flach and Todd Witsken.

In the women's event, there were fewer changes with Katrina Adams and Manon Bollegraf, and Anke Huber and Claudia Kohde-Kilsch dropping out. They were replaced by Conchita Martinez and Mercedes Paz, and Alexia Dechaume-Balleret and Florencia Labat. Three players, Sandy Collins, Elna Reinach and Elizabeth Smylie, teamed up with new partners. By the end of the third round, half the seeds were gone. Clare Wood, partnered with Tracey Morton, won their first-round match against Caroline Kuhlman and Lupita Novelo. However, in the second round, they were beaten by Patty Fendick and Andrea Strnadova.

In the mixed, the draw was thirty-two teams, half the size of Wimbledon's sixty-four draw and also smaller than the forty-eight team draw in Paris. There were eight as opposed to sixteen seeds with five seeded teams from Wimbledon and two seeded players with new partners, including Arantxa Sanchez Vicario who had teamed up with Todd Woodbridge. By the end of the second round, four pairs were already out including Arantxa and Todd who were the top seeds. My preferred pair from Paris, Bryan Shelton and Lori McNeil were wild cards and reached the quarter-finals. Byron Talbot and Isabelle Demongeot won their first match but lost in the second round.

Goodbye Mac
In the fourth round of the men's singles, the tournament said goodbye to another icon in the form of John McEnroe. He had first played in the Open way back in 1974 as a fifteen-year-old in the men's doubles, partnered by his then coach, the ex-

player, Tony Palafox. He'd played in doubles again in 1975 and 1976 and gone on to play fifteen times up to and including 1992, winning the title on four occasions, losing in a final once. In singles, McEnroe played for the first time in 1977 and played sixteen consecutive years. The Open had been his best Slam in singles when defined by win ratio which was eighty-five per cent; he won sixty-six of the seventy-eight matches that he played. McEnroe was a New Yorker and the crowd loved him, pretty much whatever mood he was in. As a player, he seemed to be able to do things others couldn't even contemplate with his ability to play both power and touch tennis, often in the same point, let alone game, set or match. However, in this tournament, a pumped-up Jim Courier proved too much for the former champion, beating him in three sets. Four of the eight men's matches went to five sets including Ivan Lendl's defeat of Boris Becker, in the longest match in the Open's history to that point, lasting just over five hours and finishing just before one o'clock in the morning. Michael Chang beat Malivai Washington and Pete Sampras beat Guy Forget. The fourth match was Stefan Edberg's win over Richard Krajicek, a match I watched in the Louis Armstrong Stadium where Edberg's amazing all-court agility overcame the Dutch player's huge serve.

On the women's side, again Monica Seles and Steffi Graf won easily in straight sets. Seeds Mary Pierce and Zina Garrison were beaten by fellow seeds Mary Joe Fernandez and Arantxa Sanchez but Helena Sukova was beaten by unseeded Patricia Hy, extending the Canadian's good run. The only match which went the distance was Maggie Maleeva's victory over Chanda Rubin, 6-1 in the third set. Maggie joined her sister, Manuela, in the quarter-finals.

Approaching the finals
We were down to the last eight in the singles. On the men's side, two matches went to five sets including another one for

Stefan Edberg in beating Ivan Lendl 7-3 in a final set tiebreaker, a match I was fortunate to watch with Edberg again a break down in the final set. Michael Chang, Pete Sampras and Jim Courier who won the all-American battle against Andre Agassi, advanced to the last four. In the semi-finals, Stefan Edberg survived his third five-set match in a row in defeating Michael Chang after the American had led 3-0 in the final set. In the all-American clash between two friends and at times, doubles partners, Pete Sampras beat Jim Courier in four sets.

In the women's singles, Monica Seles dispatched Patricia Hy but Arantxa Sanchez Vicario played brilliantly to beat Steffi Graf in straight sets, preventing the chance of a third final in a row at the French, Wimbledon and now, in New York between the two top-ranked players in the world. Mary Joe Fernandez put out Gabriela Sabatini and in the sisters' match-up, Maggie Maleeva had to retire allowing Manuela through to the semi-final. Monica beat Mary Joe Fernandez relatively easily in their semi-final and Arantxa beat Manuela Maleeva-Fragniere in straight sets too.

A long, final weekend
The last weekend began on the Friday. As sometimes happened at the Open, especially in the day session, when one of the doubles finals was on, hardly anyone was watching. I had a ticket for the Louis Armstrong Stadium court and watched as Jim Grabb and Richey Reneberg, no doubt having discarded his pimple-soled grass-court shoes in favour of something more suitable to the Open's hard courts, played their men's final against Kelly Jones and Rick Leach. Here were two American teams competing for their home title. In the semi-finals, Jones and Leach had claimed the prize scalp of the Woodies who had beaten Jacco Eltingh and Paul Harhuis in the quarter-final. Grabb and Reneberg had disposed of the dangerous partnership of John McEnroe and Michael Stich, after beating Borwick and Youl in the quarter-final. I sat high

up in the seats and watched a four-set win for Grabb and Reneberg which hopefully was a salve to the wound of losing the marathon final at Wimbledon before against McEnroe and Stich. I didn't know it then, but my interest with Jim and Richey on this trip was not yet over.

In the women's doubles final, Gigi Fernandez and Natasha Zvereva had come through after beating Lori McNeil and Rennae Stubbs in the quarter-finals and Sanchez Vicario and Sukova in the semi-final. Their opponents were Jana Novotna and Larissa Savchenko-Neiland who had beaten Mary Joe Fernandez and Zina Garrison, and Martina Navratilova and Pam Shriver. Gigi and Natasha were too strong in the final, winning in straight sets. This was the third Slam in a row that they had won in the three Slams that I had attended so far on my journey. If they could win in Melbourne in the coming Slam in January, they would win a non-calendar year Grand Slam in that event while I would complete my spectator version of that Slam.

In the mixed doubles, Mark Woodforde and Nicole Provis beat Cyril Suk and Helena Sukova to win the title.

In the junior girls' event, the winner was Lindsay Davenport who was at the upper end of an age group which often included players much younger than its U18 designation. Her parents had insisted that Lindsay complete High School before joining the tour full time. If it could be said that anyone on the junior circuit had experienced a relatively normal existence up to the point of winning a Slam title, Lindsay had, it seemed.

When it came to the men's and women's singles, in 1992 what had become known as 'Super Saturday' was still being played. The men's semi-finals would top and tail the day on the Louis Armstrong Stadium Court with the women's singles final being played in the middle.

Monica Seles and Arantxa Sanchez Vicario came on court to play their final in mid-afternoon in between Edberg and

Sampras's semi-final wins. Unlike the final in Paris, which had been a battle, and more like the one at Wimbledon, which hadn't, Monica beat Arantxa in straight sets 6-3, 6-3. Monica had not dropped a set throughout the tournament.

It was now the final Sunday and I had a ticket and so did Peter. Again, I was sitting high up in the stands, a view of the tennis that some called these seats, the 'nose-bleeds'. I actually liked these seats. Also, I had that magnificent view of the Manhattan skyline across to the west as the sun set, one removed in later years when the huge Arthur Ashe stadium was built to take over the centre court role for the tournament. It was a wonderful final for me as both players preferred playing serve-volley tennis. Despite what must have been some fatigue from his three previous matches, all of which had been five setters, Stefan Edberg prevailed over rising star, Pete Sampras, who had already won the Open in 1990 and would win it again. My favourite player at the time had won in an exciting setting. It was just about a perfect end to the tournament for me.

With the Open now over, I got ready to start the trip across the country. There was a lot of planning to do for what would be a lot of travelling. But so far, my plan had unfolded without a hitch and I didn't even envisage one. I carried on regardless. The next stop would be Washington D.C. I had many things in my mind that I wanted to do and I intended to enjoy each one. But the excitement at attending the Tennis Fantasies week down in Texas towards the end of October, was starting to build inside me.

Chapter 9

Tennis Fantasies at Newk's

Train trips, rental cars and football games
Thinking back to that afternoon in Bruges when I sat down and planned out the rest of my European trip, I realised that the next few weeks would need similar meticulous planning. I had to be in San Antonio by the third Sunday in October for the start of the Tennis Fantasies week at John Newcombe's Tennis Ranch in New Braunfels, a few miles north towards Austin. So, I sat in my room in the Days Inn and mapped out how the trip might work considering my aim of visiting some of the nation's major cities and wherever possible, watching some American football. Armed with the Amtrack timetable brochure and the *Street and Smith* guides, one for college football and the other for the NFL, I began planning.

Most of the major train routes across country had at least one, if not two services each day, leaving in the morning and the evening, for overnight travel. For the slightly shorter trips, I would take the morning service. For the journeys of the longer duration, I would travel overnight. For any location not involving American football games, like my visit to the Grand Canyon, I would try to complete that part of the trip in midweek.

Counting down to Tennis Fantasies
I stayed on in New York a few days more. When Saturday arrived, I went uptown to Columbia University to watch their football team, the Lions, play rivals, Harvard. The people I sat with were really friendly, chatting to me, offering me food and drink. It was a really pleasant experience.

With the aim of being in Boston by the following weekend, I left New York and boarded a train down to Washington D.C. I booked a day trip to the location of the iconic 1863 American Civil War battle of Gettysburg, via the site of John Brown's insurrection at Harper's Ferry, and after a few days of sightseeing around the political buildings and museums of the nation's capital, I got back on the Yankee Clipper and headed back through New York and on to Boston.

I was staying only a short distance from the iconic baseball field of Fenway Park, home of the Boston Red Sox, who were playing a game the evening I arrived, one I attended. I spent a few more days looking at the sights, including the location of the bar in the famous television show *Cheers*. At the weekend, I watched Boston University against Michigan State on the Saturday, and on the Sunday, the New England Patriots against the Buffalo Bills at Foxboro.

The weekend over, I was off again bound for Chicago on the Lakeshore Limited, this time, an overnight journey. It was baseball again as I attended another game in another iconic stadium, Wrigley Field. I watched the Chicago Cubs sitting next to a man who owned his own marketing agency but was considering giving it all up so he could concentrate on his true passion, which was fishing. We had a lot in common, it seemed. As the weekend approached, I started the short journey back east towards Ann Arbor, the home of the University of Michigan, and also, John Kosta. On the train, I spotted an attractive young woman who was trying to put on nail polish as the train rumbled along. She was very good at a task I perceived to be absolutely impossible to do without getting the varnish everywhere. I started up a conversation and Leslie and I are friends to this day.

I checked in at the University Alumni Hotel and went in search of the enormous football stadium. I had been told that due to the huge demand for tickets, I would never be able to get one but I couldn't believe it as I was able to pick one almost exactly where I wanted to sit. I made my way to John Kosta's travel company, passing the Permian High School where I saw a band practice going on for a game that evening – Friday night lights. Speaking to John on the phone, sadly, he had experienced a family bereavement and would be away for the weekend. But he said that his wife Jan, would love to see me on the Sunday. I walked back towards my hotel and came across my second band practice of the afternoon. This time, it was the huge University of Michigan band having their last rehearsal. After dinner, I returned to Permian High and watched the Panthers play their game

Saturday dawned. Everywhere was a sea of fans covered in the Michigan Wolverines' colours of dark blue and yellow. As kick-off approached, I walked towards the stadium with the band I had watched the day before. The hairs on the back of my neck stood up when the drummers started. Sitting in the stadium was another breath-taking experience. The attendance was over one-hundred and six thousand. Like the Foro Italico, once you were inside, part of the stands and field were down below as if the land had been excavated. Once in my seat, I sat in awe of the sight.

The next morning, Jan Kosta picked me up as promised and I had breakfast at the Kosta house with her son, a committed junior tennis player. She dropped me at the car rental place and I drove to Detroit, watched the game in the Pontiac Silverdome between the Lions and the New Orleans Saints, drove back, Jan picked me up again after I had dropped the car back and drove me to my hotel. I was very touched by her selfless kindness. In the morning, Leslie and a friend picked me up, drove us to the station and we returned to Chicago.

An amazing coincidence
I only had a few hours to kill before boarding the Southwest Chief overnight service to take me across country towards Los Angeles. However, on this occasion, I would be stopping off at Flagstaff in Arizona so that I could see the Grand Canyon, and

Monument Valley. It would be a wonderful stopover, staying in perhaps the funkiest guest house of the trip so far.

On the small bus taking us to see Monument Valley, where so many famous Westerns had been filmed, there were four women who were obviously from the UK sitting just in front of me. I got chatting to them and asked them where they were from. One of them said, "Cheltenham." I responded by saying that my mum lived there and without missing a beat, one of the women said, "Sheila Cripps", the name of my mum. I couldn't believe it and when I told them who that was, neither could they and nor could my mum when they returned and told her. These women were in one of the various groups my mum was a member of back at home and here they were, thousands of miles away from Cheltenham in the middle of the Arizona desert and the one British person on the bus was the son of their friend from back at home.

When it was time to move on, I picked up the Southwest Chief again and headed off to Los Angeles where I was treated to the wonderful hospitality of Bob and Pat Fairbanks, the parents of Bill, a friend of my friend from Bahrain and Paula Abdul days, Michael Hosking. The Fairbanks welcomed me in, gave me a key and left me to my own devices offering to help me if needed. I rented a car to get around Los Angeles as it's a huge area. Another weekend arrived and on the Saturday, I drove north to the Rose bowl, where the final of the 1994 World Cup would be held. I watched UCLA play rivals Stanford in front of another massive crowd, intrigued by Stanford's band mascot, a student inside a green tree. The next day, I watched the LA Raiders play the Bills (again) in the LA Memorial Coliseum, site of the 1984 Olympic Games.

The following weekend, it was time to head back east to Texas and the fantasy camp. I chose to travel overnight, leaving Los Angeles in the evening on the Sunset Limited which went all the way back across the country through to New Orleans. The train would arrive in San Antonio early the next morning just before six o'clock. I had phoned Steve Contardi and he confirmed that I would be collected from the station and brought up to the ranch, a drive of about thirty minutes. I couldn't wait.

Sleepless with excitement

Just when I should have been dreaming of the wonderful tennis to come, I found myself staring out of the window as the landscape passed by. After a while, time started to drag. Finally, there was a glimmer of the dawn and the train arrived at San Antonio station. As I stepped down onto the platform, a young man in tennis kit approached me, one of John Newcombe's tennis coaches, and he drove me up to the ranch as the light came up.

True to form in demonstrating fantastic customer service, Steve Contardi was there to meet me, even at that early hour. I was put into a room that was available, although not the one I would be in for the week and quite quickly, now in a proper bed as opposed to a train seat, I fell fast asleep. Once I had woken up and had a quick shower, I made my way back to reception to take in the sights, smells and sounds of the ranch. I intended to savour every minute of the week ahead.

Once a dude ranch

The John Newcombe Tennis Ranch, often known as Newk's, was not a tennis centre when John bought it in 1968 with Clarence Mabry, the tennis coach at Trinity University down the road in San Antonio. While 'Newk' was, at that time, one of the top players in the world as the game went open, his partner, Mabry, also had a reputation steeped in the sport's history, especially in Texas and in the college circuit. Clarence made you feel like smiling as soon as you saw him.

He had been born in Victoria, Texas back in 1925 and had become a player of good repute, winning a number of titles. Following this success, Mabry established the Trinity

University men's tennis team in 1955 and quickly developed a nationally recognized programme that ranked in the top four NCAA teams for eighteen of his nineteen years as a coach. Dennis Ralston, the Wimbledon finalist in 1966, had been one of Clarence's players. Mabry received many awards for his work and was well-respected. He was a family man with three daughters, including Terri, who we would all meet.

The ranch revolved around the lodge which included a reception with offices behind, a large lounge with a bar attached and behind that were the kitchens, out of sight but where vast amounts of food would be prepared throughout the week. There was a pro shop and another hall where the meals were eaten. The court surfaces were cement and in banks of four or eight, surrounded by single or double-story condominiums. The price you had chosen, would determine your accommodation, single or double occupancy, with or without lounge and small kitchen.

The usual tennis activities at the ranch, catered for adults in week-long or Friday-to-Sunday weekend programmes and also, at the other end of the site, visible as you drove up the access road before entering the main drive, there was an international junior academy with its own accommodation. Here, top local, regional, national and international players across all the teenage junior age groups lived and developed their tennis, going to schools locally every morning in the ubiquitous yellow school buses used nationwide. On their return, they would be out on the courts. Often, the juniors would be up early and with the floodlights on, they would complete all sorts of footwork drills under the watchful eye of Phil Hendrie, an amazing head coach.

Into this world, every October, an important man would bring his event to the ranch. He would be calling the shots to keep us all happy and provide us with a week to remember.

The man with the clipboard

Originally from Wisconsin, Steve Contardi was always a tennis fan. He went to college at Northern Michigan University where he was a four-year tennis letterman. After college, Steve went into school teaching but stayed involved with tennis, at one point, working with Nick Bollettieri, helping him to structure his summer camp programme. Steve changed to coaching full time and took up an opportunity to get involved with The Club at Harper's Point, a large indoor and outdoor tennis club with swimming pools, gym and family facilities, in Cincinnati. As managing partner, while his family grew, Steve created a flourishing business with a loyal membership and staff. All the while, Steve was building his reputation as a coach receiving many awards. He was a USTA Master Pro.

A commitment to people was at the heart of everything Steve did. I can't think of anyone better at reading people and situations. He commanded the respect of those who he dealt with. Steve was a brilliant organiser, solving problems as they arose, in some cases, before they even became problems. He seemed to have a framework for analysing every situation, a system that could be applied to everything, an approach that I tried to copy. Part of his daily routine at the camp was to walk around with a clipboard that contained all his key information. It was one evening a couple of years later that one of the campers came up with a short poem about Steve which he read out to everyone. It included the phrase, 'The Man with the Clipboard'. Of course, the clipboard was not the sole source of Steve's ability to run everything so well but the words were a simple catchphrase that everyone could use and use with much respect about the person who created so much joy for everyone.

Spring break to autumn leaves

Living in Cincinnati, Steve noticed one year in the late eighties that the city's baseball club, the famous Reds, had developed a fantasy camp, called Dream Week. At the time of Spring training, the Reds would allow fans to spend five days in the company of their legend idols playing baseball. With the success of that event, Steve wondered if the same idea might work in tennis. Sounding out the idea around his extensive tennis contacts, he came together with John Newcombe and his team in Texas and they decided to give it a try.

Looking at the tennis calendar and the weather in Texas, it was decided to try out the event in October where it has stayed ever since. The week was promoted as a men-only event, although a spring-time mixed event was added later, with good success. The first year attracted twenty-five players but by the time of my visit, in 1992, the sixth version of the event, there were fifty-two players and the numbers would keep going upwards. The format would be based on a team event, one Steve had used successfully in summer camps with his juniors, where the campers would be divided into four teams, each with a couple of legend pros as their team captains.

On the middle three days of the week, from Tuesday to Thursday, each team would play each other in a round-robin format. The teams would be organised by strength with the best player at number one, the next best at two and so on. All the respective numbers would play against their opposite number. It would be singles in the morning and doubles in the afternoon. By Thursday afternoon, a winning team would emerge with much fanfare from the team captains and bragging rights by the campers. Everything would be taken seriously at the time of the matches, but once they were over, it was time for relaxation, a few drinks and fun with friends.

Grand Slam title custodians
The big attraction of the week was not just being introduced to a great group of top players from the past but spending time with them from when a camper arrived to when he departed. As the event developed, the number of legends that Steve had

to have at the week increased. But as this relatively early stage of the event's development, there were eight legend pros, every one, a significant name in the game's past and in the minds of the campers who now looked forward to interacting with their idols, myself included.

John Newcombe, was one of the most iconic players of the era that transcended the changeover from amateur to open tennis. Using Wimbledon as an example, in 1967, in the last amateur year of the tournament, he won the title. But after Rod Laver had taken the first title of the open era in 1968, there was Newk again, in three more consecutive finals, losing to Laver in 1969 but beating Ken Rosewall in 1970 and Stan Smith in 1971. Indeed, along with Rod Laver, Newk is the only player to have won both Wimbledon and the US Open in the amateur and open eras. Born in Sydney, he was the top junior in the world before his adult career began in 1960 and he would go on playing until 1981. He won twenty-five Grand Slam titles in singles, doubles and mixed and was ranked No. 1 in the world in both singles and doubles. Overall, he won sixty-eight singles titles and thirty-three in doubles. He was a key member of the successful Australian Davis Cup teams between 1963 and 1967. He would captain the side between 1995 and 2000. In 1977 and 1978, he was the President of the ATP (the players' union, the Association of Tennis Professionals). He used his image to maximise business opportunities, not only buying the tennis ranch but marketing himself using a logo based on his distinct moustache, especially in conjunction with the Maggia brand of tennis clothing, a range I had bought back in the mid-eighties. That moustache was part of the logo of the ranch. Newk was a larger-than-life character with tremendous presence and he welcomed everyone to the ranch as if he really was taking you into his home.

A Queenslander keeping an eye on us at the camp was Mal Anderson, known as 'Country' or just 'Mal'. He concentrated on tennis from when he was a teenager and became good enough to win the US Championships unseeded, in 1957. Turning pro, he won the Wembley Professional Tournament in 1959. He played in Davis Cup for Australia in 1957, 1958, 1972 and 1973, the year he won the Australian Open doubles title with John Newcombe. In 1972, Mal had been awarded an MBE in recognition of his services to lawn tennis. He was a lovely man, very gentle but with a keen sense of humour and was always willing to have a laugh. Mal had endless patience when explaining strokes to campers.

Neil Fraser or 'Frase', as he was called, was a former Wimbledon champion in 1960, when he beat the up-and-coming Rod Laver. A left-hander with vicious topspin and kick serves, he won two US Championships in singles, as well. But in doubles, he won a Career Grand Slam while capturing eleven titles. Fraser is one of the twenty men to win all four majors in doubles. He also won five mixed doubles Grand Slam titles. Like John Newcombe, he was ranked No. 1 in both singles and doubles and won thirty-seven singles titles.

Roy Emerson or 'Emmo' was another amazing character. He played from 1953 to 1983, although for the last ten years, he was involved in Team Tennis and coaching. In his prime, Emmo was a fearsome competitor and won one-hundred and five singles titles. In Grand Slams, he won twenty-eight titles including twelve singles and sixteen doubles. He won a career Grand Slam and while he was an aggressive serve-volley player, nonetheless, won the French Championships twice in singles and in the doubles, he won every year in Paris from 1960 to 1965, an amazing achievement. Like many of his Aussie team-mates, he loved a beer but was regarded as the fittest of them all and was willing to work extra hard to shake off any after-effects of having a good time. He played in a record eight Australian Davis Cup winning teams between 1959 and 1967, many times as the lead singles player and often, playing doubles too. Like Mal, Emmo showed tremendous patience when teaching the lower-skilled players. The word was that

Emmo couldn't remember people's names and called everyone, 'Blue'.

As for Fred Stolle, 'Fiery', another Aussie, he had been born in Hornsby, New South Wales. Fred began his career as an amateur in 1958, becoming a pro in 1966 after winning the US Open. He retired officially in 1976. He was called Fiery due to his strongly held views. Arriving at the US Championships in 1966, after winning the German Open, finding himself unseeded, he quipped that the committee must have now regarded him as an old hacker. After winning the tournament, he stated that the old hacker could clearly still play a bit. He played an aggressive serve-volley game at a time when three of the Grand Slams were played on grass but he could be patient too on slower surfaces, as his other singles Slam win the year before in Paris proved. He had appeared in eight Slam finals, but in five or them in a row, he faced his friend, squad mate and at various times, doubles partner, Roy Emerson who prevailed in each match, although Fred has a winning record against both Emmo and Newk at the US Open. He won seventeen other Grand Slam titles in doubles and mixed doubles. Including his two singles Grand Slams, Fiery won thirty-nine singles titles across the amateur and professional eras. He was part of the Hopman years of top Australian players and teams in the Davis Cup and part of the successful squads which won the cup in 1964, 1965 and 1966. After retiring, he coached in Team Tennis and on the tour, he coached Vitus Gerulaitis. He was a much-respected television commentator for over twenty years. His son, Sandon, was playing on the tour at the time of the camp.

Fiery ran the team, which I joined, with fellow captain, the South African, Cliff Drysdale. 'Cliffey' was a tall man of good looks which certainly qualified him to sit under the banner of the WCT's original 'Handsome Eight' alongside Newk and Roger Taylor too. Cliff had a long career beginning in 1962 as an amateur in South Africa, where he was born, the country that he would represent in forty-five Davis Cup matches. By 1980, his official retirement date, he had won thirty-five singles titles and twenty-four in doubles, including the 1972 US Open men's doubles, partnering Taylor. Cliffey was known for his double-handed backhand long before the times when this was the standard way of playing the shot. Occasionally, he wore a glove with the fingertips cut off, on his right hand. He was a respected top ten player ranked No. 4 in 1965, the year he reached the final of the US Championships. He had been the first president of the newly formed ATP in the seventies. He was now beginning to get involved not only in television commentary, where he would work for ESPN for many years, but also in resort, hotel and tennis club management which he did very successfully. When he played during the week, I loved watching his topspin serve which had a vicious kick to it and was almost impossible to return certainly by most of the campers. I imagined how it must have been a nightmare to face when he was in his prime.

Back to the Aussies, the man often talked about as the greatest mixed doubles player ever was Owen Davidson. 'Davo', as everyone called him, was born in Melbourne. He had an outstanding junior career ending up number two in the world to John Newcombe before entering the adult ranks. Like the other legends, his career started in the amateur era and ended in the open one. Another player from the Harry Hopman stable, while a Grand Slam singles win evaded him, he reached the quarter-final of all the Slams, advancing to the semi-final at Wimbledon in 1966. But in doubles, he won two Grand Slam titles in Australia in 1972 and the next year, in the US. In mixed doubles, he was outstanding, reaching twelve finals and winning eleven of them, including a Grand Slam in 1967 with Lesley Bowery and then Billie Jean King. In the middle of his career, he took time out to fulfil the role of head coach at the All-England Club as well as the manager of competitive tennis for the LTA. After his playing days were over, Davo held a number of senior coaching positions at respected clubs and resorts. At the time of the camp, he was also the chief operating officer of Grand Slam Sports, the management company that represented and promoted all of the legends and their work at events, clinics and public appearances. They always said that there was no point lobbing Davo as he had the best overhead in the game. I never saw him miss a single one.

The American, 'Marty' Riessen, was known by his first name. Marty had been a student at Northwestern on a basketball scholarship. Marty's tennis career on the tour began in 1959 and he played as an amateur, turning pro when the game went open in 1968. He retired in 1981 after winning nine singles titles and fifty-three doubles titles in the open era with more prior to 1968. His highest rankings were No. 9 in singles and No. 3 in doubles. In Grand Slam singles, he reached the quarter-finals in the Australian Open, the US open and at Wimbledon. He won two doubles titles at the French Open and the US Open, although he reached the final at Wimbledon and at the Australian Open too. In mixed doubles, he won seven titles, including a Career Grand Slam. Marty was in the US Davis Cup squad in 1963, 1965, 1967, 1973 and 1981. Although not on his team on this week at the camp, I would be seeing more of Marty later in my trip and years later, he would be the legend pro who said one of the most important things to me that I had heard in my tennis journey.

Trainers, masseurs and the dean of tennis photography
In addition to the support of his wife, Debbie and kids, Mario and Katie, Steve Contardi and the ranch staff, managed by the boss, Jeremy Fieldsend, were supplemented by some important people who were integral to everyone's enjoyment of the event and in many cases, the ability to finish it.

If you were worried about a nagging injury, the first place you would head for was the open-sided tent next to the court where each day's activities began. There, you would put yourself into the hands of the amazing Larry Starr. Something I didn't quite pick up for a few days was that Larry was actually taking part in the event as a player, but would somehow, still be at the tent in charge of all the treatments, application of ice packs and diagnostic processes where limbs would be lifted and swivelled carefully to try and work out what was going on with campers hamstrings, calf muscles, shoulders, elbows and just about every other part of their bodies.

Larry was a trainer of considerable experience. He had been involved with major league baseball as athletic trainer for the Cincinnati Reds and would move on to the Florida Marlins. He was not only a master of diagnosis after years of treating top athletes but also, the wizard of rehabilitation. He would later get a doctorate at the age of sixty and work in academia as well as running his own health and fitness consultancy. Larry was integral to the running of the camp and never, ever gave you less than his complete attention as you returned, often with the same problem as before. He would patiently explain what was going on with your leg, or arm, or shoulder and then work out the plan to keep you playing while telling you what you should do once the camp was over and you had returned home. In years to come, Larry would be assisted by Jason, a lovely guy and just as trustworthy as he helped you deal with another strain, sprain or cramp.

As well as Larry and Jason's top expertise, there was always a crew of local masseurs who could be booked to provide a restorative massage. When you walked through the door into the room, the often, macho atmosphere of the camp had shifted to a calm, spirituality with soothing music interrupted by the odd grunt as each new knot was exorcised on some poor camper's body. The masseurs draped white sheets over their patients, leaving just their heads poking out at the end. Campers had been miraculously transformed from their ultra-competitive stances on the courts to looking like pods out of the film *Invasion of the Body Snatchers*. I tried to book sessions during the lunch break. But the massages were so relaxing that often, all I'd want to do would be to go back to my room and sleep. However, even catching just forty winks would slow down your metabolism and make it even harder to crank everything up into competitive mode for the afternoon doubles. The therapists used lots of antiseptic, medicine-based cream and after a while, everyone you walked past or sat next to at mealtimes had that faint whiff of liniment about them. In the years ahead, Vanessa Carpenter would be a friendly face scheduling us into our cameos as pod people encased in sheets.

The final key person in Steve's team was a man you could almost miss. Of course, as the camp's photographer, Russ Adams was trying to take his brilliant photos of you, without you realising that he was there. Russ also took all the photographs of each camper with all the legends and the team photos as well. It would be later that I'd discover that this unassuming man was regarded by his colleagues on the international tennis press corps as the dean of tennis photography. He was superb at his job and while you were playing, often in tight situations, you'd never know he was there, just a few feet away clicking at the point you hit that winning shot or as the ball passed your lunge at the net. Russ worked in the sport for fifty years winning many awards and held a massive archive of tennis photos. Once you got to know who he was, you realised that Russ was a great in his field.

Carry on campers
Getting to know my fellow campers through the week, I would meet academics, administrators, attorneys, businessmen, doctors, entrepreneurs, inventors, politicians, professional sportsmen (current and retired), property developers, realtors, retailers, surgeons, tennis coaches and writers, in fact, people from all sorts of job backgrounds. Campers were mainly American and from all over the country. There were a couple

of Australians, including the amazing Angus Deane whose family had begun the first cattle ranch in Queensland back in the nineteenth century. Angus's ranch was so large (over three hundred thousand acres) that to check out its farthest perimeters, he would fly around the outskirts in a small plane. Driving was left for more local tasks. Angus was like a real-life Crocodile Dundee with craggy looks and a charming smile. When he shook my hand, it felt like I had placed it into a vice made of rock. From that moment, I was certain that he had not been born but quarried. His toughness didn't just apply to his physical demeanour and his home environment. A few years on, when bad injuries meant that he couldn't play right-handed anymore, he taught himself to play with his left hand, an amazing achievement.

There was also, usually, a Brit or two. In the first couple of days, I noticed one tall player wearing a cap with a Union Jack design. I introduced myself to Howard Rogg. Although we were on different teams and didn't play each other, we would have a quick chat whenever our paths crossed.

Howard later told me about a hiccup with his wife Desi that occurred due to a simple misunderstanding. This trip to Texas was the first time Desi and Howard had been apart in their marriage. Desi had promised to call Howard to check he had arrived safely. The problem was that with the time differences, when Desi called, the women from the weekend group who would be just vacating the rooms, were still in them. When Desi asked for Howard Rogg's room, the receptionist looked up Howard's room number and put the call through, forgetting that as yet, the previous occupants were not yet out of the room and Howard was not yet in it. Hearing a female voice must have been confusing to say the least for Desi, so far away on the end of a phone. Thankfully, everything was sorted out and Howard and Desi were reunited with each other on the next phone call.

Play, move, split

From the moment campers arrived, the schedule had a structured timetable which had already become a tried and trusted formula. On the opening Sunday, after registering and collecting a bag including various T-shirts and a tracksuit, all suitably branded with the Tennis Fantasies' name and logo, the campers would get ready for the afternoon start, either resting in their rooms, chatting to old friends or making new ones. Some would just get straight to it, get onto the courts for a hit whether with friends they were accompanying, players who were already waiting to practise or Newk's ranch pros.

At four o'clock, the event began officially. Steve Contardi and John Newcombe welcomed everyone. Then, it was straight into some playing where the legend pros walked around watching the campers, rating their level of play. We played something called an Aussie mixer where each court had four players and everyone served a game. If the score was two games all, a sudden death point would be played to decide the winners. Then everyone moved court with the winners moving one way and the losers moving the other. Also, each pair split up to play on opposite sides of the net. This format meant that everyone played against lots of different opponents and provide an idea of the various standards of the players to the legends and Steve as they watched.

While the mixer was going on, I could tell that although there were a few players of a better standard than the rest, just about everyone could play well. The older players, understandably, played a bit slower than the younger ones. I felt I was in the right company, neither too good for anyone nor too weak either, except for maybe, one or two exceptions.

When we had played for a couple of hours, the campers went off to have a shower and then a drink in happy hour while Steve and the legends went into a conference to complete the camp's very own player draft. At dinner, the legend team captains stood up and read out their teams. There was much back-slapping and high-fiving and then we all went back to the bar and had another drink or two before bed and a much-needed sleep in preparation for the demands of the next day.

By now, I had met Fiery and Cliffey whose team I was in. I'd had a quick chat with Marty Riessen too. As we shook hands, I blurted out how back in 1968, my mum had taken me to Wimbledon and we had watched him and Tom Okker play Lew Hoad and Owen Davidson. Before I could add anything, he replied, "Lost 6-4 in the fifth," giving a frown, as if he had just walked off the Centre Court that very Saturday.

Where's that cat food?
On Monday morning after breakfast, where you could eat pretty much what you wanted from a large selection, things got underway at about nine o'clock. One of the legends gave a quick stroke demonstration with a few key tips. Then, after a warm-up by Larry Starr, each team moved to a bank of courts and in our case, Fred and Cliff started getting us organised. It looked like I was going to play quite high up in the team order where the players were rated from number one down to number thirteen, as the fifty-two campers were split four ways. For doubles, a ranch pro would partner the thirteenth player. The practice involved short sets of doubles and a few games of singles too. Just before lunch, four of the legends played an exhibition set, which we all watched and enjoyed.

After lunch, the afternoon was spent in more practice until about four o'clock. Next on the schedule were the fantasy sets. During the week, from Monday to Thursday at this time of the day, Steve Contardi had to organise things so that every camper would have at least one set through the week, where he would play with a legend against another camper and legend team. This was a time for relaxation and there was an endless supply of drinks, including beer, for people to drink. After another happy hour, dinner would take place.

When the eating was finished, Steve put on what were called rap sessions, where some of the legends, usually led by John Newcombe, would sit in front of us all and tell stories from their time on the tour and take questions about the game back then but also about the modern era too. Emmo and Fiery told some lovely stories about their time travelling together in the amateur days before the game went open. They related how they stayed together during Wimbledon, when they both reached the final in 1964 and 1965. They spent the evening before the matches together, travelled to the All-England Club together, changed together, warmed up together and were only parted when the final began and they were at opposite ends of the Centre Court. That, of course, was in a different era and wouldn't happen today. But the story I loved the most and one that campers requested again and again, was about an incident at a tournament.

After a late night, playing in a WCT tournament at the Spectrum in Philadelphia, Emmo and Fiery arrived back at where they were staying and grabbed a couple of beers to help them relax. Emmo went off to watch a late-night movie, while Fred went into the kitchen in search of a bite to eat. He found some spread in a Tupperware container which he put on some toast. Next morning, their hosts, who were great supporters of Tournament Director, Marilyn Fernberger, called out to their cat while asking Emmo and Fiery if they had seen the container. Fiery confessed that he had opened it and enjoyed his snack, concluding that the cat ate pretty well.

Two matches; two defeats
On Tuesday, things on the court shifted into the team competition where each team would play all of the others. The singles matches were played in the morning with the doubles in the afternoon. Opponents were selected depending on the team order worked out by the captains on Monday. If team A was playing team B, both number one players would play

against each other and the same would apply to all the other numbers. In the doubles, number one and two would usually team up and play the same pair from that day's opponents. The legends' ability to match up players was almost uncanny. Whichever number I played at, my opponents were carbon copies of me. I had my strengths and weaknesses but so did they. The question seemed to be who could make the most of their strengths while exploiting their opponent's weaknesses. There were no easy matches.

My first match was against an inventor from New York City, Marc Segan, whose brother Larry and father Irwin, were also at the camp. Our match was very close and at every opportunity, I tried to get to the net where I was most comfortable. But ultimately, Marc was too steady and after a long three-set match, he emerged victorious. This match was, in many ways, a perfect example of what competition was like at camp. After a short, late-morning clinic given by the legends for those who wanted to keep playing, it was time for lunch and a short rest. In the afternoon, I played doubles where again, after a close fight, my partner and I ended up on the losing side. So, after the first day of competition, I had played well, experienced two tight matches but lost both. After fantasy matches, happy hour and dinner, there was karaoke in the bar.

Show a bit of enthusiasm, Blue
On Wednesday, the stiffness was beginning to kick in. It was getting increasingly difficult to pull my tennis socks on, always a good indicator of how tight my muscles were. With the day pretty much a repeat of the one before, while playing well again, I lost again in my morning singles.

When the pre-lunch, late morning clinics began, because I wanted to experience everything the week had to offer, despite feeling tired after my singles match, I wandered over to Emmo's clinic where he was giving tips on how to return serve. Once we started to practise the moves, Emmo arrived on my court as I came to a standstill. After witnessing my almost stationary reaction to a serve coming my way, he called out, "Show a bit of interest, Blue." All I could do was stare blankly at him and then we both burst out laughing.

In the afternoon, again despite playing well, my partner and I lost the doubles. My record was now four matches played and four defeats. Then, although it was just a set, my record became won zero, lost five after I was teamed up with Davo to play a fantasy set. This was great fun but I became aware of how self-conscious I was about my game despite the fact that I was playing amongst friends with no-one taking notes. I think that my body was beginning to give out and what would normally be easy tasks all became much harder after three days of non-stop play in the heat on hard courts.

In the evening, we all went out to a local Mexican restaurant. There was talk of a trip down into San Antonio for a continuation of the evening in some clubs and a small group of night owls headed off in taxis. Relieved to be just about in one piece, I dragged my aching limbs into bed.

The good doctor
The climax of the Mexican night had been an Australian Boat Race, a drinking game where two teams compete to drink down their glass of beer in a relay, the winning team being the won who successfully downed all their beer first. I stood back and watched the action, preferring to enjoy the fun as a spectator. The boat race was the platform for one of the most fascinating characters who attended the week to make his presence felt.

By the time of my visit, Al Eden was already an established veteran at the camp. When Steve Contardi had set up the week originally, Alvin's wife, Elaine, had spotted the advertisement and signed up her husband as a sixty-fifth birthday gift. Al had always loved tennis and played at his club regularly. As one of New York's top paediatricians, he ran a very well-established practice. He lived on New York's Upper East Side, bringing up his son, Robert. In fact, he was so well thought-of professionally that he had published a book on child obesity and had appeared on national television. This background made it all the more amusing that at camp, for one week of the year, this upstanding, gentle and empathetic doctor would adopt the role of an administrative bureaucrat who told naughty jokes as he ran a raucous drinking game better suited to a frat party at spring break.

Many pro sports in the US appoint a commissioner. So, Al became the self-styled Commissioner of the Australian Boat Race and took his job so seriously that he appointed assistant commissioners, including Larry Starr. The 'Commish' as he would become known, would also send out a letter between camps to give everyone who had attended the previous year a report of the boat race and remind everyone of the rules and transgressions which should be avoided at all costs in any future holding of the race. The letter came across s extremely serious, although it was all tongue in cheek. I think the most hilarious aspect of how Al played out this role was the jokes he told every evening at dinner. These were hard-hitting and very near-the-knuckle. But for me, it wasn't the details that were amusing, but Al's performance. He delivered his words in a recognisable New York accent with an absolutely straight face and with perfect comedy timing. He would have been ideal for the stand-up circuit, I reckon. It would only be at the end of one of his announcements to the campers after dinner and the completion of the daily joke that his face would break into a beaming smile.

Do you beat them?
All of the legend players were now approaching, or in, middle age. However, after a lifetime playing the game at the highest level, they could all still play beautifully, efficiently and if required, ruthlessly. In the years to come, I was fortunate to

play with just about all of the game's former stars who were the team captains in that first year. On a few occasions, I was asked by people back at home if I could beat the legends.

The first thing I had to point out was that the way the camp format was set up, there wasn't time to play singles with them. But based on the fact that when playing against them in doubles, it was usually difficult to win a single point, unless you relied on a mistake by the fellow camper who would be playing opposite you, I dreaded to think what the score might have been in a singles match. Club players like me and most of the other campers with the odd exception, even ones who played reasonably high up in the team order, were tennis civilians. The legends lived in a different tennis universe.

My aim, as the years went by and I played more fantasy sets, was just to get the ball back to the right place. I would find that mysteriously, when I went on the court to play a set involving the legends, my legs felt heavier, my feet moved slower, my decision making became confused, my hands also slowed and the timing of all my strokes seemed to have been re-programmed for the worse. Often, the harder I tried, the worse I played.

One year, I was partnering Tony Roche, often called 'Rochey'. We were playing another camper and John Newcombe. Newk still had that wonderful rocking motion on his serve and just as he swayed forward, he would look at you for a split second before placing the ball toss up and making contact. He must have spotted that on the first point, I was standing just a bit too far towards the centre of the court. As he hit the serve, he hit a slice which landed on the inside tramline on the service box in a place that meant, even if I moved for it, I was never going to get it. I stayed rooted to the spot. After Rochey won the next point for us, Newk served again to me and as I compensated for what had happened before, I must have shifted myself just a bit too far over towards the outside. This time, Newk hit the serve right down the centre but to my left. Again, I didn't even move. In a split second, the ball was hitting the fence behind me. I tried not to look at Rochey, but I couldn't stop myself. He raised an eyebrow at me quizzically. Again, with a good return from Rochey, we were even. On the next serve, I did manage to make contact, but floated a return straight into the oncoming path of Newk as he bore down on the net to hit his still devastating forehand volley. He crunched the ball away for a winner. Tony called me over.

"Crippsey (as I was called at the camp), the bloke at the net is an orthopaedic surgeon from Philadelphia. The other bloke is the former world No. 1. Hit it to the orthopaedic surgeon."

"Right, Rochey" I confirmed.

On the next serve, Newk out-thought me again. As I stayed to the right, he served to the left. With the game over, I considered how I'd been swept aside. In a weird way, it felt like nothing had happened. Well, on my side of the net, nothing had!

In all the visits I would make to the camp, there was only once when I became involved in a decent cross-court groundstroke exchange with a legend. This involved Mark Woodforde, usually referred to as 'Woody'. I hit seven or eight forehands in succession before making a mistake. But throughout, I felt as if Woody was really only in first gear while I was straining every sinew of brain and body to concentrate and stimulate muscle memory to get my hands, feet and racket into the right place to keep the point going. When it was over, I felt like going for a sit-down on one of the chairs at the side of the court simply to get over what had just happened. That was just one rally.

Another good doctor
One of my opponents on the last day, Mike Lawhon, was a well-respected orthopaedic surgeon from Cincinnati. Known as 'Doc', he was one of the big characters at the camp. 'Doc' had

been the club physician for the Cincinnati Reds and had also been the doctor for the ATP Tour. He was a good friend of Steve Contardi and the Cincinnati crowd at the camp and he took his enjoyment of the weekend seriously, arriving before anyone else and leaving after most had departed. Outside his condominium, he would erect a sign which read 'Margaritaville!' in honour of the song by country music star, Jimmy Buffet. As well as the song, Doc also loved margaritas and would drink plenty of them, especially on Mexican night. He lived life to the full, partied hard off the court and played hard on it. Doc always co-ordinated a collection made amongst the campers where everyone would give $50 to a nominated person in their team and the money would be pooled and then split up to provide decent tips for the staff at the ranch. He hated to lose and often seemed quite stressed on the other side of the net if things didn't go to plan. But this was his way of playing. This approach helped him to compete. He could play well and was deserving of his place in his team's top doubles pair, partnering the best player at the camp across all four teams, other than the legends, someone I was about to play.

Better late than never
Before meeting Doc on the court in the doubles, I had my last singles match to negotiate. I was forever positive about my chances. After all, although everyone was taking the competition seriously, we were all there for fun and enjoyment. You could do no more than give everything your best effort and with one day's competition to go, that's what I did. Unfortunately, as per the rules, my team captain had moved me up a slot in the team order to the number one position. Captains could shift their players around because they were keeping a close tab on who was doing well and therefore, they could take a view on how they might obtain the most points for collective match wins from all their team members. I was a bit bemused to have been moved up considering that I had lost

two matches, not won two, but the way this worked was if our number one player had played their number one player, Fred and Cliff must have thought he would lose. Plus, if I played against my counterpart at number two, they must have thought I might well lose too. So, we would have lost both matches. However, if our number one played their number two, he would probably win while they would sacrifice me by playing me at number one. With this second option, we would be more likely to earn one point for our team from the two matches as opposed to none with the previous team order.

The good news about my opponent, their number one, was that he was one of the small group of campers who had gone on to sample the San Antonio nightlife and he was clearly the worse for wear due to a lack of sleep as well as too much booze. The bad news for me was that this number one player was John Lehmann, who was the chief executive of the legends management company, Grand Slam Sports, but had been a touring pro in his time and had been ranked in the world's top two-hundred and fifty. He was also still a relatively young man and despite his hangover, a fit bloke. I'm afraid that there were memories of my matches against Frank Sabaratnam in Bahrain and Simon Ickringill at Ilkley that came flashing across my mind as John beat me with relative ease 6-0, 6-0. The problem with tennis scoring is that you can do well for a couple of points in a game but if that's all you've got, it won't be enough. So, despite the odd, good bit of play from me here and there, I'm afraid that it was another double bagelling to start the final day of competition.

The morning had started a bit murky but then the weather cleared up for the afternoon and the last match of the competition. I was teamed up with a new partner, the tall, big-serving Bill Druckemiller. We were playing my morning opponent, John Lehmann who was partnered with Mike Lawhon, Doc. I didn't think we had a chance but somehow, we split the first two sets and then finally, things really started to come together for Bill and me. My serves went where I wanted them to go, my net play became sharp but most important, my return of serve started to win point after point from the advantage court. Maybe, that clinic with Emmo was paying off? Combined with Bill's excellent serving, and a stunning return which helped break serve as the set came to a climax, the momentum shifted our way. Finally, after that break, we served out the match. At last, with Bill's help, I had clocked up a win and it felt good, especially considering the quality of our opponents.

With the competition over, after dinner, awards were given out and a small, personalised package of photographs taken by Russ Adams.

Farewells but not for long
Although people started leaving on Friday morning, for those heading off a bit later to catch their flights home, the legends and the ranch pros put on clinics with drills for those who still had the legs, body and mind for it. By lunchtime, people were leaving in groups, taken back to San Antonio Airport at regular intervals. I found the energy to take part in the morning clinics and after lunch, I had booked a rental car as I wanted to go to see the University of Texas play Houston in a football game the following day and was under no time pressure.

As I said goodbye to everyone, after telling them my travel plans, Fred Stolle and Cliff Drysdale told me to look them up at the Hilton in Melbourne in the New Year when the Australian Open was on. Marty Riessen had also told me to stay with him in a few weeks' time when I would be on my way down from San Francisco to fly out of Los Angeles for Hawaii en route back to Australia.

After thanking Steve Contardi, I drove up to Austin where I found a motel for Friday night. I spent an enjoyable evening on Six Street in Austin where all the bars and clubs are located and the next day, saw the game, accompanied by Terri

Mabry. Driving back down to San Antonio afterwards, I stayed in a motel close to the railway station on Saturday night. I dropped the car off early Sunday morning, picked up the Sunset Limited and headed for Houston where another NFL game was on my agenda. I sat on the train thinking about the amazing week I had just been through and how and when I would return.

Chapter 10

Remembering Hop

Billie Jean and Bobby's battle
I was now moving into the final stage of my time in the US. While the main focus of my activities would involve more playing with a return to Harry Hopman Tennis, now located in the Saddlebrook resort, north of Tampa, I also planned to visit a number of other cities, including Houston, New Orleans, Atlanta and then Dallas on my way back west. Once back in Los Angeles, I would drive to Las Vegas and then on to San Francisco before heading back south, hopefully seeing Marty Riessen in Santa Barbara on the way before flying out to Hawaii and then on to Australia. Three of these cities, Houston, Dallas and Las Vegas were linked to the sport's history in significant ways. But first came a stop in Houston, although this would be another quick one. The location I was heading for was where an important step in the development of the women's game had taken place two decades before.

Arriving in Space City, the home of Zena Garrison and Lori McNeil, I checked into a motel near the Astrodome stadium, another huge and impressive indoor arena where that afternoon's NFL game was being played. Unlike the Pontiac Silverdome in Detroit, which I had already visited, and the Superdome in New Orleans and Georgia Dome in Atlanta, both of which I would visit soon, the Astrodome had tennis history significance. It was here back in 1973 that the 'Battle of the Sexes' match was held between Billie Jean King and the former player, six-Slam winner, Bobby Riggs, then in his mid-fifties, a self-claimed hustler. Riggs had already challenged and beaten Margaret Court and Billie Jean now felt that she had to accept another challenge from Riggs having rejected previous overtures from him. While Billie Jean was heavily focused on building the women's tour and its presence in the sport, she felt that to reject this new proposal from Riggs would not help the cause. In fact, she believed that is she could win, the cause would be enhanced, even though the challenge match was clearly a promotional event, a Riggs concoction and nothing to do with the mainstream pro tour. Aggressively promoted, the match, watched by a television audience claimed to be in excess of ninety million people, went ahead and Billie Jean did win, in straight sets in a best-of-five-sets encounter.

Just under twenty years later, there was no sign of any tennis court, which had looked tiny when laid out in the huge floor-space of the Astrodome, surrounded by a few bleachers and dwarfed by the surrounding stands. On my visit, only gridiron markings were visible as the Oilers came out to play the Cincinnati Bengals.

Saved by the human lizard
The following day, as I wanted to spend a bit of time in New Orleans, I carried on across country on the next train and took up the offer from one of the campers back in New Braunfels that I should stay in his house; he would be away working for a few months. I met his neighbour who gave me the key. All was well until the following day. Returning from a few hours sightseeing in the city, I checked in my pocket for the key. To my horror, it wasn't there. Somehow, I'd lost it. When he returned from work, the neighbour did not like the idea of my sleeping on his floor until we could work out how to get a new lock and key organised, so he performed what looked like an impression of a human lizard by climbing up the door, opening a window above it and somehow, sliding through it, dropping down to the other side and letting me in. I was most grateful to him and slept with one eye on the unlocked front door all night before sorting out the lock and key situation at a local store the following morning. After a long-distance chat to my camper friend, once I'd sorted it out, I breathed a huge sigh

of relief. The whole incident had been a bit too stressful and far too embarrassing, for my liking.

At the weekend, holding obsessively onto my new key, it was back to American football with two games played inside the huge Superdome that would be in the news as a refuge for many people after Hurricane Katrina hit New Orleans in 2005. I watched Tulane play Memphis State on the Saturday and on Sunday, the Saints played against the first team that Kyri had taken me to see on my visit to Florida in 1984, the Tampa Bay Buccaneers. Then, it was time for more tennis. I flew down to Tampa, picked up a rental car and drove a few miles north of the city to the Saddlebrook resort, located in a small town called Wesley Chapel. This was new home of Harry Hopman Tennis. After Hopman's death, his wife had made the decision to complete the relocation to Saddlebrook.

Posing without realising it
I was keen to sample another dose of Hopman-style training, the likes of which I had experienced back in 1984 and 1985 in my two annual holidays spent visiting Kyri. Back then, Hopman's was based in Bardmoor, close to where Kyri was working and living in St Petersburg. Harry Hopman and his coaching methods were inextricably linked to Australia's domination of the Davis Cup and the tennis development of the top Australian players, including all the Aussie legend pros I had just spent a week with back in Texas.

Harry Hopman was called 'Hop' or Mr Hopman, especially if you worked for him, although Vitas Gerulaitis, in his slightly contrarian way, called him 'Mr H.' Harry was a former Australian tennis player himself whose career was in the thirties. He won quite a few tournaments on what was then, an amateur circuit. His best results in Grand Slam tournaments were in doubles where he won seven titles in men's and mixed. In 1939, he became the Australian Davis Cup coach-captain at a time when the Davis Cup was the flagship event in the sport. He would remain in that post for around three decades, winning the cup twenty-two times, although perhaps his notoriety was as much down to the large number of top players he helped to create, making Australia the power in world tennis. But, as far as his training academy in Bardmoor (and then Saddlebrook) was concerned, it was the type of training a player would receive that was the attraction.

Hopman's method, used with all his Australian Davis Cup squads, was based on hard physical work combined with a Spartan attitude to things off the court. He expected his players to live according to a strict discipline. Most of the time on the court, players worked in teams of three with one player doing all the work while the other two recovered from their turn, feeding or rallying balls to the working player. The drills were designed to stretch that player physically in every way. This was the type of thinking that believed if you worked much harder in practice than you did in matches, when you actually played in the matches, things would almost seem easy. One drill I remember involved hitting an overhead smash time after time. This was a drill used elsewhere in tennis coaching around the world. But the difference was the intensity with which the drill was executed and the long length of time that the working player had to hit balls. There were numerous drills like this which his instructors all knew and would execute in the same way across all the courts of his facility. The other attraction for me was that whoever was on the courts, from world-ranked players to beginners, you all did the same drills.

So it was, back in 1984, once I'd arrived in Tampa, I booked a couple of days at Hopman's. The daily rate was quite expensive and even though I was well-paid at American Express, I still had my budget to meet. As it turned out, the cost of two days was what I felt comfortable to afford. Once on the court in a small group of four players with instructor, John, the hitting, running and gasping for air all began on legs turning quickly to rubber. The way the day was organised, you were on the court for five hours from eight-thirty to eleven o'clock in the morning followed by a much-needed lunch break and then, the same again from one o'clock to three-thirty.

In a water break, I looked around and spotted Andres Gomez, a future Grand Slam winner at the French Open in 1990. He was training two courts away, doing all the same routines we had been doing. Mima Jausovic, the top Yugoslavian pro was also there. This was a place the pros respected and valued. The Australian player, Paul MacNamee would spend six months based at the academy converting his single-handed backhand into a two-hander. Coach John also told me about the time when the young American pro, Kathleen Horvath, was training and when she hit the first ball of the day down the court to her practice partner, they kept that ball going non-stop for fifteen minutes before one of them made a mistake. That is a very long time and a lot of hits without a mistake in anyone's book.

At the lunch break, everyone ate what I thought was a healthy meal with lots of salad. There was no bar at the facility and the drinks were all non-alcoholic. Players and coaches would spend the rest of the two-hour break relaxing from what had just occurred, preparing for what was about to happen again. During the afternoon, I noticed Mr Hopman walking down all the walkways between the courts. John told me that this is what he did all day. He was keeping an eye on things but also ensuring that spare tennis balls were thrown back onto the courts. Balls cost money and he was running a business. Returning to Kyri and Mike's apartment, I was ravenously hungry and completely exhausted. After stuffing my face with whatever food I could find, I collapsed onto my bed. I didn't even have the energy for a shower, which is exactly what I needed in order to assist my aching limbs to recover. The following day, it was rinse and repeat but I loved it at Hopman's and knew I would return.

Return I did the following year in 1985 and completed another couple of days of exhausting but enjoyable practice. On this occasion, after lunch in the afternoon session, there was video analysis completed for each participant. But the highlight of this exercise was that while one of the instructors was on camera duty, Mr Hopman actually fed the balls and barked out instruction. He didn't hold back in his criticism. In one sequence of shots that he wanted me to hit, the last one was a backhand volley. I kept hitting the ball cross-court and after the fourth one, 'Hop' called out, "When are you going to stop hitting the easy one?" What could I say? I tried to hit the remaining volleys down-the-line. Then, when we moved on to hitting backhands, I held my follow through with the racket up high, as a coach back in the UK had advised me to do. I had been dumping too many balls into the net and this slight pause at the top of the follow-through was a suggestion to help correct that problem. This particular way of doing things was too big an opportunity for Harry to miss. "Stop posing," he barked down the court. Seeking to please this great tennis training guru, I did as I was told.

Sadly, a few weeks later, Mr Hopman would ascend to that great tennis academy in the sky. I felt fortunate to have been coached by him, albeit for a few minutes where I doubt that I brought him much joy.

Hopman's in all but name
Seven years on and Hopman's had moved. Wesley Chapel had a small population but the town had really started to grow in the time of the Civil War. It was named after the chapel that had been built there and probably, unsurprisingly for this part of Florida, it had been known as Gatorville.

The land on which the Saddlebrook resort now stood had been a ranch but in the late seventies, a businessman, Charles Dempsey, had a vision for the site and built the resort focusing on golf and tennis. With two golf courses, extensive meeting facilities and a golf training range, the resort soon appeared on the lists of top golfing resorts in the US. The integration of the Hopman programme onto the tennis courts did the same for the resort in the tennis market. A school was built, the Saddlebrook Preparatory, and amongst others, it accommodated the educational needs of the players who attended the junior academy side of the tennis programme.

The resort also offered a fitness centre and a spa and today, offers team building activities too, ideal for the sort of corporate convention and meeting business that the resort targets. All I really cared about was the tennis, although while there, I was aware of the considerable commitment to golf evidenced by the constant stream of golfers walking by the courts. Anyway, I had been looking at photos of Saddlebrook in *Tennis* magazine since my visits to the original Hopman's at Bardmoor and now I was going to spend five days there.

Too much cranberry juice
After landing at Tampa Airport with all the memories of my earlier visits flooding back, I picked up a rental car and headed north of the city up Interstate 75. Arriving at the Wesley Chapel intersection, I decided to stock up on some supplies to eat in the small condominium apartment room I had booked. I turned into the car park of a massive supermarket which in return visits, would become an Albertsons, one of the largest supermarket retailers in the country.

As I entered the store, my jaw dropped at the size of the place. The range of products in every area was enormous and the choice extensive. I started to fill my shopping cart with what was going to be far too many items for the odd snack that I was going to need in my room. Seeing a carton of cranberry juice, I added it to the growing collection. Then, walking a few yards further on, there was more cranberry juice, this time, in large glass jars. What was the difference? Should I take that bottle too or replace the carton I'd already taken? Even after putting a few items back, as I put the purchases in the car, I realised that I still had way too many items, probably half of which I didn't even take out of the fridge in my condominium by the time my visit was complete.

Shopping over, I drove the short distance to the entrance of Saddlebrook and was given a card with a number to display next to my front window through the duration of my stay. Then, I drove to the main building, checked in and found my room.

Enjoyable tennis masochism
I awoke early the next morning and with plenty of time to spare, I wandered over to the main building where in various places, pots of coffee seemed to be on the go. I did not fancy having a big breakfast as I knew the type of experience that I was about to be taking part in. However, it was unwise to train on an empty stomach, so I had eaten some fruit and a bagel in my condominium washed down with some cranberry juice, of course. Having poured myself a cup of coffee, I headed for the courts where I could take a few moments to sip my brew and wait for the day to start.

As I would soon find out, reassuringly, despite the absence of Harry or Nell Hopman, the system that I had experienced before back at Bardmoor was still the way things were done on the courts. Howard Moore had been the director at Hopman's since 1986 and he was at Saddlebrook providing the continuity in what was on offer now that Mr H. was no longer there. Looking back to my brief time at the Bardmoor facility, it really was as if there was hardly any difference in the daily routine then and now. Obviously, the surrounding environment with the resort's buildings, restaurants and condominiums was different, although even back then and especially today, Bardmoor is a well-developed place too.

Saddlebrook was attractive to all sorts of players. As well as helping to develop many juniors many of them with a college scholarship of some type as a goal, many top pros had trained there too. The resort was also attractive as a place to live as well as one to use as a training base. Jennifer Capriati owned a condominium with her family and on a return trip a few years later, I spotted Martina Hingis riding around on a bicycle reminding me just a bit of the lovely Katherine Ross, playing Etta Place, doing the same in the iconic film, *Butch Cassidy and the Sundance Kid*. Of course, unlike in some of the locations that Butch, Sundance and Etta hung out in the film, here in Florida, raindrops rarely fell on anyone's head. It was sun and heat most of the time. Great for hitting tennis balls.

Once on the courts, you had to be prepared for a lot of hard work. As well as working a lot on technical aspects of stroke-production, there was a strong focus on fitness. Indeed, the promotional literature of the resort would claim that using your own natural style, the coaches would help you to develop the stamina, speed, agility and endurance you needed to play at your very best.

The daily timetable was the same as it had been years before. Once organised into your court allocations, the hitting began from around eight-thirty and the drills would come thick and fast. The promise was that there would never be more than four players to a court although the reality was that in all my visits both back at Bardmoor, this current visit and a few repeat trips in the future, other than the very first time I went, there were usually, no more than three players on my court. On one occasion, in the afternoon session, I was the only player and had the luxury of spending the time with a personalised programme on my backhand drive. Ironically, the instructor and I discovered that if I held my follow-through with the racket quite high up above my head for a split second longer than usual, this seemed to help create more topspin and excellent net clearance. But this method was quite close to the style that I had been using back in 1985, a method that Hop made it clear that he didn't like. I could imagine him looking down from his heavenly location and tut-tutting in disgust. I'm sure I could hear, through the lilting tones of singing angels somewhere above, a growling voice stating the words, "stop posing."

By the time the mid-morning drinks break came around, you had hit literally hundreds of balls under the close supervision of your coach. The last hour of the morning was spent doing more drills and playing a few points using the 'King of the Court' format, where the winner of the point always stayed on the court, at the far end of the server. By eleven o-clock, your mind, body and strokes really did feel like they had been through a tough workout, just as Harry always had planned. In most of the places I went for a tennis holiday, other than the Tennis Fantasies week where the format was different, the Hopman-style morning session alone would have been enough tennis for the day for most people. But here, you were going to repeat it in the afternoon.

From eleven o'clock, there was a two-hour break and I always went straight back to my room and had a shower, as I would be literally, soaked in sweat from all that training in a hot and humid environment. Then, I'd delve into my supermarket supplies and eat; I'd eat a lot and keep going on that supply of cranberry juice. Then, I'd rest on the bed and watch television, even dropping off for a short nap. As one o'clock approached, I'd repeat what I'd done in the morning and head back to the reception or the pool area and get myself a coffee before the afternoon session began. Then, it was more sweat, toil and hitting until three-thirty. While it was really tough, there was a huge sense of achievement just to have got through the day and feel like you had given your best, especially when you felt like giving up. But even after five hours, for those who wanted to play some more, the coaches would organise these super-humans into pairs to play sets. Not many people took up that option.

A league of their own
In the evenings, there were restaurants and bars you could visit to replenish your depleted reserves as well as to relax in and enjoy yourself. I spent most of my time off the courts back in my room, not so much because I was in an anti-social mood but because, quite simply, I was exhausted. One evening, I watched the film, *A League of Their Own,* starring Tom Hanks and Madonna, about the professional women's baseball league that was established during the Second World War in the US. I really enjoyed it.

The next morning, as I was walking past the huge swimming pool on the way to the courts, I fell into step with an older woman who reminded me of Monique from Roland Garros. We shared some pleasantries and I told her how much I had enjoyed the film the night before. The hairs on the back of my neck went up again as she said to me, "I played in that league." She went on to tell me a bit about her experience as a young woman back in the early forties. Another intriguing coincidence, I thought, as I walked over towards the sweat and suffering that was about to unfold on the tennis courts.

The Andy Roddick impersonator
Sometimes, the groups you were partnered with might stay the same or they could change, even for the afternoon session as the resort was catering for a wide range of visitors with many different lengths and types of stay. There were people visiting for a morning meeting which would enable them to do one afternoon session and there were those like me, who were involved in a week-long tennis-only programme. There was even a retired businessman from Germany who was in the middle of a month-long stay. Either he would be a complete wreck physically by the end of his visit or he'd be ready for the legends pro tour, I wasn't sure which.

Accordingly, for a couple of days in the middle of the week, my group included a husband-and-wife team from the

Chicago area, both of them good players. The husband was a stocky but muscular build while the wife was quite petite. They could both hit the ball well and we all worked efficiently together in the drills which were fed by the coach and involved us all playing out the point with each other. But it was at the end of the first morning that I came to appreciate the husband's strength which was his serve. Usually, towards the end of the morning session, everyone would not only practise their serve with the coach giving instruction along the way but to finish off the session, you would play some points. This was all well and good until either the wife or me had to face the husband. He had an unreturnable serve. He hit it so hard and so accurately that after a while, I limited my attempts to just getting my racket on the ball as it came thundering across the net and fizzed into the fence behind at the back of the court. Years later, whenever I watched Andy Roddick - who periodically, trained at Saddlebrook - smash another ace, especially on the courts in the grass-court season building up to Wimbledon, I'd think about the husband back at Saddlebrook and think, Andy, I've faced your serve or at least a Chicago businessman-version of it.

Close Encounter of the Beadle Kind
Saturday arrived and although I could have played tennis; it was my final day, for once, I gave up the opportunity because I wanted to return to the place where I'd seen my very first college football game back in 1984. I was also physically exhausted after the combined effects of the week in Texas and then four days of hard training Hopman-style. I headed north for Gainesville to watch the University of Florida play their college football game. There, the Gators were playing against Southern Mississippi University. Due to my location at ground level in the end zone, I became aware of a few more details about the game-day routines, especially all the middle-aged men, alumni I presumed, who greeted the team as the players

came onto the field. The fans were wearing puppet-style gator heads but heads created by putting one green sleeve with pretend teeth attached on one arm and another similar sleeve on the other arm. Placing both arms together and then snapping them open and closed, it looked as if their arms had indeed turned into a real-life snapping gator. After the game, I found my car and headed south for Saddlebrook where I had a dinner date with some friends from New York I'd made on the next court over.

It was on the drive back that my imagination got the better of me. I was listening to the radio, eating up the miles when over to my left, up in the sky, I saw some lights. There were four shafts and they seemed to be moving in a particular way, in and out and then across each other. It started to cross my mind that I had become part of a real-life scene from the film, *Close Encounters of the Third Kind*. Were the aliens finally making themselves known to the human race? Perhaps, although quite why they had chosen the residents of Florida, probably over in the Orlando area, I had no idea. But what should I do? How could I tell the world that this amazing moment had arrived?

I pulled over at a service area and stopped in the gas station to fill up. I looked over at another driver, smiled and asked if he had seen the lights. "Yes," he replied and then added that they were part of a display at a large car showroom at a town a few miles away. Yes, of course. How could I be so easily deceived? I didn't dare tell this complete stranger that I believed that the aliens had arrived. I carried on my journey back to Saddlebrook a bit self-conscious about my own stupidity, and how I had let my imagination get the better of me. Memories of a Jeremy Beadle spoof in his programme, *Beadle's About* in which he had convinced a poor woman that an alien had landed in her back garden, came to mind. In that episode, called *Close Encounters of a Beadle Kind* on one website, I had always been impressed how the terrified woman, who ultimately, not only got the joke but adopted the alien in question, had offered the celestial being, which was a blow-up plastic figure available from joke shops, a cup of tea!

The *right* trousers

On the next court from me at Saddlebrook, there was a group of women who all seemed to know each other. Sure enough, it transpired that they were a group of friends from New York who were spending a long weekend break away from the city in the Florida sunshine. Coincidentally, their last night was the same as mine on Saturday and we all agreed to go out for dinner at a recommended restaurant not far away in Wesley Chapel, once I had returned from Gainesville.

So, on my return from avoiding the car showroom alien invasion, I met up with the ladies from New York and we went to the local restaurant they had suggested. For a change, I didn't wear tennis kit which had been my uniform of choice throughout most of the year but put on some decent trousers which had been hiding at the bottom of my bag. Made of a mix with wool in them, at this time of the year, especially in Florida, they were not the ideal choice to match the heat and humidity which were still high, even in the evening.

This slightly inappropriate choice of clothing was a blessing in disguise. After we'd finished our food, coffees were ordered. As they were being passed around the table to ensure everyone got the correct one, someone knocked my mug over and all the contents poured over the edge of the table onto my right thigh. It was hot but the thick trouser fabric made it bearable. Tissues were produced, another mug poured and the conversation continued despite my wet leg. I was relieved to get back to tennis kit on returning to my room.

The following morning after checking out, I walked around to the ladies of the court and said goodbye. They had given me telephone numbers and I promised to call when I was next in New York. Then, it was off back into Tampa where

I had arranged to meet and stay a night with Larry and Sherrie. I had met this charming couple at the Tennis Fantasies week. Although the camp was a males-only week, due to some complications with trying to book a previous, mixed incarnation of the event, Steve Contardi's solution to the problem was to invite both husband and wife to the autumn event instead. When they found out that I would be coming to Tampa, they insisted I stay with them on my last night.

We met up, attended the Buccaneers game against the Minnesota Vikings, without being thrown in Tampa Bay, the Bucs stated intention in the words of their song, had a nice dinner and I was put up in the guest room. The following morning, my travels continued as I said goodbye to Larry and Sherrie, dropped my car off at the airport and boarded my next flight, this time up to Atlanta.

Free at last, free at last ...
Atlanta had not only long been known as the unofficial capital of the South but also had a more recent good name for being a hotbed of club team tennis. In the Civil War, the city had been almost raised to the ground in the later stages of the conflict by the Union forces of General Sherman as he tried to destroy the South with a scorched earth policy. But in the reconstruction years up to and after the turn of the twentieth century, the city's location as a rail hub meant that it became a focal point of life in Georgia and across the region. By the time of my visit, Atlanta was a thriving city in arts and culture, commerce, education, sport and politics.

Having checked into a Motel 6 recommended in my *Let's Go USA 1992* guidebook, I found the Georgia Dome, home of the Atlanta Falcons. I also booked a tour for the following day. I spent the evening watching two NFL teams, I hadn't yet seen on my travels (the Falcons and the San Francisco 49ers). But it was to be the tour I took the next day, which was the outstanding memory. The places visited included the headquarters of Coca-Cola, CNN and a museum on the city's involvement with the Civil War. Then, we visited the Martin Luther King Jr museum and stood silently looking at a plaque put up in his honour with the famous words which I've always found really moving, *Free at Last, Free at Last, Thank God Almighty, I'm Free at Last.*

Muscles forgets his cheque
It was now the middle of November and I had been in the US for nearly three months. Dallas was my next main stop as I headed back west in preparation for flying to Hawaii and then on to Australia. Dallas is known for many things including oil; the iconic television programme about the oil industry, *Dallas*, with its cult characters, including J.R. Ewing; the city's NFL team, the Dallas Cowboys; and for being the location of the assassination of President John F. Kennedy back in November 1963.

In tennis, the list of home-grown tennis professionals includes Anne Smith, winner of ten Grand Slams in doubles (with Kathy Jordan and Martina Navratilova) and mixed (with Billy Martin, Kevin Curren and Dick Stockton). But perhaps, the most important tennis event which is associated with Dallas is the final match of the 1972 WCT Finals played in the Moody Coliseum between Rod Laver and Ken Rosewall.

WCT (World Championship Tennis) had grown up as a concept as the sport began to open itself up to full professionalism in the late sixties. Lamar Hunt, who was from a wealthy Dallas family became involved (as he did in soccer and professional football) as an early, major investor. After Jack Kramer's initial attempts to create a tour structure for his contracted professionals through the fifties and sixties, WCT built on the concept and offered a schedule of tournaments to its professionals, one distinct to the Grand Prix circuit (run by the ITF and ultimately, the ATP). The WCT season usually ended with an end-of-year finals tournament, the likes of which became adopted by what have now become the ATP and WTA tours.

The 1972 finals, held in Dallas in May culminated in a magnificent five-set match between the Rocket and Muscles. The match was watched by a reported television audience of over twenty-one million people and a view has been stated that this match was the one which really fuelled national interest in the sport. The impact of the match was heightened because the broadcast was about to finish but because the tennis on offer was so good, the station extended the coverage allowing the viewers to experience and enjoy the superb contest. Certainly, the match would have contributed to the US boom in tennis in the seventies which saw many new courts opening and players taking up the sport with all the concurrent growth in associated aspects like increased sales of rackets, shoes, clothing and club memberships.

After Rosewall's victory, I heard one anecdote which talked about Muscles, so drained after such a demanding match, leaving the changing rooms and forgetting the winners cheque for fifty thousand dollars, a huge amount of money at the time and the single largest prize ever awarded in the sport for a tournament win to that point. He left it on the bench and had to return for it.

On gameday Sunday, I headed for Texas Stadium to watch the Dallas Cowboys. The car park was absolutely huge. There were the usual clusters of fans holding up tickets for sale and I bought one from the first couple I spoke to. The Cowboys were playing the San Francisco 49ers, who I had just seen play in Atlanta. But the highlight was the half-time show which was a celebration of thirty-years of the Cowboys' cheerleaders. Out on the field, almost every blade of grass, synthetic or otherwise, was taken up by a cheerleader. It was an impressive sight and the routines were executed perfectly by an array of women of a variety of ages.

Before flying out, I visited Dealey Plaza and stood in a variety of locations taking it all in. I looked up at the sixth-floor window where Lee Harvey Oswald was located, or was alleged to have been placed, as he performed the shooting. It was a bit odd being there in person. I had seen this location so many times across the years, it felt like I had been there before.

Flying back into Los Angeles, I stayed with the Fairbanks but this time, not with Bob and Pat but with Bill and Susannah and their growing family. They also made me feel really welcome. On the next Saturday, I drove down to San Diego to see a college game between San Diego State and Fresno State. On another day, I headed back down to see the famous Zoo. The NFL game I took in was another 49ers one and I began to feel like one of their fans. This time, the game was against the Los Angeles Rams who played in Anaheim at the Angel Stadium. Another highlight of my second stay in Los Angeles was a visit to the famous Beverley Hills Tennis Club where I did a quick walkabout, although I'd have loved to play there.

Home to two great tennis stars
Next, I drove across to Las Vegas. I had not booked ahead but was pretty sure of getting a room at this time of the year. I am not a gambler but it was fun to wander around the casino at my hotel, *The Mirage* and in other hotels too watching everyone else at the tables. I spent just two days in Vegas from start to finish but it felt as if I'd been there much longer. On the second evening, I went to see the impressionist, Rich Little, whose take on Richard Nixon was so good, you could almost believe that the disgraced president was actually up on stage. Of course, the city is well known worldwide for its gambling but it is where two of tennis's greats were born.

Jack Kramer is the man who sowed the seeds for the modern professional game. Born in the city in 1921, Kramer became a good junior player in the thirties. By the end of the Second World War, he had become an experienced competitor in the US Championships, going on to win in 1946 and 1947. He also won Wimbledon in 1947, and nine Grand Slams in all, including six titles in doubles and mixed. These wins were supplemented by two victories in professional majors and two wins in Davis Cup. It was in his post-playing days that Jack had a massive influence on the sport. As a professional, he began to play in the tours where two top players would compete nationwide in large numbers of matches night after night, often playing in obscure out-of-the-way towns in poor conditions and on questionable courts. He remained a player but bit by bit, took over the role of promoter and through the fifties, expanded his troupe of professional players. It was the type of tournaments, formats, points systems and prize money allocations he created to meet the needs of his players that ultimately, were used the basis for what was implemented by the WCT, the Grand Prix, the Virginia Slims tour and finally, the ATP and WTA tours. He was also a BBC television commentator on Wimbledon, a smooth, knowledgeable voice I recall from my childhood as he sat next to Dan Maskell. Also, he owned and ran tennis clubs and golf clubs back in the US. The tennis racket named after him was an incredibly popular one for many years.

In more recent times, Andre Agassi, known for his fine career in the sport, began life in Las Vegas where he grew up after his parents had moved there when his father, so integral to Andre's early tennis experience, was offered a job at one of the big hotels. Andre's story has been told extensively but his career, in which he won eight Grand Slam singles titles, including a career Super Slam, had many ups and downs. Thankfully, in retirement, living back in Las Vegas, he has found happiness in his marriage to Steffi Graf. They have their own family and are involved in various businesses and charity work making significant contributions to the well-being and education of children.

For me, the city now has an added tennis significance because of a short video available on the internet which shows an exhibition played there at Caesar's Palace in 1975 between Rod Laver and Jimmy Connors. What this clip shows is an ageing Laver; he was in his mid-to-late thirties, playing Connors, then in his early twenties. Rocket plays a serve and volley style and although Jimmy plays more from the back of the court, he attacks the net at every opportunity. The tennis is an exciting watch on every point and to my eyes, Rod looks incredibly fast, especially around the net. Jimmy is relentless in coming forward. Also, his passing shots look as if they have been literally blasted past the Rocket. If you were an opponent of either, Peter Burwash's concept of playing 'in emergency' comes to mind again. When anyone asks about Rod Laver and how he played, I refer them to this clip and tell them that although there are others available, I think it is this one which will give them the best idea, especially considering that a low camera angle used for many of the points provides a really good view of what both players were doing and just how fast they were.

After a final morning in *The Mirage*, where I allowed myself to bet fifty, luckless dollars on the slot machines, I headed for San Francisco.

Ramen with the Riessens

Heading west to Bakersfield, it was then a direct drive northward and I arrived in the middle of the evening with a stunning view of the city, as the road swung around some hills revealing the lights below. I found my hotel which had all sorts of art painted on the walls both outside and inside my room.

San Francisco is the home of Brad Gilbert and his siblings. When he was at school, Brad had to contend with the reputations of his brother and sister who had all played for the team before him. Gilbert retained his desire to succeed, worked on his talent and went on to a highly successful career as a professional. Brad's sister, Dana, just happened to be friends with Leslie who I had met on the train doing her nails as we sped towards Ann Arbor back in early October. Through Leslie's connection, I tried to meet Dana to say hello but we couldn't find an appropriate time, unfortunately.

As well as driving around the city, I went over to Alcatraz and at the weekend, watched the 49ers play again, but this time, in their home stadium. As I looked out over the field before the game against the Philadelphia Eagles, Luther Vandross belted out the National Anthem. However, the man next to me muttered to his wife, "Ruined again." Inquiring what he meant, he said that he was fed up with all the renditions he kept hearing where many well-known singers, like Vandross, added all sorts of extras to the song. He just wanted the anthem sung without any frills.

Leaving the city, I had been told by a few people about the picturesque drive down the coast from San Francisco to Los Angeles, using the coast-hugging Highway 1. This was my route on my way down to see a legend. They were right.

Back in Texas, I had told Marty Riessen that I wasn't sure when I would be coming down past Santa Barbara on my way to Los Angeles Airport prior to my flight across to Hawaii. He said that it didn't matter as he and his wife, April, were very flexible. He told me to let him know when I was close by and he would tell me how to find his house. So, as I approached Santa Barbara, I pulled in at a truck stop, found a phone – no mobiles back then – and called Marty's number. However, I wasn't sure that I had dialled the number correctly with the right area code sequence. Someone answered and I assumed it was an operator. Immediately, I started babbling about the number sequence and that I wasn't sure what to do and could this person help me. It then struck me that I recognised the voice of the man on the other end. It was Marty. I had, after all, dialled the correct number. Embarrassing start to the call over, I told Marty where I was and he told me how to find his home.

On arrival, I was very impressed. Marty and April's house was beautiful and they showed me to a spacious guest room where I dumped my bags. They asked me if I liked Japanese food and when I told them that I did, they suggested we go to their favourite local place. I was very happy with this plan. So, off we went and halfway through the meal, a new party of people sat down at the table next to us. I did a double take and then asked Marty if indeed, it was the British actress who now lived in the US and had made a successful career there, Jane Seymour? On confirmation that it was her, I spent a large part of the rest of our meal trying not to look at her which meant that I did exactly the opposite and found myself staring at her at just about every opportunity. Anyway, during the moments when I could break my attention away from Jane, the Riessens were the perfect hosts listening attentively to the tales of what I had been up to since the start of the year, let alone just since leaving Tennis Fantasies, a few weeks before.

In the morning, after some breakfast, Marty looked at me and said, "Fancy a hit?" I nearly spat out my coffee. While I was not even thinking about playing tennis at that point, I could not think of anything I'd like to do more. It was a beautiful day and when we stepped out at the back of the house, there was a tennis court. So, we had a hit and did so for at least forty-five minutes. I probably could have gone on longer as I'm sure Marty could have done. But I did not want to overstay my welcome. So, we called a halt. But it was a lovely end to a short stay. After giving Marty and April my thanks for their warm hospitality, I got back on the road heading southwards in time for my early evening flight to Hawaii.

Airplane re-created

I thought I'd walked into the opening scene of the film *Airplane*. As I entered the departures terminal at Los Angeles Airport, I was approached by some form of monk in orange robes. Unlike in the film, I didn't use a martial arts move to send him flying but seeing a thick book in his hands, I dispensed with the inevitable selling process I knew was about to take place.

"How much do you want?" I asked.

"The book is ten dollars," he said.

With a couple of long flights ahead of me, I took out a ten dollar note and handed it to him. The book was about the philosophy of his guru, a being with an unpronounceable name and many arms. I really intended to have a look at the mighty tome that my orange-clad friend had sold me but that moment never arrived, although it took me a few years to discard it from my book collection. That delay in getting rid of it was due to a sentimental attachment to my year-long trip, not to the contents of the book.

I was off to Hawaii and when I arrived, I stayed in a reasonably upmarket hotel for the first night but moved out for the rest of my stay. I walked the strip in Honolulu and found a cheaper option, more suitable for my budget. I found the main tennis club in Honolulu and spent some time there, although again, there was no-one around to play. From here, after a couple of days, I boarded the next plane. I was Australia bound.

Chapter 11

Musch, Milton and Martinez

Honeymoon without a wife
Just over a year after leaving, I touched down in Cairns, back in Australia, where the idea for my trip had taken root. I had flown to what the British used to call Trinity Bay back in the nineteenth century. If you wanted to see the Great Barrier Reef, this is one of the main places that you would head for. Although the city's population has grown since I was there, at the time of my visit, once I had arrived and settled into my hotel, Cairns had a smaller town feel about it, compared to the other Australian cities I had experienced - Sydney, Melbourne with a bit of Adelaide and Perth thrown in. What was not a surprise from my previous year spent in the country was the heat, which was excessive.

My plan was to do a few tourist things in the city like a trip to see the reef. I would then head down to Sydney where I would stay with my friends, Mark and Susie Dalton. From there, in the New Year, I would head up to Brisbane to spend a week watching the Danone International, a WTA warm-up event to the Australian Open. I would stay with my former sales manager for Queensland, Barry Musch. After that, I would head back to Sydney and spend a week at White City watching the Peters NSW Open, another build-up tournament which was for men and women. This was the last tournament prior to the Australian Open, so once it was over, I'd fly down to Melbourne, get established and complete my Grand Slam (non-calendar year version, that is) by going to Flinders Park every day. I'd also try and find both Cliff Drysdale and Fred Stolle and take them up on their offers of dinner.

I booked a trip out to the reef but as the morning progressed, I began to feel as if I was at a party but hadn't been invited. While the focus of the trip was on what was underneath the boat, I started to focus on what was happening on deck around me. The group that morning were all couples who seemed far more interested in each other than the spectacular views in the sea around us and from the reef below us. It was only when I disembarked that someone told me that I had somehow found myself on the Japanese honeymoon junket where all of the passengers were newly married couples. Well, that explained it!

I also booked a trip to see examples of the rain forest which exists up around Cairns but throughout, I was struggling with the heat and the humidity. Evenings were spent in search of Asian food as usual and that wasn't difficult to find. But I spent a good amount of time just sitting in bars drinking cool beers, a very Australian pastime and now, I knew why. After a few days, I was back at the airport, on a plane heading south to Sydney. It was time to get back on the tennis tour.

Checking in with the Daltons

I had worked with Mark Dalton at American Express in London and he and his wife, Susie, lived in a really nice unit, as flats are called in Australia. It was in Mosman, not that far from Neutral Bay where I had lived during my year in Sydney. This part of the North Shore was fantastic for pubs, bars and restaurants, especially my favourites, those serving Asian food. You could get all types from Japanese, Korean, Chinese, Vietnamese, Malaysian, Singaporean and Indonesian. There were some really good Indian restaurants too. It was perfect for me as most of these different types of cuisine were available in abundance in cafes and restaurants along Military Road, near where I had lived and Mark and Susie now did live.

Once back in Sydney, I organised a few meetups with former friends and colleagues from American Express. But I had no desire to go back to the offices, as I had done in Zurich earlier in my trip. I had to get organised for my week in Brisbane at the start of the New Year. I contacted Barry and as I expected, he immediately offered me the spare room in his house for my stay.

A first trip to Brisbane

Strange as it may sound now, in the year I spent with American Express based in Sydney, considering my job responsibilities covered the state and that I had a state manager and a team, I didn't visit Brisbane once. But that was an indication of what was going on back in the North Ryde headquarters as I have described earlier. Also, more than once, Barry had flown down to see me. It seemed easier that way.

Amongst other things, Brisbane, established in 1825, since 1859, had been the capital of Queensland, located north of the state's second city, the Gold Coast, a really popular holiday destination. Brisbane and Queensland had a long history with sport including rugby league, cricket, tennis and others. The great Roy Emerson, who I had spent the week in Texas with, was from Blackbutt, west of Brisbane; Mal Anderson was also from the state, born in a town called Theodore, north-east of the capital; and Rod Laver was also a Queenslander coming from Rockhampton, south-east of the capital.

Although there was plenty to see in Brisbane, as you might expect from a flourishing state capital city, arriving just before the start of the tournament, I did not have time for the type of sight-seeing tours that I had taken in many of the American cities I had visited in the latter part of the previous year. My time would almost exclusively be taken up watching the women play at Milton, a location which encapsulated the state's long commitment to tennis.

Rotating venues and surfaces

The tournament in Brisbane that week was sponsored by Danone and had grown out of the Australian Hardcourt

Championships, a tournament for men and women which began in 1938. The tournament had been hosted on a rotational basis in various cities around Australia throughout its history, including the Queensland locations of Toowoomba, Brisbane and Gympie from 1939, in rotation with other state venues. The tournament was played on clay courts until 1977. In 1978, the event switched to hard courts and continued to be played on that surface until 1987. In 1988, the men's event had been held in Adelaide while the women's event was not held at all. From the following year, the men stayed in Adelaide while the women's event was held in Brisbane and called the Danone Australian Hardcourt Championships. This was the fifth year of a run which would last until the following year's tournament. The event would not be staged in 1995 and 1996 but would re-emerge as a women's only event called the Thalgo Australian Women's Hard Courts which was held until 2002. The tournament would have various sponsors into the twenty-first century and would be merged with the men's event into a new combined tournament called the Brisbane International.

This year's tournament was a Tier III event, one above the lowest on that year's structure. While it might not attract many of the top players who might be spending the week practising or waiting elsewhere for the event in Sydney the following week, it was an attractive proposition to many of the players just below the top rankings because it was a build-up event to a Slam with a reasonably large-sized draw in both singles and doubles.

Home of the huge racket
The home of the tournament had an important place in Australian and Queensland tennis history. The Milton Tennis Centre had been opened in 1915. The current incarnation of the centre is called the Roy Emerson Tennis Centre in recognition of Emmo. But the park is now called Frew Park, in recognition

of the President of the Queensland Lawn Tennis Association, Alison Frew, the original driving force behind the centre. There was a large centre court stadium which seated seven-thousand spectators. It had been used for three Davis Cup Finals. The first time was in 1958, at a time when the Challenge Round was often a battle between the United States and Harry Hopman's strong Australian teams. On that occasion, the Americans came out on top. In 1962 and 1967, the final was again played at Milton and the Australians beat Mexico and Spain. The site was also the venue for the Australian Open on a number of occasions, prior to the fixing of that Slam's venue location in Melbourne and ultimately, Flinders Park.

By the time of my visit, the place looked a bit tired but this was partly due to the impression given by the wooden stands. Just about everywhere else I had been on my trip had been concrete jungles and exuding a more modern, if at times, soul-less feel. In 1999, the centre would be closed and then the land was sold in 2002. But in 2014, a new, smaller incarnation was built, including the twenty-three-foot racket which had been part of the original site, erected near the entrance.

Seeds, nationalities and early rounds
A Tier III event, the tournament was for fifty-six players in the main draw and thirty-two in qualifying. The doubles event was a twenty-eight-team draw. In singles, the top seed was Spain's Conchita Martinez, a woman who has had a long relationship with the game and one that is still going today. 1992 was still quite early in her playing career which would last for eighteen years, from 1988 to 2006, one with many highlights. Her thirty-three tour wins in singles would include the 1994 Wimbledon title where she would beat Martina Navratilova and become the first Spanish woman to win that coveted Grand Slam. She was a finalist and semi-finalist in other Slams and she won thirteen doubles titles too. She would reach career highs of No. 2 in singles and No. 7 in doubles. She

won medals in doubles at three Olympic Games and she was part of five winning Spanish Federation Cup teams. She would perform not only the Federation Cup captain role but also the same position for the men's Davis Cup team as well. In more recent times, she has become involved with coaching some of the top women on the tour. At the time of the tournament, she was the highest ranked woman in the draw, a top ten player.

Following her in the number two seeding spot was Maggie Maleeva who was the youngest of the three Maleeva sisters and the only one of the family playing in Brisbane. She would have a sixteen-year career as a pro. In 1992, she was into her fourth year and ranked in the top thirty at the time. Maggie would reach a career high of No. 4 in the rankings with ten singles titles from twenty-one final appearances. She was a solid performer in Slams and would reach the fourth round on twelve occasions. In New York, back in September, she had reached the quarter-finals. In doubles, she was consistent too, reaching a ranking of No. 5 and winning five titles from ten appearances in finals.

The third seed was Belgium's Sabine Appelmans, another good player who would end up with a similar record to Maggie Maleeva. In a slightly shorter career, Sabine would reach No. 16 in the rankings and win seven titles from twelve finals. She would also be a consistent achiever in Slams, reaching a number of fourth rounds and one quarter-final. In doubles, she reached a ranking of No. 21 and won four titles from fourteen finals. When Sabine started out, she was a right-hander but insisted on playing left-handed in order to stay in a left handers' group with a best friend. She played her whole pro career as a left-hander.

The other thirteen seeds included a number of solid players whose rankings at the time stretched down to just above No. 60 in the world. Julie Halard, the number four seed, had a respectable career-ending list of achievements. Many of Julie's successes would come towards the end of her career and especially, in her final year on tour in 2000, when in doubles alone, she reached a staggering twelve finals, winning ten titles, most of them with Ai Sugiyama.

Most of the seeds, along with many of the competing players at the event had begun their tennis journeys in their childhood. Tenth seed, Debbie Graham was one such player. From California, she progressed through local competitions into regional and national events winning the US Nationals at U16 level in 1986 while playing school tennis too. She played in college at Stanford where she was an award-winning player in 1990, before going on the tour full time. She won the 1990 NCAA singles title as a junior and was a member of three NCAA championship teams. Debbie earned all-American honours four consecutive years and was ranked No. 1 in singles and doubles during her collegiate career. In a twelve-year pro career, Debbie reached a career high of No. 28 in singles and in doubles, won five WTA Tour events and six ITF level events. In Grand Slams, she reached the third round in Paris and a doubles semi-final at Wimbledon. After retiring, she would go into coaching as part of the USTA structure. She would also specialise in teaching the game to small children in a mini tennis environment, giving back to young juniors the passion for the game that she had experienced at their age and trying to instil that love for the sport in them.

When looking at nationality clusters, it was no surprise to find eight Australian women in the draw, led by seventh seed, Rachel McQuillan, who seemed to be the poster girl for Aussie tennis at the time. There were seven Americans in the draw, led by Debbie Graham. Italy was well-represented with seven players, the highest being Federica Bonsignori, the fourteenth seed. Clare Wood was the only British representative at the tournament. She beat Canadian Rene Collins in straight sets, a good result for her. Clare's ranking had been on a steady rise throughout 1992.

The draw size meant that the top eight seeds received a bye through to the second round. But there were some casualties amongst the seeds who had to play in first-round matches, including Ros Fairbank-Nideffer, Debbie Graham, Alexia Dechaume-Balleret, Federica Bonsignori, Karina Habsudova and Nanne Dahlman.

Daily routine
Barry lived to the east of the city centre, a train ride in for me. But the local service was very good and it was a nice trip through some pretty suburbs into the centre. I could walk to the courts once in the city and getting in was easy. So began another daily routine which was like the ones before. Although the tournament had a reasonably large draw, it had an intimate feel about it.

I spent a lot of time watching the matches on the famous stadium court for no other reason than I could sit in the shade of the main stand, even though the blistering heat kept the temperature up at a very high level. I can't imagine what it must have been down on the court where the Rebound Ace surface, the same one used in Sydney and Melbourne for the Australian Open, tended to become sticky in such heat.

The matches began in the late morning and went on all afternoon. But with the good weather, the schedule was completed without any difficulties. Making the return journey, I was usually back at home in time for dinner with Barry and his family. It was all very relaxed and laid back. If it was possible to live, stress-free, even for a short while, this was probably the time. Nonetheless, now that we were in January, I could see an end to my trip and that would arrive sooner rather than later after the end of the Australian Open which was at the end of January and into the start of February. Originally, I had considered visiting countries like Nepal but I'd been away from the UK for nearly six months and was beginning to look forward to arriving back at my flat. I decided that the experience of travelling through the infamous Charles Sobhraj's hunting grounds could wait!

A round of straights
Two more seeds fell in the second round when the top eight seeds joined in and played their first matches. Third seed, Sabine Appelmans, was beaten in three sets by Australian, Michelle Jaggard-Lai. Sabine had won the second set 6-1 but the home player came back to take the match. Michelle was a good example of a player who did exceptionally well as a junior, winning Australian age group national titles and appearing in a number of junior Slams, surviving on the tour for a decade. She began playing as a small child and was a pro from a young age, starting on the tour from the age of fifteen. Although she retired when only twenty-five years old, Michelle had effectively been playing in one form or another, for twenty years. At Brisbane, she was coming towards the end of her career and like Julie Halard, experienced some of her better successes in the final stages of that career. This success, she told me, was a lot to do with having her new husband on tour with her which helped provide her with company, and a more stable existence as she dealt with the rigours of tour life. In fact, this tournament in Brisbane was the start of a new regime for Michelle and things went well from the start. She was happier, played better and the results started to improve. She went on to achieve her top ranking of No. 83 later in 1993, a year before her retirement. Michelle did win three WTA Tour singles titles and at ITF level, she won two singles (one in the event before Brisbane securing her a wild card into the tournament at Milton), and seven doubles titles. She played in the Federation Cup for Australia and received an award for her contribution to Australian sport.

Also, sixth seed, the Czech player, Andrea Strnadova lost to the Dutch player, Stephanie Rottier. Strnadova was a pro for eight years, slightly less than many of the other women she competed with. She reached a career high in singles of No. 33 and appeared in five WTA finals, a runner-up on each occasion. In doubles, she reached three finals and won all three and her highest doubles ranking was No. 14. Stephanie Rottier, another hard-working pro who was also on the tour for eight years reached a career high of No. 30 in singles.

In other matches, top seeds Conchita Martinez and Maggie Maleeva both won in straight sets. All the other matches were also won in straight sets other than the one between Sabine Appelmans and Michelle Jaggard-Lai and one between eighth seed, Manon Bollegraf and the young American, Chanda Rubin which Bollegraf won 6-4 in the third set. Unfortunately for Clare Wood, young Lindsay Davenport was too strong, winning their match 6-3, 6-2.

The next round proved to be the last for three more seeds. Julie Halard and Radmira Zrubakova were both beaten in straight sets by fellow seeds, Shi-Ting Wang and Florencia Labat respectively, while Manon Bollegraf was beaten by Noelle van Lottum in a longer, three-set match. Rachel McQuillan won an all-Australian encounter against Nicole Pratt and top seeds Conchita Martinez and Maggie Maleeva, who beat Lindsay Davenport, both progressed.

Number one seed doubles up

In the doubles, as ever, there were players in the draw who had not qualified for the singles or whose ranking allowed them only to try for qualification or inclusion in the doubles main draw. There were eight seeds and again, Conchita Martinez was the top seed in a team with Larissa Savchenko-Neiland who had not played in the singles. Manon Bollegraf was also in the doubles with her usual partner, Katrina Adams. They were the second seeds. The other pairings included players who had played in the singles like Barbara Rittner and Julie Richardson. With this size of draw, some of the higher seeds received a bye to the second round, meaning that they would have to win four matches to secure the title, while first round participants would need to win five.

In the first round, seventh seeds Rachel McQuillan and Noelle van Lottum fell at the first hurdle, beaten by Louise Pleming and Maria Strandlund although that team were then beaten by Clare Wood who was playing again with Tracey Morton, another of the Australians. The second round was also the end of the road for a few more seeded teams. Katrina Adams and Manon Bollegraf were beaten by the Dutch team of Miriam Oremans and Monique Kiene. Next, eighth seeds, Barbara Rittner and Karina Habsudova were beaten by the American team of Kimberley Po-Messerli and Shannan McCarthy. Finally, the fifth seeds, Ros Fairbank-Nideffer and Julie Richardson, were beaten by another American team, Jessica Emmons and Nicole Arendt. The top seeds came through easily in straight sets.

A question of motivation
As I sat in the ferocious heat as the week progressed, watching the players fight it out in the gladiatorial way that singles, especially, sets two players against each other, the question of motivation came to my mind. Why would these young women, most of them at this tournament in their early or mid-twenties put themselves through such gruelling experiences on such a gruelling tour?

Looking at the backgrounds of most of the players, many, if not all of them, had begun their tennis journeys as young children at a time when tennis would have been a fun thing to do. For many, playing tennis may have been wrapped up in their relationship with their parents, as often, players might begin playing the game with their parents at their tennis club or were coached by their mother or father at some point, including on tour, as they travelled, if money was tight and the player could not afford to pay a team of support staff, including a coach.

I would later find research that highlighted - if young children and teenagers were learning in groups - the attraction of sport and especially tennis, would revolve around the social aspects of the experience. Remember how Sabine Appelmans had even decided to play with the wrong hand, being with her friend in the group lesson was such a priority. The focus would be on seeing the friends they had made at lessons and enjoying the atmosphere of the activity. On the tennis side of things, interestingly, when starting any form of organised, competitive activity, winning was a side benefit to be enjoyed as and when it occurred, not the goal of their involvement. Learning new skills, practising existing ones and getting better as time went along were important to youth sport participants in general and junior tennis players specifically. It was the excitement of competition that was as important as the result for many youngsters. In this sense, ironically, if left to process the results themselves, juniors could often handle both winning and losing better than their parents.

With juniors who decided to take the path of the competitive journey in local, regional and then national and international competition, as most of the pros I had been watching all year had done, initially, they would have enjoyed all the benefits of participation experienced by those not seeking to go the distance in the sport. But things would be a bit different once they did make the decision to go for it. Although not always a healthy aspect of their development as a junior player, the focus of the adults involved, parents, coaches, National Association representatives and even agents and tournament directors, tended to focus on results. Winning became the currency of development, even though the word in the coaching world amongst those that really understood the development process was that the experience of the performance, or how the player played, should be the focus, not just the end result. In competitive junior tennis, it became about the winning. Winning would determine your ranking and which tournaments you could enter or might be invited to enter. This would be the case all the way through the junior years and as and when the junior player entered the pro ranks, winning became even more significant.

Winning would mean prize money. Prize money would be needed to fund the daily business of playing on tour, paying off debts, paying back sponsors or investors or giving back to mum and dad who had probably expended considerable amounts of money on lessons, equipment, stringing and clothing, travel to and from tournaments, accommodation and food once there. Alongside these financial considerations, there were usually the additional organisational issues relating to family life where often, disruption to the lives and sometimes, the aspirations of siblings and their goals, could be anything from minor at best to extreme at worst.

This focus on winning meant that it really helped if the professional player loved the sport. Most of them would tell you that they did, although for some, what had once been a fun activity and then turned into the pursuit of a dream, had become a job and often, a tedious one, but without the type of stability that the rest of us might experience working and returning home every day would provide. Many players talked about how living out of travel bags, checking in and out of hotel rooms, might have sounded different from the norm, fun even, but after a while, became tedious and wearisome. The motivation needed to dig deep to work at achieving the best results possible when the family, not just the player, might depend on the result of a match or the overall performance at a tournament, had to be strong. Andre Agassi, a top star of the sport once talked about how he played tennis for all the wrong reasons throughout his life. Agassi's story is a sobering one to say the least. Maybe, its saving grace was that at the back end of his career, despite playing with almost constant pain from a terrible back condition, he played for his reasons, not those dictated to him by others.

This was a complex subject. For some, the pursuit of the dream, to experience the glory and prestige of winning the big tournaments like the Grand Slams, would keep them going through all the daily grind and everything that went with it, like playing in tremendous heat here in Brisbane. For others, the fact they were providing for their families might be a pressure, while for others, it would set the purpose for what they were doing. Some would say that they enjoyed the life and the fact that they were playing a sport they loved and that all the things that people outside the sport might see as being negatives were in fact positives.

In some ways, the pressures, however defined by a player, would be easier to handle if they were able to win enough to get their ranking up to a point where they were experiencing direct entry into the top tournaments and doing well enough to secure decent prize money. Getting into Grand Slam singles events was always a big priority not just because of the prestige but because the levels of prize money, even for losing in the early rounds, was significantly higher than in tour events at the lower tiers of the ATP Tour or in this case in Brisbane, the WTA Tour.

Then again, in many cases, it seemed that the more a player won, the more the expectations from everyone around them would increase, from family, sponsors, the tour, agent, the media and tournament directors. If you became a star, everyone around you and involved with you, more often than not and for many good reasons, would want you to stay as a star. But these expectations could often create a never-ending pressure to succeed to keep it all going.

Endorsement contracts were another opportunity and if a player could rise above the basic level of receiving free rackets, clothing and shoes to a level where they were being paid to play in particular brands or to wear logo patches of the company sponsoring them, then this would provide added income over and above prize money earnings. Players at the very top could earn endorsement contracts which would pay them many times more than their prize money. This meant that how players conducted themselves on and off the court, could pay big dividends. Ultimately, sponsors in the commercial marketplace would be wondering if they could sell more of their products and services by associating themselves with any given player.

Living as a pro involved more than just hitting tennis balls, either in endless practice or in stressful competition. Dealing with motivation, the highs and lows, the joy of success but often the fear of failure were constant companions and part of the job.

Conchita summits
Back on the courts, the quarter-final matches were relatively straight forward other than the match between Michelle Jaggard-Lai and Noelle van Lottum which the Australian won 7-6 in a third set tiebreaker. Conchita Martinez beat Angelica Galvadon; Maggie Maleeva beat Rachel McQuillan and Shi-Ting Wang beat fellow seed Florencia Labat, all in straight sets, to progress to the semi-finals.

In Sunday's final, the two top seeds came through to meet each other. In the semi-finals, Conchita Martinez had beaten the unseeded Michelle Jaggard-Lai while Maggie Maleeva had been too strong for thirteenth seed, Shi-Ting Wang, beating her, also in straight sets. The final was another relatively straight-forward affair with Conchita beating Maggie.

In the doubles quarter-finals, the top seeds, Conchita and Larissa Savchenko-Neiland beat Clare Wood and Tracey Morton, bringing their run to an end. In the semi-final, they beat Alexia Dechaume-Balleret and Florencia Labat to advance to the final where they played the Americans, Kimberley Po-Messerli and Shannan McCarthy. The final was relatively straight forward with the top seeds winning the title. It had been a very good week for Conchita Martinez.

Chapter 12

Return to White City

Back to Port Jackson

Many of the players and their support teams, if they had them, had already travelled south either to Sydney for the next warm-up tournament or down to Melbourne for a week of practice prior to the start of the Australian Open. On Monday morning, I said my thanks and goodbyes to Barry and family and flew back down to Sydney where I re-established myself in the Dalton's spare room. Then, I made my way straight back out across the Harbour Bridge to Rushcutters' Bay and my former tennis club, White City.

While things had not been what I would have wanted in my year working in Sydney with American Express, they had ultimately led to something really good. After all, here I was back in the city after an amazing nine months of travel and a wealth of new experiences and contacts with so many interesting people along the way. At least now, I could spend a bit of time appreciating the city for all it had to offer, without the work situation dominating my time like before.

I had educated myself on Sydney's recent history, especially after moving to live there. Originally, Captain Cook had landed in Botany Bay in 1770. Then, in 1788, Captain Phillip chose Port Jackson, now known as Sydney Harbour, as the place to begin the establishment of a penal colony. Years later, that colony became the modern city. Military Road in Neutral Bay, close to where I had lived in my unit, was named that way because it was the road used originally by the British troops when they were going about their business on the North Shore. The historic old buildings in the city were a throwback to that time as well. Ever since I was a child, I'd been interested in history and in this city, there was plenty of opportunity to look back just a couple of hundred years, never mind the long history of the country and its indigenous people before that, right back to pre-historic times.

Sydney was a city, like New York amongst others, often in the news and featured frequently in popular culture as well. Photographs and film clips of the Harbour Bridge alone had certainly made an indelible image in my mind. However, as in all the locations I had visited where tennis was the priority, this time around, as in the previous week up in Brisbane, I could not spend too much time musing about the past. I had a tennis tournament I wanted to watch and White City was calling.

The Championships of New South Wales
The event I was now going to watch had a long history. In fact, in its original incarnation, it was one of the oldest and earliest tournaments held in the world with its first edition in 1885 around a similar time to the British tournaments mentioned above, including those at Wimbledon, Eastbourne, Manchester, Ilkley and the Queen's Club.

The tournament had been held in various locations including a part of the Sydney Cricket Ground, a ground at Double Bay and from 1922, at the White City Club in Rushcutters Bay. It had only been held annually from 1935. Its name had been the Championships of New South Wales but by the early nineties, it had become the New South Wales Open. It stayed at White City until 1999. After the Sydney Olympics in 2000, the tournament would be moved from White City to the Sydney Olympic Park Tennis Centre.

The tournament catered for men and women and included singles and doubles for both. Until the sport went open, the winners of the singles and the doubles events had been Australian with one or two exceptions. In the men's event in the very early years, Britain's Wilberforce Eaves had twice been a winner and the better-known Americans, Ellsworth Vines, Tappy Larsen, Vic Seixas and Dennis Ralston had won in 1932, 1950, 1951 and 1965 respectively. In the women's event, Britain's Dorothy Round had won in 1934 followed by Americans, Doris Hart, Maureen Connolly and Althea Gibson winning in 1948, 1952 and 1956, respectively. South Africa's Renee Schuurman won in 1957. Through the seventies, beginning with Billie Jean King in 1970 and Alex Metreveli in 1972, as Australia's dominance of the world tennis stage gradually diminished and participation from other countries increased, winners from those places gradually took over the honour roll. However, these were an assortment of players, as it wasn't until the eighties when the Australian Open was re-launched with the opening of Flinders Park in Melbourne, my port of call the following week, that the gradual return of all the top men and women to Australia to start their year with the Australian Open and its build-up tournaments began.

Here at White City, at the previous year's tournament, the winners had been Emilio Sanchez and Gabriela Sabatini. This year's event was a World Series tournament in the ATP Tour hierarchy and there were two other tournaments of similar size that week, one in Auckland and another in Jakarta. In the WTA schedule, the tournament was a Tier II event, one up from the previous week's tournament in Brisbane. There was also a Tier IV tournament down in Melbourne.

One of Hop's old training grounds
Returning to White City felt just a little bit strange. I was coming home in one way, but in another, it was no longer home. I was no longer a member and the place had been taken over by the tennis circus, now in town in the form of the Peters NSW Open. The tournament was at the White City I knew but the atmosphere was different and the activities I had known every weekend in my year before were not going on this time.

White City was an iconic part of Australian tennis history, something I had always been aware of during my one-year membership. The courts had been built in 1922 although the club was created in 1946. By 1992, there were six hard courts using the Rebound Ace surface used in Melbourne. These were the courts the tournament would be played on. But in addition, there were rows and rows of grass courts too, the ones that I played on as a member. It was these courts on which the Australian greats I had watched at Wimbledon back when growing up, had played, preparing for their domestic competitions and also, for their overseas trips when it became time to take part in the northern hemisphere's summer season.

Rather like at Milton up in Brisbane, White City had hosted a number of important Davis Cup ties, including the Challenge Round final where the previous year's winner played the country who had emerged from all the zonal competitions and pre-final rounds. White City was used five times, in 1951, 1954, 1960, 1965 and 1977. Extensions were added to the existing stands on the Centre Court where in 1992, there was a grass court next to one of the Rebound Ace ones which the tournament used. In 1954, for the final against the US, a record for a sanctioned tennis match was set with 25,578 people watching. There are photographs of those stands rising up into the sky, absolutely packed with tennis fans.

Fred Stolle, a former winner of the NSW Championships in 1964 and 1966 when he beat Roy Emerson and John Newcombe respectively, has told me that as the players went around the country playing in all the state championships and in the Australian Open, they could practise under Harry Hopman's critical eyes, continuing to work on their games and getting themselves ready for the challenges ahead. Long before I walked on to the banks of grass courts at White City, Hopman had been training his teams there as hard as ever.

As I had experienced in my visits to Bardmoor and my week at Saddlebrook, Hopman's methods revolved mainly around work on the court. There was very little of the modern gym work players complete today. While the players did go for runs, most of the work involved a lot of lung and leg-busting drills, just as I had experienced. Fred once told a group of us at

Tennis Fantasies that the definition of fitness that the players and coaches used as their benchmark (remembering that most top tennis was played on grass at the time) was that they should be able to play a five-set singles match and then, on the same day, play a five-set doubles match. They should then be ready to do the same again on the following day. After a day's matches, relaxation with a few beers would have then been earned. Roy Emerson, a player renowned for running in the early mornings if his lager consumption had been a bit high the night before, always said that if a player walked on to court to play, then they were saying that they were fit to play. Injury niggles they might be carrying or, presumably, headaches they might have been dealing with as a result of too many beers consumed the night before, didn't matter or count. If you won the match, that was fine but if you lost, there were no excuses.

Seeds, nationalities and early rounds
Looking at the seedings for the men's event, the top seed was Pete Sampras and the others were all top twenty players including the last and eighth seed, Sweden's Henrik Holm who had been rising up the rankings steadily over the previous year including that good run at Wimbledon. He had also entered the draw as a wild card, but also, straight into the seeding list. The others were well-known from the seeding lists of the recent Slams including, Richard Krajicek, Guy Forget, Wayne Ferreira, Carlos Costa, Sergi Bruguera and Thomas Muster.

As far as nationality clusters, on the men's side, it was the Swedes who made up the largest contingent from one country. In addition to Henrik Holm, there was Thomas Enquist, Nicklas Kulti, Magnus Gustafsson, Christian Bergstrom, Magnus Larsson, Jan Apell and Jonas Svensson, making a contingent of seven of the thirty-two players in the first round. As expected at a home tournament, the Australians were well-represented with Mark Woodforde, Sandon Stolle, Michael Tebbutt, Grant Doyle, Wally Masur and Richard Fromberg.

The French and Italians were also well-represented but there were no British players in the draw. Harking back to my first tournament on the trip, in Rome, amongst others, Amos Mansdorf was competing. Who would bring him his supply of bananas here at White City?

In the opening two rounds, Amos did well, beating Carlos Costa in three sets and then Christian Bergstrom. Guy Forget was beaten by fellow Frenchman, Cedric Pioline, who was beaten in turn, by David Wheaton. Henrik Holm came through the first round but was beaten by fellow Swede, Nicklas Kulti, in round two. In the bottom half of the draw, Sergi Bruguera and Richard Krajicek were beaten by qualifier, Michael Tebbutt and Emilio Sanchez, respectively. The remaining seeds, Pete Sampras, Wayne Ferreira and Thomas Muster progressed to the third round.

In the women's singles, although Monica Seles and Steffi Graf were absent, Gabriela Sabatini was the top seed and like the men, the rest of the list was made up of well-known names including Arantxa Sanchez Vicario, Mary Joe Fernandez, Jennifer Capriati, Anke Huber, Helena Sukova and the friends who had developed their junior careers together, Lori McNeil and Zina Garrison.

On the nationality front, Gabriela Sabatini had fellow Argentinian countrywomen, Florencia Labat, down from Brisbane and Bettina Fulco-Villella as well, to keep her company. In a strong group of Americans, Capriati, McNeil and Garrison were joined by Patty Fendick, Pam Shriver, Tami Whitlinger, Amy Frazier and Ann Grossman. The Australians were represented by Rachel McQuillan and Michelle Jaggard-Lai, down from Brisbane and also, Elizabeth Smylie, a solid player who reached No. 20 in singles with three tour titles but was also known for her excellent doubles play where she reached a high of No. 5 and won thirty-six tour titles and four Grand Slams in doubles and mixed. Clare Wood was not in the draw. There were no British players competing in the singles, as in the men's event.

In the first round, Helena Sukova had to retire while facing Barbara Rittner and Sabine Appelmans upset Zina Garrison, although in the second round, the Belgian would lose to Tami Whitlinger. At that stage, Lori McNeil was beaten by Pam Shriver. Ros Fairbank-Nideffer had two long three-set matches, one she won against Michelle Jaggard-Lai and the other she lost, against Jennifer Capriati. Another player from Brisbane the week before, Stephanie Rottier, not only came through qualifying but beat Bettina Fulco-Villella before losing a hard-fought match in three sets to number two seed, Arantxa Sanchez Vicario. All of this meant that of the eight seeds, Gabriela Sabatini, Jennifer Capriati, Anke Huber and Arantxa Sanchez Vicario, progressed to the quarter-finals.

Going to the tennis by boat
During this week back in Sydney, I made my way across the harbour to the city centre from Mosman where Mark and Susie lived, by ferry, one of the wonderful aspects of life in the city. Arriving at Circular Quay, I could take a bus or a cab to White City but at least once, I walked to Rushcutters Bay, although it was a bit of a slog in the heat at just under three miles. But Sydney is a marvellous city with so many interesting buildings, different areas with different architecture, each with its own feel and the weather was superb, so it was an opportunity for a great walk, too good to miss.

On arrival at White City, I'd go through my tried and trusted routine of checking the order of play and deciding which matches I wanted to focus on that day. This was all very flexible at a slightly smaller tournament, unlike at a Slam where there were around twenty courts with matches on them. Here at the NSW Open, there were just six courts and I knew the orientation of the grounds extremely well.

Returning the same way that I had come earlier, I'd either spend the evenings with Mark and Susie or on a couple of occasions, I met up with friends I had made previously in my year in the city or with members of my team from my time in North Ryde with American Express.

Quarter-Finals

In the men's event, Pete Sampras beat Nicklas Kulti quite easily in straight sets. Amos Mansdorf also won in straight sets against David Wheaton. The second set score of 6-1 suggested a slightly easier path than the first set which Mansdorf won in a tiebreaker, 7-2. The only three-set match was between Omar Camporese and Wayne Ferreira with the Italian coming out on top. Finally, Thomas Muster beat Jonas Svensson in two tough sets, winning the second one 12-10 in a tiebreaker.

On the women's side, all four matches were straight sets affairs. Gabriela Sabatini beat Barbara Rittner and Jennifer Capriati beat Pam Shriver, allowing her fellow countrywoman just one game in the second set. In another all-American affair, Amy Frazier beat Tami Whitlinger and finally, fifth seed, Anke Huber beat Arantxa Sanchez Vicario.

Seventh game or ninth?

In Brisbane the week before, while watching the matches and trying not to melt, I had considered the motivations of the players. Here in Sydney at White City, after watching a few more matches, the thought for the week was about the situation, often in the first set where, usually commentators but also, journalists, coaches, players and then fans, inadvertently influenced to do so by all these others, talked about the important seventh game in a set. While a literal interpretation of the seventh game might see a variety of scores before that seventh game took place, like 2-4 or 5-1, for example, the score most people were referring to when they talked about the seventh game was when the score was 3-3. It was often at this point where up until then, each player had won all their service games, that the serving player would break that established pattern and lose their serve, giving their opponent a chance to pull away and after another couple of service games, assuming they held them, to win the set. Perhaps it was just the matches I had watched over the last ten months, but it seemed to me that it was not the seventh but the ninth game, at 4-4, where one of the players would be just as likely to crack in some way and lose their serve.

I did not have any empirical data to prove if I was right or not. This was just a feeling that I sensed after watching a lot of matches. In a way, it didn't matter if it was the seventh or the ninth game. What was interesting for me was why the phenomenon of one player pulling away after both seemed so equally matched up to that point existed. Trying to analyse it a bit as I sat in the shade of one of the covered stands on White City's centre court, it seemed to me that the offending player who cracked was usually the lower-ranked one but it could be the higher-ranked one too. The thing was that to the uneducated or even the casually observing eye, there didn't seem to be anything that had changed in the play. Usually, both players seemed to have carried on with the same tactics that had taken them through the first six or eight games on an equal footing. But the service break occurred on too many occasions for me not to notice it.

I concluded that both players' minds must, almost inevitably, seeing as they were human and not robots, have been considering the situation and as the opportunity came to pull away to win the set, that this must have been triggering subtle changes in what the players were actually doing. Maybe, they tried harder and this could mean too hard, whereby they would hit the ball just a bit wider or deeper and therefore, out? On the other hand, they might have been trying not to hit so hard, effectively adopting a more conservative approach, believing that this would maintain the performance level as it had been so far, while all it did was to make their shots land too short or too central, providing opportunities for their opponent to exploit the new position? Possibly, the reason that the higher ranked players were in that position was because they possessed the combination of mental skills, including confidence in their game, combined with their tactical choice of shot and more reliable technique to take those opportunities more often and more effectively.

Whatever it was, the differences in point construction or execution usually seemed subtle to me but exist they did.

Guy's serve exhibition
Quite possibly down to the heat, the atmosphere at White City for those of us not out on the courts in the baking sun, putting our tennis playing expertise on the line, was very relaxed. These were days still prior to the terrible day in Hamburg when a deranged spectator would leap from the seats behind the umpire's chair and stab Monica Seles. While the spectators respected the players and their privacy and space, the players didn't seem to mind wandering around the club in a relaxed way. Mind you, for most of these players, this is what they would have been used to for many years since beginning to compete in junior tournaments. From this year of travelling, it had become noticeable that it was at the Slams where things, understandably, were a bit more pressurised and where the demarcation between pros and those involved working in the tennis circus were separated more distinctly from us fans.

On one occasion, I stood at the back of one of the practice courts with a few others, watching Guy Forget practising his serve. The ball seemed to disappear to the other end in a split-second and there was an amazing noise like a rifle-shot when Guy made contact with the ball. He proceeded to hit what appeared to be first serves and then went on to hit second serves. The amount of spin seemed to be the difference between the two. Many club players would imagine that the first serve would be hit hard and flat without any thought of spin or effort to impart it on the ball. Indeed, this was what many, if not most club players did, often because they didn't use the proper serve grip, thereby limiting them to be able to only hit the ball flat with the variable of how hard they hit it as their option differentiating first and second serves. Many club players would simply hit a softer second serve often meaning that the ball just stood up waiting to be smacked back past them by their opponent. With the pros, of course, things were done a bit differently. Forget's first serve was closer to a slice than topspin but hit very hard so that for a right-hander, it would curve away from the backhand with irritating evasiveness, a bit like I observed with Roger Taylor's serve back in Vale de Lobo a decade before. The second serve was closer to a topspin one but it was also hit hard. Because fellow pros were so good technically on their returns, you could not afford to hit slow serves. Some degree of risk had to be taken. Hence double faults at this level.

At this stage of his career, Guy was a top player. That week in Sydney, he was ranked No. 12 and would go into the top ten the following week. He retired in 1997 after a fifteen-year career. In singles, he reached a ranking high of No. 4, winning eleven titles in nineteen appearances in finals. In Slams, he reached the fourth round in all of them, going on to two quarter-finals in Melbourne and three at Wimbledon. In doubles, he reached a ranking high of No. 3, winning twenty-eight titles from a staggering fifty-five appearances in finals. In Slams, he was a finalist at Roland Garros twice with Yannick Noah in 1987 and Jacob Hlasek in 1996, although he did win the tour finals with Hlasek in 1990. In his post-playing career, like Conchita Martinez, he would become the captain of his country's teams in both Davis Cup and Federation Cup. He went on to become involved in the administration of the game and in 2016, he became the tournament director of Roland Garros, a position he held for five years.

After enjoying Guy's serve display for twenty minutes or so, I continued to meander around the show courts watching the matches while often bumping into friends from the club members who I had known in my stay before.

Two American title-winners
The men's final was between Pete Sampras and Thomas Muster after both players had dispatched Amos Mansdorf and Omar Camporese, respectively. The American won the title in another match where it was a case of the player winning the first set going on to win the match. After a long first set tiebreaker which Sampras won 9-7, he won the second set and the tournament, 6-1.

On the women's side, in two more straight sets semi-final matches, Jennifer Capriati knocked out top seed Gabriela Sabatini and in the final, she faced Anke Huber who had despatched Amy Frazier. Capriati won the title after beating the young, German star, 6-1, 6-4.

The men's doubles was won by the Australian pairing of Sandon Stolle and Jason Stoltenberg who beat the Jensen brothers, Murphy and Luke, a player who could play right or left-handed and switched between the two, especially when he was serving, in order to maximise the impact of hitting a slice serve out wide in both the deuce and the advantage courts, one hit right-handed; the other hit left-handed.

The women's doubles final was fought out between two Australian-American pairings. Elizabeth Smylie and Pam Shriver beat Rennae Stubbs and Lori McNeil in straight sets.

So, it was time to say goodbye to my old tennis home at White City and head south, down to Melbourne for what would effectively be the beginning of the end of my trip.

Chapter 13

Happy Slam at Flinders Park

Man climbs into car boot, twice!
My plane landed at Melbourne airport. I had visited the city once in my year with American Express, although at the time, that first trip was one I wanted to forget. Its purpose was to impart some not-so-good news to one of my sales managers about changes taking place in the company that would affect him and his team. The visit was also made at a time when I was probably at rock bottom in my motivation, my outlook on the job, my stay in Australia and my career overall with American Express. On the return from Melbourne on that trip, an event occurred on my arrival back at Sydney that night which added to my growing sense of frustration and disappointment at how things were working out. Looking back, it was mildly ludicrous, surreal, bizarre, and totally unexpected at the time, although actually, quite amusing.

It all concerned my company car, a big Holden saloon with a huge V8 engine, far too powerful to drive legally on Sydney's roads if you really wanted to let the engine do what it was built for. Nontheless, this beast of a machine was a smooth ride, as I made my way back and forth from Neutral Bay to North Ryde every day. The problem was that the battery kept going flat. On a couple of occasions, I'd taken the car into a garage near the American Express offices and they had given everything a clean bill of health. But on returning to Sydney on a blustery and rainy evening after my day trip to Melbourne, to my great frustration, as I tried to start the car, it was clear that the battery had gone flat again. I knew that sorting the problem out would take up valuable time in my evening and that in all probability, by the time I returned home, I would have to get to bed, accelerating the arrival of the morning and another stressful day being increasingly ineffective at work. I called the road assistance number and waited about half an hour before a mechanic showed up. To my non-Australian eyes, he looked the epitome of the Aussie working man with his short-sleeved shirt, tailored shorts, long thick woollen socks and heavy-duty shoes, all topped off with a semi-wide-brimmed hat. I explained the problem and how it had been repeating itself but that so far, no-one had come up with a solution, evidenced by the fact that he was there with me in the airport car park. He checked a few things and then suggested that he knew what the problem was.

"Mate, I'm going to get in the boot and I want you to shut me in," he announced. I was speechless but he was moving quickly to execute his plan. I had little choice but to follow his instructions. After he clambered in, he showed great trust in me, as I shut the boot. He knocked on the inside of the tailgate and immediately, I opened the boot back up again.

"Yup," he announced, "That's it. He explained that there was a switch that made the light inside the boot go on so that you could see inside when you needed to use it. This switch should have made the light go out when you closed the boot and it had become broken, meaning that while you couldn't see it, the light inside the boot had been on all the time and when the car was parked and not in use, the light had been draining the battery. He fixed it and in order to test his theory, he repeated his act of climbing into the boot and my shutting him in, so that he could check that the light was now going out. He gave a couple of bangs on the inside of the boot and I released him. With a big, beaming smile, he confirmed that the light now did indeed go out as soon as the boot shut. He told me to take the car for a drive to re-charge the battery but that everything would be all right from then on.

Despite my frustration at the infringement on my ever-shortening evening time, some good then came out of the escapade as on my drive up the coast to re-charge the car's battery, the first thoughts entered my head that my time was up with the company and the job, and it was time to move on.

A year or so later, now back in Melbourne, as with Cairns, Brisbane and Sydney, I was looking forward to experiencing the city without the demands of work clouding everything. Melbourne was a vibrant place, one with a lot to offer. Named after one of Queen Victoria's prime ministers, Lord Melbourne, the city had been incorporated in 1835, becoming a city in 1847 and in 1851, the capital of the new colony of Victoria. It had developed quickly from this point onwards, growth that was stimulated by the discovery of gold and this led to a massive increase in the population. These new citizens had come from all over the world, although especially from Italy. I had heard people talk about Melbourne as being one of the most European cities of the Australian state capitals and after all my travels through many well-known European cities back in the early stages of my trip the year before, I could see what they meant. Melbourne was renowned for its coffee, café and restaurant culture as well as for many famous museums, art galleries, street art and a fine state library. Like the other states, Victoria had a serious commitment to sport and Melbourne was the venue for many top professional teams and stadia including the Melbourne Cricket Ground, situated right next to where I would be going every day for the next fortnight to watch the tennis.

My very own Bates Motel
Although the relatively new tennis centre at Flinders Park was close to the city centre, I had booked a hotel for my two-week stay (again found with the help of a *Let's Go* guide, this time for Australia), a bit further out in the suburbs in St. Kilda down by the seaside. It was only a fifteen-minute tram ride but I had been attracted to the place by the fact that it was incredibly cheap. Although I still had enough money back in my bank account at home to last me some time, I reckoned that as all I'd

be doing was sleeping in the place, so long as it was clean, safe and had a shower, at that price, what could go wrong? Well, when I arrived, I gulped a few times as this place looked like it had not been touched in ages. The room looked like something stuck in a fifties time-warp and my eyebrows were raised even more by the fact that although I had a wash basin in my room, the showers were communal, reminding me of what we had at my school back in the early seventies. In the heat of the Australian summer, showers were essential. Would I be putting my life on the line, forced to take part in communal showers? I wasn't in prison, although images of Alcatraz came back to me as I walked up and down my corridor with the facilities at the end of it. But it was so cheap, I decided to give it a go and if it turned out to be Melbourne's version of Bates Motel with Anthony Perkins lookalikes or Norman Bates-type characters wandering around, I could always find somewhere else. The added benefit of the place was that there was a superb café next door which served great coffee and food. Next to that was a terrific pub which had a great atmosphere and easy-going staff. I was all set.

A Slam reborn
On the first Monday, I arrived at Flinders Park and just like at Flushing Meadows, when I found the ticket office, I was able to buy a batch of tickets for every day of the two weeks of the tournament including the finals day weekend. I bought tickets for the day sessions, as the Australian Open was like the US Open in that it held a night session which was ticketed separately. I thought that bearing in mind my experiences in Brisbane and Sydney in the previous two weeks, and in New York before that, a day of tennis watching in the heat would be enough. I would use the evenings to relax in the pub before I locked myself in my room, barricading the door and preventing any forced entry from Melbourne's answer to Norman Bates or marauding gangs of Zombies!

The tournament I was about to watch had a long history. It began in 1905 as the Australasian Championships and was held in Melbourne, Brisbane, Sydney, Adelaide and over in New Zealand in Christchurch and Hastings in 1906 and 1912, respectively. As competitive tennis developed in the country, the state championships were also held and became established too. Some people even felt that those tournaments were more important than the continental championships.

Due to long travel times from the Northern Hemisphere by boat, in its early years, the tournament often catered mainly for local players. But even in Australia, where a long train journey was required to get from coast-to-coast, either east-to-west or north-to-south, this limited the involvement of local Australian players as well. The organisation of the pro game after 1968 influenced the entry of some of the top Australian players too, when in 1970, George McCall's troupe of professionals, including Rod Laver, Ken Rosewall, Roy Emerson, Fred Stolle in addition to Andres Gimeno and Pancho Gonzales, were prevented from taking part.

It was in the eighties that things began to change with improved air travel links and better prize money attracting some of the top players to the tournament. This trend was accelerated when in 1988, the Open was moved to Flinders Park, close to the centre of Melbourne. What had always been a grass-court event was changed to hard courts and Rebound Ace became the new surface. Sweden's Mats Wilander was the only player to have won the Open on both grass courts before the move and on hard courts as well, after the move had taken place. Also, in the year before the move from Kooyong, the date of the Open was changed from late December to the end of January. The Open became the first Slam of the new year, as it had been many years before, as opposed to the last Slam of the previous one.

There is a long and distinguished honour roll for the Open. On the men's side, I love it that across the amateur and open eras, the youngest and oldest male winner is the same player: Ken Rosewall, who was just over eighteen-years of age when he beat Mervyn Rose in 1953 and just over thirty-seven-years old, when he beat Mal Anderson in 1972. Novak Djokovic has won the most Open-era singles titles while in the amateur era, Roy Emerson won the most times with six titles. Adrian Quist won the largest number of total titles with thirteen in singles and ten in men's doubles. In the Open era, Bob and Mike Bryan have won the men's doubles six times. Harry Hopman, Hop, is the leader in mixed doubles wins, sharing that accomplishment with Australian player, Colin Long, both players winning four titles, all in the amateur era. On the women's side, it's Margaret Court who has won eleven singles titles across eras while since 1968, Serena Williams has won most titles with seven victories. Another player who stands out is Australian, Thelma Coyne Long, who won most doubles titles, most consecutive doubles titles and most mixed doubles titles too, all in the amateur era. She was also the oldest singles champion, winning in 1954 in her thirty-eighth year. Martina Hingis was the youngest singles winner at sixteen years and four months old in 1997. As far as titles across events, another player from Thelma's time, Nancy Wynne Bolton won twenty singles, doubles and mixed between 1936 and 1952. In the open era, it is Martina Navratilova who has won twelve titles in singles, doubles and mixed between 1980 and 2003.

To Flinders via Kooyong
There are two sites, which are associated strongly with the Open, certainly in more modern times. From 1972 to 1987, the Australian Open was held at Kooyong Lawn Tennis Club in Melbourne. Before that, all the way back to the start of the tournament, other than the two years it was held in New Zealand, the various top tennis venues in each state like Milton

in Brisbane and White City in Sydney, were used to hold the tournament on a rotational basis.

When the decision had been made to pick one venue to hold the tournament, Melbourne had been chosen over the other state capitals due to the perceived potential to attract the largest crowds and Kooyong was the obvious choice in the city. The Victoria Lawn Tennis Association had been created all the way back in 1892. Then, with the growth in the interest in the sport, helped by Norman Brooks, a Melburnian born in St. Kilda, winning Wimbledon in 1907 and then, after the Great War, another Wimbledon win in 1919 by another Melburnian, Gerald Patterson in 1920, land was bought with a large tennis facility in mind. Patterson won Wimbledon again in 1922 and in that year, a clubhouse was built at Kooyong, twenty courts laid out and a stadium built which initially, could hold 5,500 spectators. The look of the centre court stadium and outside courts was not dissimilar to that of the West Side Tennis Club in Queens at the time it held the US Championships.

Like Milton and White City, Kooyong had a historic association with the Davis Cup and beginning in 1946 was the venue for seven finals, the last one staging Sweden's defeat of Australia in 1986. While it was a purpose-built tennis venue, in the seventies and eighties, the stadium was used to stage some of the world's top rock and pop stars including Elton John, Led Zeppelin, Black Sabbath, the Rolling Stones, Bob Dylan and David Bowie. By the mid-eighties, the feeling was that the Australian Open had outgrown Kooyong and plans were made to move the tournament to another site capable of accommodating larger crowds.

The newly opened Flinders Park not only delivered on the hopes of higher attendances by nearly doubling them in the first year, but the quality of the site helped to kick-start renewed interest in making the trip to Melbourne from overseas. Also, right from its opening, the site and how the players were looked after, received positive reviews from the players and coaches. Spectators loved the site too. As I would experience, it was easy to locate, access and get around, once inside. This was a fine example of how to cater for a major event with large numbers of spectators while never giving the feel as if things were crowded. The place almost had the feel of a smaller tournament while the reality was that you were amongst a very large crowd indeed.

At the time of my visit in 1993, there was one main centre court. Officially, this was known as the National Tennis Centre at Flinders Park but its name was changed to Centre Court in 1996 and recognising the Rocket, the Rod Laver Arena, in 2000. The seats felt as if they were slightly wider and more comfortable than any other stadium I had visited on my trip and the views from every seat were superb. There was the added attraction of the concourse being air-conditioned when you fancied a break from watching in the heat.

There were two other show courts with major seating in addition to the other outside courts, some of which had seating. The courts were the Rebound Ace brand and I had played on this type of court in my time in White City. Although hard courts, they were ever so slightly soft on the surface due to the final coating consisting of paint mixed with tiny pieces of rubber and some players described the courts as feeling sticky when the temperature really heated up.

The combination of the time of year that the tournament was played in January, the excellent facilities for the players, their entourages and those working at the event (let alone the fans) combined to create a very good image and perception of the tournament. It would be Roger Federer who would coin the phrase, 'Happy Slam' to describe the tournament but the seeds of that catchphrase were sown back in the late eighties when Flinders Park was created to try and offer the best facilities and services to everyone associated with it.

Imagining Norman
By now, my daily routine for these tournaments was a tried and trusted one. Once I had got myself up and dressed including a shower in the communal area where, for two-week duration of my stay, I didn't see a single soul, I went next door to the trendy café where they served great coffee and all the types of bread and pastries which were just becoming trendy then but which would be seen as normal today.

Next, I walked over to a tram stop and took the next one into the city centre. Then, I'd walk the mile or so into the park to the tennis. As I had done in New York, bearing in mind that there was an evening session here at Flinders Park, I stayed as long as I could before heading back to my strange hotel. Most evenings, I'd end up in the pub next to the café and got chatting to a few of the staff and some of the regulars.

Then, I'd head back to my room and prepare to sleep with one eye open in case Norman Bates or one of his mates decided to enter my room and attack me with a huge Psycho-style knife. Throughout the two-week stay, once I'd drifted off, I slept soundly every night as if I didn't have a care in the world. The imaginary Norman clearly had other priorities than terrorising me, whether in real-life or even in my dreamworld.

Seeds, nationalities and early rounds
Although the 1992 US Open had been played five months before, the seedings for the Australian Open were pretty similar to how they had been back in New York.

On the men's side, there were just two changes with Andre Agassi and John McEnroe out, and Sergi Bruguera and Alexander Volkov back in, as fifteenth and sixteenth seeds. The top three seeding positions were the same as in New York with Jim Courier, Stefan Edberg and Pete Sampras taking those places.

On the women's side too, there were very few changes compared to the list in New York. Martina Navratilova and

Helena Sukova were both out because, like Agassi and McEnroe, they weren't present in Melbourne. Lori McNeil and Maggie Maleeva returned to the list. As in 1992, the top two slots were taken up by Monica Seles and Steffi Graf and with Martina's absence, Gabriela Sabatini moved up one position to become the third seed.

Looking at the nationality clusters, on the men's side, as would be expected, the Australians were well represented. Including those who had received wild cards, there was a group of seventeen players. The Americans had twenty-three players in the draw. After these contingents, the Swedes contributed twelve players, the Germans nine, the Spanish seven, the French six and the Italians just four. There were two British players in the draw: Jeremy Bates and Chris Bailey. Going all the way back to the players I had watched in Rome, Ronald Agenor, Jaime Yzaga, Fabrice Santoro and Amos Mansdorf were all competing.

On the women's side, there were twelve Australians, although again, the biggest contingent was from the US with twenty-nine players. There were ten Germans, eight French, and five each from the Netherlands and Italy. The Japanese group was strong again with seven players. The British had Monique Javer and Clare Wood in the main draw. Clare had done well in winning three qualifying matches.

The biggest surprise in the first round of the men's singles, was the defeat of Boris Becker by Anders Jarryd, a match played on the main show court and one I watched. It just wasn't Boris's day and everything went well for Anders. The only other seed departing was Ivan Lendl, beaten by Christian Bergstrom. Bates and Bailey were both beaten and Pete Sampras and Charlie Steeb were drawn against each other again. As in Paris on the Bullring, Sampras won in straight sets. Fabrice got through the first round but lost to Michael Stich in the second. Both Ronald Agenor and Jaime Yzaga lost in the first round but Amos Mansdorf won his first two matches.

In the women's singles, the only seed to depart early was Jana Novotna. Debbie Graham, who I had watched in Brisbane, beat fellow American, Pam Shriver, and Jennifer Capriati beat Linda Harvey Wild easily, 6-0, 6-1. Of the players from *Courting Fame*, Camille Benjamin had qualified but lost in the first round and Stephanie Rehe won her first-round match but was beaten in the second. Of the Japanese contingent, Kimiko Date was thumped by Mary Pierce 6-1, 6-1. Monique Javer also lost, beaten by the Danone champion, Conchita Martinez.

I watched Clare Wood's first-round match on an outside court. It was blisteringly hot, over one hundred degrees and I had difficulty following the play. What it must have been like to play in that heat I could only imagine by thinking back to my time in Bahrain where I'd played a few times in really high temperatures. But back in Manama, most of the tennis was played in the late afternoon and early evening, thereby sparing the players from the sort of exposure that Clare and her fellow pros were experiencing here in Melbourne in the daytime. I found a narrow area of shade where if I stood bolt upright with my back and head pressed against the fence of a nearby outside court, I could get out of the sun and just about see the court. One man walked by and looked like he wanted to give me his loose change, possibly thinking that I was a street performer doing one of those stationary poses. Unfortunately, Clare lost in the furnace to Barbara Rittner in straight sets.

Wally and mates

All pro tennis players practise. The need to put in time on the court often begins right from when a player falls in love with the sport. A simple love of tennis usually motivates young players to spend as much time as they can whether taking group or individual lessons, practising or playing matches. When they are developing and the realisation arrives at some point that not only are they capable, but that combined with their love of playing, they also want to develop their abilities as far as they can go, then a player's commitment to spend time on the courts intensifies and the hours increase. Once they start to compete, if results go well, players and coaches want to take things to the next level. Often, this will cement the commitment to practise. But if things have gone badly, practice time becomes even more important as mistakes or inconsistent aspects of a player's game are focused on and improved, hopefully to the required standard. Either way results-wise, the process requires time on the practice court.

People outside the tour might regard the players lifestyles as glamorous as they fly in and out of a range of locations. For the players though, things have to be all business. Arriving at a tournament location is not an opportunity to go sight-seeing, as I did as a traveller, but the time to check out the practice courts and book one. Practising becomes as routine as brushing your teeth.

Here in Melbourne, I spotted Wally Masur practising a lot. Wally was a good example of a solid pro with good habits. His career lasted thirteen years and in singles, he reached a career-high of No. 15 with three titles and in doubles, he reached No. 8, winning fifteen. In Grand Slams, he had reached a singles semi-final in New York (after winning a previous round match from 0-5 down in the fifth set) and the fourth round at Wimbledon on three occasions. Here in Melbourne, he had been knocked out in the first round but other than that, he carried on with his normal routines, including practising. He was in the doubles with Mark Kratzmann too. Wally would be on the court usually, with a couple of mates from the Australian team and they would always have their shirts off, a bit like Jim Courier in Rome. They worked hard too.

Everyone seemed to know the routines and focused on the task at hand. The practice would start slowly, after a few stretches, with groundstrokes but after a while, transition play would come into things ending with lots of volley drills close to the net. Often, the session would be completed with a few singles points played out with the players rotating every point with team-mates at their end of the court if there were more than three players involved, so that there would be one-against-one situations. In a way, this routine was like a shortened version of a Hopman-style session at Saddlebrook. At the end, while towelling down and drinking as much as possible, more stretching would take place.

Despite the somewhat obvious need for it, over the years, practice had always been a very personal thing with the likes of Jimmy Connors never staying on court for more than forty-five minutes, while someone like Guillermo Vilas seemed to stay on the court for hours, as I had seen back in Rome. John McEnroe was known for using the argument that playing lots of doubles was better for him than hours spent on a practice court. His appearance practicing on the back courts in Paris was probably an example of the exception proving the rule.

On the way to the second week
Two seeds were beaten at the third-round stage: Carlos Costa and Alexander Volkov. Elsewhere in the draw, Todd Witsken, Todd Woodbridge, and David Wheaton all lost. Christian Bergstrom continued his good run.

On the women's side, sixteenth seed, Zina Garrison was beaten. But other than that departure, all the remaining seeds went through to the second week. Steffi Graf progressed after Claudia Porwick had to retire injured. Nicole Provis, who had beaten Lori McNeil in the second round, continued her good form in beating Isabelle Demongeot.

Gigi a Natasha compare notes
As usual, as the days went by, the number of doubles matches gradually increased on the courts as the singles events worked their way towards a conclusion with fewer and fewer players remaining as each round went by.

In the men's doubles, the top four seeds were the same pairings as in New York five months before with the Woodies at number one and Jim Grabb and Richey Reneberg at number two. Although there were some changes in other pairings and seeding numbers, the pool of players was very familiar. Wayne Ferreira and Piet Norval, and Kent Kinnear and Sven Salumaa were returning to the list and new additions included Patrick McEnroe and Jonathan Stark, Danie Visser and Laurie Warder, Jacco Eltingh and Paul Harhuis, and Hendrik Davids and Libor Pimek.

In the first two rounds, the biggest surprise was the defeat of the Woodies. Also, the seeded teams of Kelly Jones and Rick Leach, Tom Nijssen and Cyril Suk, Sergio Casal and Emilio Sanchez, David Adams and Andrei Olhovskiy, and Hendrik Davids and Libor Pimek were all beaten. Brad Pierce and Byron Talbot had a good win but were knocked out in the second round. In the third round, with seeds now facing each other, Kent Kinnear and Sven Salumaa, Jacco Eltingh and Paul Harhuis, Steve Devries and David Macpherson, Wayne Ferreira and Piet Norval, and Patrick McEnroe and Jonathan Stark, all departed.

One aspect of the way players do things now was not nearly so evident back in the early nineties. Now, doubles teams fist-bump and talk to each other after every point. In 1993, this was rare. Gigi Fernandez and Natasha Zvereva did do it, but because they were one of the only pairs who did, the behaviour seemed both interesting and even, a bit odd, purely because it was not the norm. They would congregate for their team meeting in the middle of the court after every point and start chatting, often looking away from each other, as if they were trying to spot and incoming plane or a face in the crowd. Once they had agreed on their plan, they would smile, give a little skip and go to their court positions for the next point. Nearly thirty years on, all doubles players do this routine in between points.

Gigi and Natasha were a highly successful team. By the end of their partnership, they had won thirty-one doubles titles together including fourteen Grand Slams (Gigi won three more and Natasha four more with other partners) and two year-end Championships. Here, they were the top seeds and they had won the previous three Slams. Could they win one more? The others seeded teams were the usual suspects and not that different from the Slams in 1992. The biggest omission was Martina Navratilova but Pam Shriver was still in the event, seeded tenth with Elizabeth Smylie. A few other pairings changed but it was pretty much the usual pool of players which made up the list.

In the first two rounds, the casualties included seeds Nicole Provis and Elna Reinach, Rachel McQuillan and Claudia Porwick, Sandy Collins and Mary Pierce, and Sabine Appelmans and Isabelle Demongiot. Clare Wood was playing with Australian, Tracey Morton again and they won their first match but lost in the second round. In the third round, when the seeds started to come through to face each other, Ros Fairbank-Nideffer and Julie Richardson, Florencia Labat and Andrea Strnadova, Katerina Maleeva and Natalie Tauziat, and Katrina Adams and Manon Bollegraf, all lost.

As with the other doubles events, the seedings for the mixed doubles included many pairs I had watched in the previous Slams. Of the eight seeds, two were new when compared with the list in New York with Danie Visser and Stephanie Rehe, and Steve Devries and Patty Fendick coming in. The event was a thirty-two pair draw and as was usually the case with this size of draw and number of seeds, there were many strong, unseeded pairs. Seeds began to fall including Steve Devries and Patty Fendick, Cyril Suk and Larissa Savchenko-Neiland, and Patrick Galbraith and Elna Reinach who all lost and in the second round, and these teams were joined by Danie Visser and Stephanie Rehe, and Mark

Woodforde and Pam Shriver. Byron Talbot and Isabelle Demongeot had lost in the first round.

Stay fresh - Don't watch the others
Into the second week and one match away from a quarter-final and even bigger prize money, the fourth-round matches began in each draw involving the last sixteen.

On the men's side, three more seeded players were beaten. Sergi Bruguera had come through to play Jim Courier and lost in three sets. Malivai Washington also met another seed, Pete Sampras and also lost in three sets. Wayne Ferreira became another victim of Christian Bergstrom's good run. The two qualifiers who had got this far, Chris Garner and Kelly Jones, were both beaten. Stefan Edberg and Michael Stich came through unharmed.

On the women's side, probably the biggest shock was Julie Halard's defeat of Conchita Martinez. Seles and Graf came through easily and Mary Pierce blitzed Gigi Fernandez 6-0, 6-0. In the other matches bar one, seeds played seeds and Mary Joe Fernandez, Arantxa Sanchez Vicario, and Jennifer Capriati all won. There was one more match in the round and for a change, I stayed on for the evening session to watch it. I found myself still in the grounds when the evening programme began. No-one seemed to be bothered about checking tickets, so I thought I'd stay and watch for a while longer. As the final fourth-round women's singles match came on court between Gabriela Sabatini and Australian, Nicole Provis, looking to my left, I realised that one of the other Australian women players, Nicole Pratt, was sitting right next to me. I had watched Nicole play up in Brisbane.

Nicole was another good tennis player from Queensland. She was born in Mackay which is north of Brisbane on the coast and known as the sugar capital of Australia. She had turned pro in 1989 at the age of sixteen and would go on to have a long and successful career, only retiring in 2008 at the age of thirty-five. At the time of our chance meeting in the stands at Flinders, her singles ranking was in the top two hundred, but it would rise to a career high of No. 35. She won a WTA title and a further five in ITF events. In Grand Slams, she reached the fourth round in the 2003 Australian Open. In doubles, where her highest ranking was No. 18, she won nine WTA and another nine ITF titles. In Grand Slams, she reached a US Open semi-final and was a quarter-finalist three times in Melbourne and once in Paris.

At an appropriate time during a changeover, I introduced myself. Although there were plenty of questions that I would have loved to ask a full-time touring pro, especially one trapped next to me for the duration of a match, I tried to control my inquisitiveness. I told myself not to interview her or become too invasive. She was obviously there for a reason, probably to watch Nicole Provis and I wanted to respect that. If she seemed happy to chat, then that was what we would do. I began by asking her how things were going and talked generally about the tournament and playing in the heat. Considering my intent to become a coach, I was generally interested in all the possible ways that players could improve, so I asked Nicole how often she watched other players. She told me that she rarely did this because the coaches had told the players not to spend time watching. The coaches' belief was that it was better if the players went off away from the site so that they would remain as fresh as possible. I could understand this perspective but also felt that players could learn by watching the methods used by their fellow pros, especially those who had made it to the very top levels. Then again, what did I know about spending every waking minute of your day training in a sport at pro level and what would maximise performance and result? Nothing. I bowed to more informed judgement.

However, all these years on, it is perhaps interesting that in the digital age, many young people use sites like YouTube to watch and learn about their interests, hobbies and passions and this includes aspiring young tennis players watching either clips of their favourite players in matches or coaching clips on how to hit certain strokes or what to do tactically in various match situations.

It was an enjoyable and interesting chat with Nicole as Sabatini beat Provis in two sets, 7-5, 6-3, to advance to the quarter-finals. I promised to keep an eye out for Nicole's results in the months ahead and wished her well.

Working hard for the new car
As the second week went by, the doubles events drew towards their conclusion, reaching the quarter-final stage.

In the men's event, Mark Kratzmann and Wally Masur, John Fitzgerald and Anders Jarryd, and John-Laffnie de Jager and Marcus Ondruska had reached the semi-finals. The last quarter-final was being played on the smaller show court which in years to come, would be converted into the Margaret Court Arena. The match was between Jim Grabb and Richie Reneberg, seeded two, and South African, Danie Visser and Australian, Laurie Warder, seeded tenth. It was another beautiful day with the heat just about bearable.

The match went to a fifth set. All four players held their serves and kept holding them. With no tiebreakers used in the fifth set, at 6-6, the games continued but then there was an announcement that the match would be taken inside onto the centre court. The night session would be postponed until this match was completed.

The games went on and on. The odd break point or match point came and went and to me, it was a marvellous demonstration of professionalism, as each serving player committed to each point, followed the serve into the net and played the first volley confidently to set up a winning shot. I didn't want it to end, if only because without the help of a tiebreaker, one of the four would have to lose their serve.

Unfortunately, it was Jim Grabb, who at 20-20, lost his, and Visser and Warder served out the match.

It had been a tremendous battle but I returned back to St. Kilda intrigued by the fact that a Holden car, probably similar to the one I had driven when I was at American Express, was being offered to the winning pair in addition to the prize money if they won the title. Maybe, I had misunderstood the prize and each player would get a car but as I sat on the tram taking me back to Bates Motel, I imagined the conversation between the winning pair.

"Let's share it through the year. You have it January to June and I'll have it July to December."

Surely, I must have got it wrong, hadn't I?

In the women's quarter-finals, other than Gigi Fernandez and Natasha Zvereva's win over Lori McNeil and Rennae Stubbs, the other three matches all saw lower ranked seeds beat higher ranked ones: Patty Fendick and Andrea Strnadova, Jill Hetherington and Kathy Rinaldi, and Pam Shriver and Elizabeth Smylie came through.

Catching up with legends
Back at Tennis Fantasies in Texas, both Fred Stolle and Cliff Drysdale had me to look them up and we would go for dinner. It didn't take long to find both Fiery and Cliffey as I wandered around the grounds. I agreed to meet Cliffey one evening in the Melbourne Hilton where many of the players were staying. I also fixed a date on a separate evening with Fred who told me to meet him in the foyer of the Hilton.

When I met Cliff, we decided to stay in the coffee shop. We sat and chatted as we ate. I was aware that other players, coaches and well-known names from the tennis world were on tables around us but I was taken by surprise when I was at the salad bar. I nearly bumped into the woman next to me but she apologised before I could. It was then that I realised that this was Margaret Court, the winner of sixty-four Grand Slam titles in singles, doubles and mixed, spanning the end of the amateur era and the start of open tennis. I enjoyed my dinner with Cliffey and we talked about my trip and about his work commentating as well as some other business interests of his.

A few days later, I returned to the Hilton and met Fred Stolle and his wife, Pat. We stayed in the foyer and had a drink before Fred told me that the plan was to walk a short distance down the road to a favourite Italian restaurant of theirs where some other people would be joining us. The other people were no ordinary folk. Firstly, there was none other than former British Davis Cup player, manager of the Barrett Boys squad, BBC commentator and author, John Barrett. Accompanying John was his wife, Angela Mortimer, the winner of three singles Grand Slams at the French in 1955, the Australian in 1958 and Wimbledon in 1961 as well as a women's doubles at Wimbledon in 1955. Angela had also reached a mixed doubles final at Melbourne in 1958 and won the Wightman Cup in 1960. There for dinner too, was Allan Stone, the former Australian pro who had played on the tour through the sixties and seventies. Allan had been a top fifty singles player with three tour titles and had reached the top twenty in doubles with fifteen titles to his name, with a variety of partners, including John Newcombe and Cliff Drysdale. Allan had won two Grand Slam doubles titles and reached the final at Wimbledon. He had also reached two mixed doubles finals. For the first time on the trip, my elation at the company surrounding me left me a bit over-excited and combining with an empty stomach, the drink I had consumed back at the Hilton and now a couple of glasses of wine really went to my head. Thankfully, bread and other food came along quite quickly and I recovered my composure. The company was really stimulating with everyone absolutely charming. Fred and Pat were the perfect hosts.

After dinner and farewells to my esteemed tennis dinner colleagues, I ended up in a bar not too far away where there was a players' party going on. We were coming to the end of the tournament and those attending could now afford, perhaps for one night at least, to let their hair down and have a drink or two. But old habits die hard. The fact was that most of the players were remarkably well behaved; no-one seemed to be the slightest bit inebriated and if anything, the atmosphere reminded me a bit of my school disco where everyone did a lot of standing on the sides waiting for something to happen. But I had a few drinks on top of the ones I'd had earlier with Fred, Pat, John, Angela and Allan and slept well on my return to Bates Motel.

The Hilton was the venue for a meeting with another tennis legend, but this time, from the world of journalism. Although I was reasonably set on my idea to become a tennis coach when my trip was over, I wanted to keep my options open in case another good avenue of opportunity arose. I'd spotted the well-known and respected tennis journalist, writer and broadcaster, Richard Evans, introduced myself to him, explained what I was doing and he had offered to meet me for a brief chat, again in the foyer of the Hilton. Richard had led a fascinating life and had been involved with journalism for some time. He had covered football, rugby union and cricket in his early days as a reporter and then, after shifting his focus onto tennis, had moved on to writing many books including a number in collaboration with top players including, Marty Riessen and Vijay Armitraj as well as biographies about Ilie Nastase and John McEnroe. He had also written a history of how the sport went open and a history of the Davis Cup, amongst many others. In the early seventies, Richard had run the press office for the early incarnation of the ATP when it was starting out as the players' union. Later in his career, as well as time spent in the US where his brief was a broader one, including politics, he had become a radio and television broadcaster and this work had involved working for the BBC on Wimbledon. He was a mine of information about the game and I was really appreciative of his time. It was a pleasure to be actually sitting and talking to the author of books that I had read and had helped to fuel my love of tennis as that sport had taken over in my sporting priorities through the eighties.

Seeds come through

As the saying goes, we were now at the business end of the tournament. Quarter-final participants had come through four tough matches competing with the heat alone, never mind their opponents. But to win the Slam, they had to win three more matches.

In the men's matches, there were all straight sets affairs with Jim Courier, Michael Stich, Pete Sampras and Stefan Edberg who ended the excellent run of his fellow Swede, Christian Bergstrom, advancing to the semi-finals.

In the women's matches, Monica Seles beat Julie Halard, the only unseeded quarter-finalist. Gabriela Sabatini, Arantxa Sanchez Vicario and Steffi Graf also advanced.

These results meant that all the semi-finalists in both events would be seeded players.

The lure of the Yarra

It was finals weekend and I was delighted to discover that a few of my friends from White City would be flying down for the women's final on the Saturday. We watched the match between Monica Seles and Steffi Graf, from high up in the stand at the side of the court and it was fascinating watching the trajectories of the players' shots as well as when and how they both tried to open up angles to create space for winners. Some used to say that Steffi couldn't hit a topspin backhand but she hit a few in this match, although she did hit her slice more often. Here we had two great players and two great champions and the match reflected this. It went to three sets after Graf won the first. Monica kept pounding those strong groundstrokes off both sides and pulled away in the final set to win, 4-6, 6-3, 6-2.

In the men's final, where my seat was on the corner of the court giving me a different but no less interesting view, the battle was between Stefan Edberg's athletic, all-court game where he tried to get to the net wherever possible, against Courier's explosive groundstrokes and passing shots. The match went to four sets but Jim prevailed as he had done the year before. Both victories were achieved in four sets with Edberg winning the second set in 1992 and the third here in 1993. The temperature was boiling hot and yet somehow, both men played as if the conditions were ideal. Despite warnings not to do so from some of the tournament officials, Jim Courier insisted on diving into the Yarra River which bordered the back of the complex near the centre court. The story goes that Jim picked up a slight infection in doing so but nothing too serious, thankfully.

The men's doubles was won by tenth seeds Danie Visser and Laurie Warder who built on their quarter-final defeat of Grabb and Reneberg. They went on to beat John-Laffnie de Jager and Marco Ondruska in the semi-final and then fourth seeds, John Fitzgerald and Anders Jarryd in the final, in straight sets.

The women's doubles was won by Gigi Fernandez and Natasha Zvereva, realising for them a non-calendar year Grand Slam in this event. Their tennis overall, including their chats either side of each point, was just too good. They beat tenth seeds, Pam Shriver and Elizabeth Smylie, in straight sets.

In the mixed, another top-seeded pair, Todd Woodbridge and Arantxa Sanchez Vicario won in another straight sets encounter, beating the unseeded Canadian pairing of Glenn Michibata and Jill Hetherington.

In the junior boys' event, there was some joy for Great Britain as James Bailey won the title.

Back home via Vietnam

It was time to head home. In my original plan, I had intended to fly from Australia up into Asia and visit Nepal, possibly Tibet, and possibly even Burma. But when the time came, I had had enough travelling. However, one opportunity presented itself which I could not miss.

My good friend in Sydney, Ted Burn, had a friend called Andrew who was trying to start up a business importing terracotta pots from Vietnam into Australia. Around the time of my imminent departure, Andrew had to make a trip to Vietnam to check on the manufacturing process of his merchandise. He would fly to Saigon, or Ho Chi Minh City, as it was now called, and spend a week there visiting his suppliers.

When I was a child, the Vietnam War was the first war that appeared on our televisions. The news coverage had a profound effect on me. When I was at university, I studied the war as part of two courses, one on American history and the other on American politics. I decided to accompany Andrew and he had no objections at all.

As far as organising that part of the trip was concerned, I was able to use my main ticket for the leg from Sydney to Hong Kong as that was what I had planned to do anyway. All I had to do in addition was to book an extra return ticket to Ho Chi Minh City from Hong Kong.

After saying goodbye to Mark and Susie in Sydney, Andrew and I flew to Hong Kong and as we lined up to check in, I spotted Grand Slam women's doubles champion, Natasha Zvereva doing the same for another flight, a few lines away. She had loads of luggage, including rackets as might be expected for a tennis pro. Through this short trip, Andrew and I got on really well and when we reached Vietnam, at times, I went with him to check on his business affairs while at others, I went off to see some of the tourist sites including the American Embassy where, in 1975, the dramatic final stages of US involvement in the war were played out as the helicopters picked up the last people to leave off the roof as the Communist forces were advancing down the streets of Saigon's outer suburbs. The embassy looked like a decaying shell, although parts of it were being used as offices. It would be demolished in 1998. I visited the zoo where the buildings and the poor animals inside were all in need of some tender loving care. We also made the short trip out of the city to where a small segment of the underground tunnels which the Viet Cong had used to fight the war from had been retained and maintained. Even managing to get down and struggle through a few yards of what was on offer for tourists like us, I could imagine how terrifying it would have been for what were called the Tunnel Rats in the US Army, whose job it was to get into the tunnels and fight the VC, many of whom, it should not be forgotten, lived down there for the duration of their involvement in the fighting to defend their country.

With our week over, it was back to Hong Kong where Andrew and I parted. He flew south back to his home in Sydney while I boarded another Cathay Pacific flight headed for London via a short stopover in the airport of my home of four years, Bahrain. A few hours later, I was unlocking my front door in Wimbledon.

My trip was over.

Epilogue

Looking Back; Moving Forward

Taking stock
It was sixteen months since I had sat on the plane going across Australia when the idea of the Grand Slam trip formed in my mind. On the one hand, I'd missed the women's event in Rome and from my original list of things to do, I hadn't made it to Montana to the site of the battle of the Little Bighorn nor some of the locations in the story of the film, *How the West was Won*. On the other, I had achieved just about everything else I had planned, including my main mission. I'd gone in pursuit of a spectator's version of the Grand Slam and completed it. However, more than ticking boxes, the trip had done far more for me from a personal development perspective. The experiences filled me with a fresh view of the world, created many new friends and instilled in me the confidence to now follow my instincts. Before beginning to work out how to become a tennis coach, I thought about the pro tours, the Grand Slams and what I had seen:

- **Relentless commitment:** I had witnessed a tremendous work ethic from the players. But that work, on the match court, the practice court and the business of travelling around the circuit, was really the tip of the iceberg when you consider the years of effort most of them had put into their playing careers since they began as a junior. Tennis may have started out as a fun thing to do at a weekly tennis lesson but the group of players that I had been watching were now professionals, playing for a living. At that level, no one was messing around. There was no time or place for coasting. The professional tours were too competitive. If you were trying to climb up the rankings, nothing less than one hundred per cent commitment would be needed just to give you an outside chance of making it. If you were up at the top level, complete commitment, including a willingness to improve further was needed just to keep you where you were, let alone enhance your status.

- **Dealing with defeat:** Winning a tournament would bring personal satisfaction, prestige, prize money and ranking points. But tournament wins, at all levels of the tour's hierarchy, when compared to the number of players out there competing, were few and far between for many, if not most players. Some completed their whole careers winning literally hundreds of matches without actually one single tournament win. Also, in any given event, there was only one winner. Far more players lost than won at any given tournament. In each draw, at some point, every player other than the tournament champion would lose. Players had to get used to the reality of defeat while striving for victory. When that defeat arrived, players had to deal with it, brush themselves down and carry on. Of course, they had experienced losing through their junior years but back then, although disappointed, their parents would have been there to help and carry the financial load as well as part of the emotional load too. But as grown adults on the tour, the buck stopped with the player. Losing and all of its implications had to be dealt with and in doing so, the reality developed resilience. If it didn't, a player would not survive.

- **Coping with injury:** Someone once said, "You're one bad injury away from the end of your career."

Although such a statement might sound harsh, it was nontheless, quite true. But if players did not receive career threatening injuries, this did not mean that they were injury free. As Jacco Eltingh and Andre Agassi to name but two, could attest, the sport made heavy demands on players' bodies, often at the younger ages, when those bodies were not yet fully developed. At any given time, most players, had some sort of niggle and the need to keep playing created pressures that might mean a decision to play on with an injury might not be the right one with rest and rehabilitation the proper thing to do. Being completely fit was actually, a rare state to be in. But being fit to play was something else. Players had to learn to compete while injured and hope that by playing, they were not going to aggravate the injury further in the short term, cause debilitating pain, a career threatening situation, or problems after their careers were over.

- **Different tennis worlds:** At most tournaments, as a fan, the experience was generally, all marvellous. You watched some top-class tennis, had something to eat and drink, and enjoyed the atmosphere. You went home surrounded by a sort of glow, like I did after my first visit to Wimbledon in 1968 and pretty much, every night after a day at the tennis on my trip. As a fan, the sport was entertainment. However, the players lived in a world with a different set of experiences and perceptions. They were workers, doing their job, earning a living. Pam Shriver's book, *Passing Shots: Pam Shriver on Tour* is a very good and particularly candid look at life on the road as a pro tennis player demonstrating how, at times, it was as if there was a parallel universe in existence contrasting the experiences of the fans outside the sport with the those of all of those inside, dependent upon it to earn their living. Also, within the insider's world, there were a number of broader issues facing the sport and how it was run. In the bibliography below, I have included some of the best books which have been written on the tour in the open era by the likes of Eliot Berry, Peter Bodo, Paul Fein, John Feinstein and Michael Mewshaw for those who want to become better informed on the issues back in the nineties in the pro game, some of which still exist and are the subject of debate nearly thirty years later.

- **Grand Slam status:** After the best part of a year spent attending the four Grand Slam tournaments, I would agree with the claim that the top tournaments are the best of the best. I was able to attend other tournaments which had places further down the hierarchy of both tours' structures and these tournaments all had their valuable roles to play as part of the tour calendar. However, the Grand Slams were the events where players' performances over their careers often determined how they were evaluated once they retired. Player legacies were often, if not usually, made by the success or failures achieved at the Grand Slams. Thirty years on, in just about every way, the Grand Slam tournaments continue to be at the top of the sport and if anything, have become even greater in their significance although the digital age and social media have helped increase fan awareness and knowledge of the tournaments below the Slams, especially events on the next tier down, like the Italian Open in Rome.

Grand Slam venues today

There have been quite a few ground developments at the venues of the Grand Slams since 1992. Here's a quick summary of the changes at the sites in the order that I visited them.

At Roland Garros, the site began a series of major developments to take it into the twenty-first century. In 1994, a second large show court was built, Court Suzanne-Lenglen, seating ten thousand fans. The Bullring was knocked down with another new show court built, Court Simonne-Mathieu which seats five thousand fans. There are now floodlights on the show courts and some of the outside courts too as well as a retractable roof on Chatrier and one planned for Suzanne-Lenglen in 2024.

At Wimbledon, things have been moved forward considerably with plans for still further major developments soon, especially on land on the other side of Church Road. A huge, new Court No. 1 was built in the nineties and both the main show courts now have retractable roofs. The Millennium Centre has extensive media and player facilities. Back in front of Centre Court, the old Court No. 2 has been moved and upgraded on the site of the old Court No. 13 and what was Court No. 2, has now become Court No. 3. The seating has been increased on a number of the other outside courts and some of the walkways widened, facilitating bigger attendances.

At Flushing Meadows, major changes have also been made. Looking at photographs of the site today, I barely recognise it. When you go through the main gates, you are now entering the Billie Jean King National Tennis Centre, a re-naming that took place in 2006. The main show court is the immense Arthur Ashe stadium which seats over twenty-two thousand fans and has a retractable roof. The Louis Armstrong Stadium has been rebuilt. The Grandstand court has been moved. All of the outside courts have been remodelled with increased seating. There are numerous new food and drink locations and the courts have changed brand from green Deco Turf to blue Laykold.

In Melbourne, since 1993, Flinders Park has been renamed as Melbourne Park. There are now three significant arenas, each with a retractable roof and all used for a variety of other sports and concerts in addition to tennis. The second main venue is named after John Cain, the late Victorian premier who played a key role in the development of Flinders Park which kept the Open in Melbourne in the eighties. The third covered arena is named after Margaret Court. The number of outside courts has increased with clusters either side of the main show court, the Rod Laver Arena. The Rebound Ace courts have been changed to Plexicushion which while still a hard court, is constructed slightly differently. These courts are blue, like the courts in Flushing Meadows, as opposed to their predecessors, the green Rebound Ace ones.

In addition to venue developments, perhaps one of the most striking changes has been in levels of prize money, fuelled by ever-increasing coverage in the digital age. At Wimbledon alone, the prize money has increased way above inflation over the three decades since, in some areas, over five times the levels of 1992. There has also been a redistribution of those funds to benefit the players losing in the qualifying events and the early rounds. These changes have made it even more important for lower ranked players to try and ensure that they are ranked high enough to secure automatic main draw places at the Slams.

Also, as far as playing formats are concerned, a major development in 2022 saw the introduction of a tiebreak (first-to-ten points with a margin of two) to be played at 6-6 in the final, deciding sets of all for Grand Slams (third for the women and fifth for the men). This new rule will make the way matches are concluded at all four Slams consistent for the first time in the open era since the tiebreak was introduced in the US Open back in 1970.

Where are they now?
It's coming up to thirty years since my trip. What happened to some of the key people mentioned above?

As far as family is concerned, sadly, dad had died way back in 1974; he was only sixty-two. Twelve years his junior, mum lived a long and very productive life until 2017 when she died at the age of ninety-three. Right up to that point, she continued to watch Wimbledon on television every year and absolutely loved Roger Federer. One year at the David Lloyd Club in Raynes Park, close to Wimbledon, I was able to introduce her to Cliff Drysdale and Ken Rosewall who were there at the time. She was almost overcome with excitement. Although more people attend Wimbledon now than in 1992, I am delighted that those attending fans have included my brother, Ben and his wife, Mary. While both had been long-standing fans, like many, their interest had been from afar via the television, although Ben did manage to see one of the late seventies finals between Bjorn Borg and Jimmy Connors when a school friend obtained tickets. Mary had been too but like many people, their visits had been on a more occasional than regular basis. They now started to use the queue and began going more regularly. My niece and nephew, Victoria and Thomas have also been and they loved it. Tom has taken up tennis and has played at various clubs since. My sister, Zoe, while more an occasional tennis fan, like mum, one who has always enjoyed watching Roger Federer, has fond memories from our childhood tennis days, and she always lends a supportive and interested ear to my tennis observations. When she has questions about tennis issues which break into the news, I try to act like a brotherly tennis oracle to answer them.

Over in the US, Simon Rogers is now living in Southern California and enjoying his life. My New York friend, Peter, still lives in the city and we are still in touch as I am with Leslie, who I met on the train to Ann Arbor. Sadly, my former work colleague, Mary Lively, died in 2017. John Kosta continued to run his family business, Huron Tours which continues to be successful. However, I was very sad to hear of his death late in 2021.

Steve McCormack is fit and well and combining his journalistic skills with his teaching experience together in his work, as well as trying to stay as active as possible with all his sporting activities, including tennis.

The friendship between my school friend, Kyri and I, is as strong as ever. After a highly successful career in IT, reaching senior management positions in a number of respected large organisations, he has now retired to enjoy time with Rosie and his three sons who are all doing well. But you can't keep a good man down and Kyri has recently become the chairman of Radlett Tennis and Squash Club in Hertfordshire. One of my biggest regrets is that due to a combination of circumstances, we have not been able to hit balls on a tennis court for far too long.

Kyri and I kept in touch with Michael and Rita Bunn, visiting them and meeting their children Jayne and Richard who now have families of their own, all these years later. Michael and Rita are still going strong and enjoying life, especially spending time with their lovely grandchildren who keep them busy.

Mark and Susie Dalton still live in Australia with their daughters, Charlotte and Molly but in Melbourne now, as does Nicky Markham, who has a family of her own after marrying Brian (she is now Nicky Saville).

Larry Gagnon is back in the US and still plays. We are in regular contact.

I am also in touch with Richard Johns who I put on those runs with playing cricket for Finchley back in 1979. I am in contact too, with other former cricket teammates at Finchley and Arkley. From my football days, I am in touch with my friends from Oakwood, Liverpool University and Winchmore

Hill. Also, I keep a close eye on the fortunes of Burgess Hill Town through social media.

The tennis pros mentioned above, especially the ones I watched, followed through the tournaments and in some cases met, have continued an involvement with tennis in one way or another. Away from tennis, Byron Talbot has done well for himself in financial services based in the US. He is a Vice President for Merrill Lynch. It has been a lovely experience to contact and speak about the book not only with Byron but also Brad Pearce, Amos Mansdorf, Debbie Graham, Elizabeth Smylie, Michelle Jaggard-Lai and Zina Garrison using the channels of social media.

Clare Wood continued to play until 1997. She reached career highs of No. 77 in singles and No. 59 in doubles. In 1993, needing a place to stay during Wimbledon, she used my spare room. I hardly saw Clare at all but watched on television when she played Steffi Graf on centre court in the second round. Clare gave me one of the Wimbledon towels for that year and it stayed with me for many years folded neatly in the airing cupboard, far too special to actually use. After retiring from competitive tennis, Clare has crafted a very successful career in officiating for the WTA. She was also involved with the tennis at the 2004 Athens Olympics and at London 2012.

While writing the book, I have also re-connected with another Southdown connection, Tony Clark, who is still heavily involved with tennis and doing well.

Sadly, Bud Collins died in 2016 but after a long life in which he made a huge contribution to tennis journalism and especially, tennis broadcasting. His book, which is in the bibliography below, *My Life with the Pros*, is one where you will be educated, informed and entertained should you read it. I smiled many times re-reading it while working on this book.

Richard Evans now lives in the US, still writes and is very active on social media sharing his views on politics and tennis. He has written an excellent memoir about his life, *The Roving Eye;* it's listed in the bibliography.

Over at Ilkley, Simon Ickringill is still coaching and the club has been developed in many ways to offer even better facilities to its members. The Ilkley Tournament is still going strong too.

Danny Sapsford is still heavily involved with the sport and runs a charity, *Bright Ideas for Tennis,* which focusses primarily on disability-grass roots level, offering opportunities to play the wonderful sport of tennis to those who ordinarily wouldn't get the chance.

Courts full of kids playing
What happened next for me? While travelling to the tournament in Manchester prior to Wimbledon during my trip, I had decided that I wanted to become a tennis coach. An opportunity presented itself almost straight away on my return home. I went to visit Steve Matthews who was, by then, the tennis director at the David Lloyd Club in Raynes Park, a short drive from my flat.

I really went to meet Steve for general advice about searching for jobs in tennis coaching, but an hour after our chat began, he was offering me a job running the junior activity at the club. He knew me from a few visits I'd made to the club since returning to the UK from Sydney back at the end of 1991 and he was aware that as a club team player, I could play the game to a reasonable level, although I was nowhere near Steve's ex-pro standard. At this stage, I didn't have a tennis coaching credential and Steve helped me, organising for me to attend the next course coming up a couple of weeks' later, run by the UK arm of the United States Professional Tennis Registry (USPTR), a tennis teaching organisation respected in the industry worldwide. However, I think it was my management experience which was especially attractive to him. As Steve talked, I looked out over the bank of courts stretching away from us and imagined them full of kids playing tennis, a vision I would realise sooner than I might have thought.

A USPTR credential obtained with the help and guidance of Clive Carrigan and Adrian Rattenbury - I would later obtain my LTA credentials and become a licensed coach when that system began, a few years later - I started the job of coaching the juniors at Raynes Park. This entailed running all the group activities in the term-time, after-school and weekend group lessons, and day camps in the holidays. I coached juniors from the ages of four to sixteen years of age and that age spread always kept the job interesting as I kept tabs on the age and stage development of my pupils, trying to match the activity we offered to those needs.

So began fourteen wonderful years. I treated the junior programme as if it was my own business. I took responsibility for everything from the programme structure, the coaching curriculum, methods and lesson plans, the equipment, the staffing, the promotion, the administration and the financial side of things too. These factors, all essential, really created a platform for the important work of connecting with the junior players both collectively, but especially on an individual level. I made it my business to know every junior's name and at the height of the programme's popularity, there were over seven hundred young players coming through the lessons each week, over two hundred alone every Saturday. After participation numbers had grown, the challenge then became to keep them there as I worked on improving the quality of what we were doing with the juniors in teaching them how to play the game. This included building up other areas of activity like in-club tournaments and junior club teams.

I had an excellent working relationship with Steve Matthews who became the general manager of the club, and went into senior management, developing a successful career at David Lloyd Leisure before setting up his own company,

Virtus Leisure Management Ltd, which runs tennis centres and clubs. This work includes involvement with the development of exciting British junior players seeking to take their game to the highest level. At Raynes Park, I worked closely with the club's tennis directors and general managers as they came and went. The programme's growth led me to some training involvement with all the other David Lloyd junior club programmes, passing on best practices. The programme I had developed was significantly larger than the activities in the other clubs. I worked hard to build relationships with the local LTA county team and head office contacts in British Tennis too. I was asked to sit on a number of LTA project teams looking at issues in junior tennis. I went on BBC5 Live and talked about junior development, did a brief appearance on a local TV cable channel and was featured in an article in a leisure industry magazine. In 2000, I received some industry recognition when I was selected for the USPTR UK Golden Eagle award for contribution to junior tennis.

Going full circle back to the first tennis holiday in 1980, I met Roger Taylor again on a number of occasions and ended up working alongside Nick Walden, who had coached me and Kyri on our visits to Portugal.

From my American Express days, Ray Pierce has continued his heavy involvement in the sport. In 1999, he was made a member of the All-England Club. But also, chiming with the theme of this book, while I focused on a spectator's Grand Slam, Ray has been achieving a playing version. As well as competing on the hallowed turf at SW19 (in one doubles match beating Roger Taylor), through his participation with AELTC touring teams, Ray has played on the courts at Kooyong and White City and representing the International Club of Great Britain, he played at Roland Garros. He also played at Melbourne Park and Flushing Meadows, both public facilities. Although the West Side Tennis Club in Forest Hills is still on his list, he did at least go there as a spectator.

Advantage International is now called Octagon and all these years later, Clifford Bloxham has risen to a very senior position. Clifford, like Ray, has become a member of the All-England Club.

Steve Contardi, Tennis Fantasies and all the legends are doing well as we shall see below.

The tennis circus comes to town
I continued to go to Wimbledon every year, usually on the two Mondays, my day off, and while there, would always try and track down as many of the legends from Tennis Fantasies as possible.

John Newcombe always stayed in a large house on the edge of the Aorangi Park practice courts and often, I would make sure to pay Newk and all the occupants of his house a visit on the Sunday evening before the tournament began to share a drink with them before they all went out for dinner.

One year, I didn't have a ground pass and was standing in the Church Road queue right where I waited on the first day back in 1992. Fred Stolle walked down the opposite side of the road. Immediately, he gave me a ticket and after thanking him profusely, there was no more standing in line for me that day. Fred was always marvellous like that. Another time down at Eastbourne, I spotted him, as he was about to be engulfed by autograph hunters after playing a legends match. I had stood well back, but on seeing me, he marched through all of them holding his hand out to shake mine. Also, one year in Texas, after I had won a long singles match, clawing my way back to win a final set 7-5 after being 1-5 down, as Fred prepared to play a late afternoon fantasy set, he was picking up a ball and he looked through the fence to where I was standing, relaxing with a bottle of beer in my hands. "You deserve that," he said giving me his huge smile. These were all magic moments with Fiery.

The Raynes Park club was open for use by the players during Wimbledon.

One year, I received a call in the office asking me if I could arrange for Brooke Shields, who was married to Andre Agassi at the time, to visit the club and use the gym, which I did, meeting and greeting her and her bodyguard.

Chris Evert once used the club to film a short feature for American TV and I helped set that up and looked after her and her crew when they arrived.

Ken Rosewall arrived at the club for a small corporate event with fellow Australian player, Scott Draper. Ken's wife, Wilma, was with him. Muscles was as humble as ever, refusing to accept a pound coin from me so he could use a locker in the changing room and when I was called away for a telephone call while sitting with Ken and Wilma, I returned to find that Wilma had placed a saucer over my cup so that my black coffee wouldn't get cold. It was a lovely touch from a lovely person, sadly no longer with us.

Albeit briefly, it was good to chat at different times with the likes of Venus and Serena Williams, Bob and Mike Bryan, Alexandra Stephenson, Tracey Austin, Patty Fendick, Barbara Potter, Brian Teacher, JoAnne Russell, Jim Courier and on one occasion, Nick Bollettieri who needed a practice court for Tommy Haas and Iva Majoli, who had just won the French Open. Running a junior group at the time, I gave him one of mine. Nick signed an autograph for every junior in my group on a photocopied tennis tip that I had taken from that month's *Tennis* magazine and was waiting to be handed out to the players. Coincidentally, the tip was from none other than Nick himself.

For a few years, at Wimbledon time, ex-player and respected coach, Nick Saviano used the club as a base for the US Boys U18 team as they prepared for junior Wimbledon. Nick reciprocated the gesture by helping me on a few coaching sessions with our top juniors. They talked about him for years afterwards, especially his amazing serve demonstrations and his slick USTA stars and stripes-adorned track suit.

Tracy Delatte used the club with some top American U18 girls and he took time out to talk to my junior group which was on the next court. He introduced each one of his players giving their name and where they were from. My young juniors sat wide-eyed.

Around the time that he became famous, I worked with Andy Murray on two promotional mornings in 2005 and 2006. Andy had to coach some juniors who had won a competition. He was brilliant with the kids.

I was also fortunate to meet and get to know Rob Koenig and his family. Rob has since become one of the sport's top commentators. Also, it was a pleasure to help John-Laffnie de Jager who brought a group of juniors he helped back in South Africa. They played at the club one morning before going to watch the tennis at Wimbledon.

Other opportunities could arise too. Through one of my contacts, I was asked at short notice if I could make up the numbers in a pro-am event that was always held around Wimbledon time at the Hurlingham Club in Putney. To my joy, I was partnered with the wonderful Vijay Armitraj who was as charming in person as he came across in public. Even more exciting was to play a set against Ilie Nastase and his partner. On one occasion, this great player really showed his class. Vijay had pushed Ilie really wide, outside his tramlines. I anticipated that his only option to return the ball into court would be to hit it back across court and moved a split-second before Ilie made contact. A second later, Vijay was grinning at me because we had lost the point. The Romanian champion had somehow, curled the ball around the net-post and still managed to get the ball into court behind both me and my esteemed partner.

Not only at Wimbledon time but during the rest of the year too, the club was often used by the top British players and on one occasion, it was fascinating watching Tim Henman practice hitting the same backhand passing shot for ages, as he tried to perfect what he was trying to achieve. Also, on another occasion, Boris Becker, who often used the club as a base during Wimbledon, played a special exhibition match with Greg Rusedski to raise money for the Omagh Bombing Disaster Fund. To watch these two top-class players compete close-up, even in an exhibition setting was a serious treat.

Back to Tennis Fantasies
Through the nineties and into the early years of the new millennium, Tennis Fantasies became an unmissable event for me. I would return each year, usually rooming with a friend made at the camp, Jack Valenti. I continued to start and end my US travels in New York and this included being in the city and visiting ground zero with Peter, just six weeks after 9/11, a sobering experience. After Tennis Fantasies, I would travel for another week or so, always picking another location from the old West and visiting historic sites as well as watching a few more college football games. In 1994, finally, I arrived in Montana at the site of the battle of the Little Bighorn and I'm glad I made the effort, although the knowledge I now have about what happened that fateful day makes me look differently at the film *Custer of the West*. In real life, things happened just a bit differently than on the silver screen but that is often the way. Mum also flew out three times and we visited some of the sites in the film, *How the West was Won* and also, in Texas, the places that influenced Larry McMurtry to write his Pulitzer Prize-winning novel, *Lonesome Dove*, its prequels and sequel. A treasured keepsake is a water-colour painting she made for me of the Palo-Duro Canyon.

At Tennis Fantasies, as the attending number of campers increased each year, so did the number of legends. It was a privilege to meet the likes of Ken Rosewall, Manolo Santana, Bob McKinlay, Charlie Pasarell, Tony Roche, Ross Case, Mark

Woodforde, Rick Leach, Brian Gottfried, Ray Moore, Sherwood Stewart, Murphy Jenson and Guillermo Vilas. Dick Stockton became a much-loved regular and as with all the legends, I particularly loved watching Dick play.

I always returned to New York for my flight home to the UK but would make a brief stop in Cincinnati to stay with Steve Contardi and his family and hang out at The Club at Harper's Point. Tennis Fantasies is still going as strongly as ever. In 2021, the camp ran for its thirty-fourth year. I am in regular contact with Steve and Debbie, and Katie and Mario as their own families grow.

Although Russ Adams sadly, is no longer with us, another good friend from all those visits, Ken Munson, took up photography in retirement with much success, and has performed the photographer role producing many terrific photographs of the action, the players and the legends as the event continues to be run, year after year.

Larry Starr still looks after everyone's injuries.

Of the other campers, very sadly, my roommate for many years, Jack Valenti, died in 2021.

I am still great friends with Howard Rogg and we visited each other frequently, playing tennis matches at Howard's local tennis centre early every Monday morning, battling it out together, often in preparation for the next visit to Tennis Fantasies.

Joel Drucker, who I met in 1993 at the camp, has become a highly respected writer about the sport and as well as working for numerous top magazines and broadcasters, including the Tennis Channel since its inception in 2003, has become an International Tennis Hall of Fame Historian-At-Large. On a couple of occasions, when working as a freelance at Wimbledon, Joel stayed in my spare room in Worple Road. On one of those visits, Joel invited me along to a party held by one of the big management agencies after play on the middle Saturday. I had a slightly embarrassing moment when I found myself seated next to rising star player, Jelena Jankovic. I had been coaching juniors all day and had not kept up with the matches. Thinking that I was being polite, I asked Jelena if she had played that day in the third round. Almost insulted, she put down her corn on the cob, just selected from the Bar-B-Q and announced to me, "I beat Venus Williams!" Suitably chastised, I said, "Well done," a bit like Hugh Bonneville's character, Bernie, in the film *Notting Hill*, when he tries to show empathy to Anna, played by Julia Roberts, about what he believes are the scandalous low wages of the acting profession, and then chokes on his drink as he discovers from her that in her last film, she earned fifteen million dollars.

Writer Bob Mitchell and I met at the camp in 1996 and our friendship continues to this day. On a stay in the UK, Mitch convinced me that it was worth my while to keep writing after I had begun some work on a book about junior tennis coaching. Bob has now had eleven of his books published and has just self-published another amazing art book with his wife, Susan, an artist herself, about Covid-19. I visited Mitch in Santa Barbara one year after the camp and still remember a fantastic breakfast we had in a marvellous café on the beach. Wherever possible, since our friendship began, I have tried to help Mitch by reading his manuscripts as he has now done with mine.

On a couple of occasions in future visits to Tennis Fantasies, I would bump into Al Eden at New York's La Guardia Airport when we were both flying down to San Antonio. Al's company was always superb. There would be no mention of the boat race. In fact, we would talk more about what I was getting up to in my coaching and on this topic, I couldn't have been chatting to a better qualified person as far as understanding the age and stage needs of the juniors.

There are many other campers and legends who I am also still in touch with mainly through social media and my friendships with all of these people have changed my life for the better immeasurably. Sadly, as well as Jack Valenti, some other friends have left us, including one of my doubles partners, Ron Davis; a fine opponent, Harry Demetriou; and the Doc, Mike Lawhon. They are all much missed.

Important words from Marty

Back at home, finding time to play while working as a coach was not always easy. Through the nineties, I worked six days a week and usually, didn't feel like playing on my one day off. But in 2001, my schedule changed and this enabled me to have Sunday off as well. That's when I started to play regularly with Howard Rogg over in Maidenhead every Monday. As my coaching experience developed, that knowledge actually helped me improve as a tennis player and wherever appropriate, I would feed aspects of my own improvement back into the curriculum of the programme that I ran.

On the court back in Texas, my successes had been mixed. Over the years, in singles, I played mainly at number four in my team. I used to play well but lost more matches than I won. In doubles, my record was better, especially if I really gelled with my partner and on two occasions, won all three team tournament matches. But I was constantly on the lookout for ways to improve my game and especially, my performances in singles. I had not experienced tennis in the junior years, the place where many players obtain their grounding, just as I had done in football and cricket. Therefore, in some ways, I was making up for lost time, effectively using the matches at the camp as my experience base to help build my game.

In 2002, I asked one of the other coaches at Raynes Park, Paul Frick, if we could take my game up another notch. We completed three really useful sessions on the basics and what might seem like small adjustments actually made a huge difference. For example, a subtle change in where I was throwing the ball up and how I should visualise the swing path of the racket when I served meant that not only did both first and second serves improve quite a bit but an added benefit was that I rarely hit a double fault from that point onwards. Also, I had been training hard in the gym, helped by fitness coach, Ian Waters. Finally, I went back to basics on the tactical side of the game and established clearly in my mind a framework on which shot I should try and execute in any given situation, something which completely changed my decision-making process as I played.

Armed with this improved array of skills, in 2002, after two days at Saddlebrook on the way to warm me up, at Tennis Fantasies that year, at the eleventh time of asking, I won all my singles matches. At the age of forty-six, twenty-two years after that first tennis holiday in Vale de Lobo, I played the best tennis of my life in ways that I would never have imagined possible at the start.

However, that end result nearly didn't happen. After winning my first two matches, it looked as if I might have to put up with a record of two wins and one defeat. My opponent, Harry Demetriou, a decent player who lived in various places around Europe and was a member at the Queen's Club, seemed to be feeding off my pace. Also, my stomach felt as if I had a slightly pulled abdomen. After losing the first set 4-6, my team captain that year, Marty Riessen, came up to me. "I want you to give him junk," he said and then, he walked away.

I felt like as if I had nothing to lose and amazingly, as I followed Marty's instruction, the slower I hit the ball, the more mistakes Harry made. I won the second set by 6-0 and resisting the temptation to start hitting hard again, I kept my no-pace strategy going. I won the super tiebreaker 10-1, converting match point with another softly hit, sliced backhand that slid past Harry's outstretched racket. To his credit, Harry gave me a strong handshake, even though I knew how frustrated he was. He returned to his room to lick his wounds. From many matches where I had been in Harry's position, I could empathise.

A few minutes later, Marty Riessen came over from the match on the next court, smiled, shook my hand and said words which meant more than I could ever describe, "Well done, Crippsey. You became a tennis player, this week." Of course, I had not suddenly risen out of the ranks of amateur campers. I was still very much a tennis civilian. But Marty's words, reinforced by the opinion of other legends at the camp that year (so Steve Contardi shared with me) were certainly a very satisfying bit of recognition about how I could now play the game. The words were a form of respect from a group of people whose opinion I valued hugely. It was a satisfying moment indeed.

Another change; another stage
Unfortunately, just after that year's camp, my body started giving out on me. I tried to keep improving my game and had sessions with fellow coach, Marc Ellis, after Paul Frick had moved on. But a serious left-knee problem led to an operation in 2004 and after eighteen months rehabilitation, the very first time I played properly in January 2006, I tore the cartilage in my right knee. Things continued to deteriorate in both knees. In 2007, I had to stop my job coaching. I was in too much pain and discomfort and I could not see any other viable way forward. Sadly, this also meant an end to playing and my trips to Texas, other than one visit in 2012 for the twenty-fifth anniversary.

Since then, while renting out my Wimbledon flat, I have moved back to living in the North-West, only this time, in Oldham on the outskirts of Greater Manchester, not too far from Liverpool, my university city. My knees continued to deteriorate. However, I remain positive because with one hip and one knee now replaced, and the other one pending, I will be able to play tennis again, something I haven't done since

2004, although I tried without any success or satisfaction in my 2012 return to Tennis Fantasies where pain and discomfort were ever-present. It's not an exaggeration to say that on completing all of these replacement operations, I will get my life back and for that, thanks are very much in order to my excellent orthopaedic surgeon, Daniel Cohen.

As far as work, with coaching no longer an option, I spent a decade working with sports memorabilia, buying and selling it and writing a blog about it but when I began to contemplate retirement, in some sad but serendipitous circumstances, as I helped my friend Phil Stevens in his final days, by liaising with his publisher about Phil's life memoir, I have ended up editing books for that company, i2i Publishing, one of the largest book publishers in the North-West region. The job has been perfect for me at this stage of my life, marrying together my life-long love of books and reading with my marketing experience with American Express and my recent blogging experience too. As noted above, when I came up with a firm plan for this book, my boss at i2i Publishing, proprietor and publisher, Lionel Ross, was insistent that if I could complete it, he would publish it. Thanks to Lionel, that has now been done and if you have got this far, you may well have read through the book. If you have, I hope you have enjoyed it.

The year off I have described and the trip that I was able to take happened because circumstances came together and created the opportunity. It would be quite possible for someone to repeat it, or their version of it, although until the Covid-19 pandemic really comes under control, world-wide travel will present far more difficulties than I ever faced. Also, although I did some research beforehand, on reflection, I didn't do all that much, especially with regard to the tennis tournaments I intended to visit. My trip took place in pre-internet days and now, it is possible to do an enormous amount of preparation on your desktop, laptop or phone. In some ways, perhaps, my attitude to it all; that I would deal with whatever situations I found in each place, helped me to get out there and experience everything. Today, if I couldn't confirm details about tickets, hotels, trains and planes, I might never leave the front door. However, at the tennis tournaments, especially the Slams and the Italian Open, I was always happy to watch matches on the outside courts; a confirmed seat on the show courts, was never essential. If I watched the big matches – and I watched quite a few - I saw that as a bonus. Luck and good fortune presented themselves in the form of Clare Wood in Paris and at Wimbledon, the queue was always a route into the grounds. Then, when I arrived in New York and Melbourne, I was fortunate to be able to buy tickets for the whole tournament at both Flushing Meadows and Flinders Park, including the finals.

Maybe, it's part of the fun to do such a trip your way? I would never prescribe to anyone how to do things when travelling and especially in making decisions about their job and career, which formed a part of my overall experience and its end result. After all, there are so many options available and decisions must be made based on a combination of personal aims, available resources and opportunities. Both head and heart will have important roles too. I hope the book will inspire people in some positive ways but even if circumstances don't allow the time and freedom that I was able to experience as I followed my instincts on my pursuit of the Slam, then hopefully, readers might still enjoy the thought of taking their ideal trip, whatever it is and wherever it might take them.

Photo Gallery:
Sport, the Slam and Me

Wimbledon 1968: Roger Taylor - British No. 1. The focus of my mum's love of tennis. Two years later, she would send a telegram to him wishing him luck against Rod Laver.

North London, 1964. Proud owner of a new ball. Interested in tennis for two weeks of the year only.

Liverpool University, 1975. 1st XI, before a cup match against Manchester University. I am back row, far left. Next year, I would be captain of the club and the 1st XI.

Finchley, 1978. 2nd XI Middlesex League Champions. I am back row, third left. Richard Johns, my partner in that big stand in the National Knock-Out, is in the front row, second right.

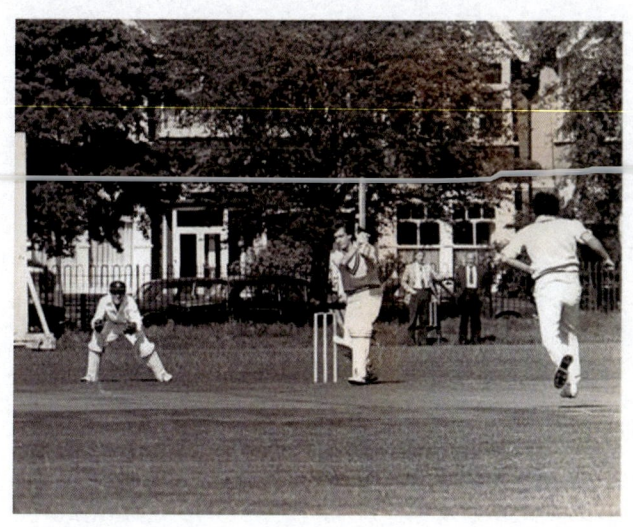

Finchley, 1979. Batting at Arden Field. No helmets in those days as I try to hit some runs.

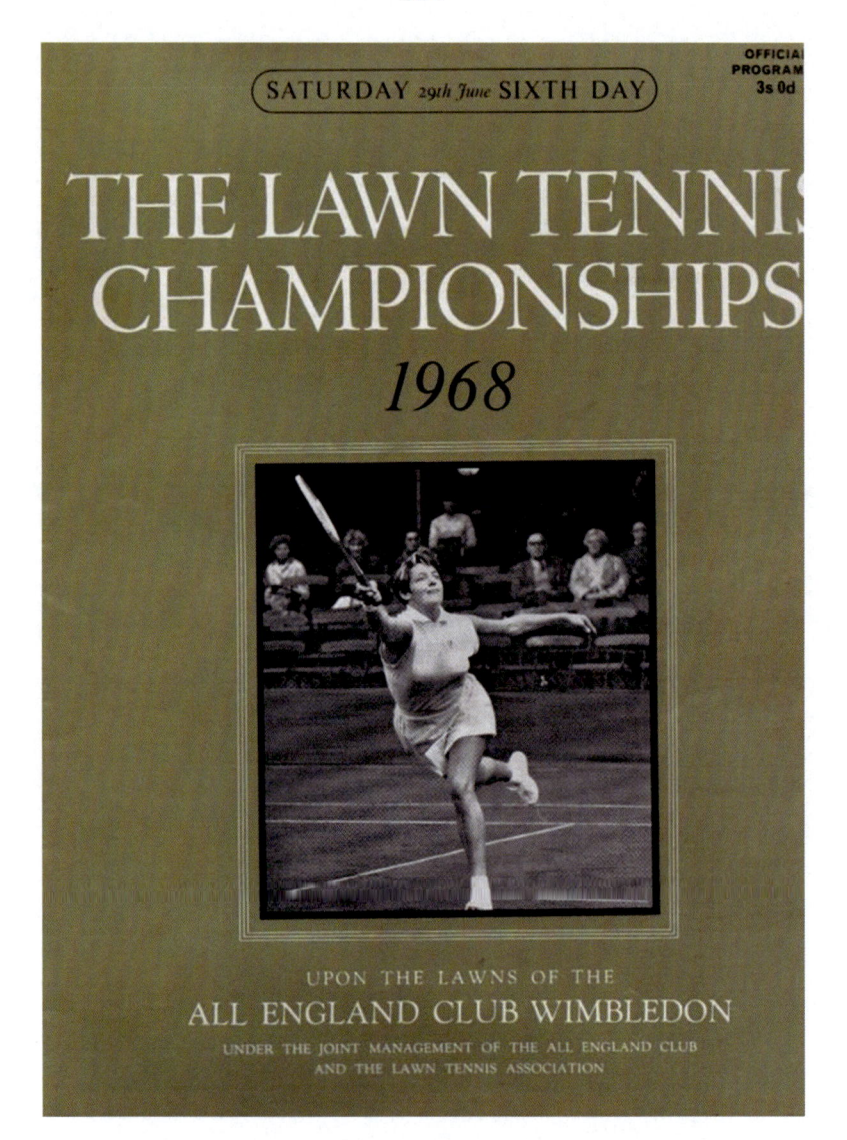

Wimbledon, 1968. Where the sport really came alive for me. The programme for my first day at The Championships.

Italian Open, 1992. Fantastico Foro Italico. The atmospheric outside courts where I spent a lot of time in my week there.

Italian Open, 1992, Brad Pearce and Byron Talbot warm-up under floodlights after the burning sun had gone in.

French Open 1992. The crowd shows its approval as Nicklas Kulti and Michael Chang shake hands on the Bullring.

French Open 1992. Pete Sampras hits a forehand as he beats Charlie Steeb, again, on the Bullring court.

French Open, 1992. John McEnroe practises on an outside court as I chat with Monique.

French Open, 1992. Clare Wood strikes an aggressive backhand. Charlie Beckman looks on, ready to intercept.

SATURDAY
20th JUNE

CENTRE COURT PROGRAMME
COMMENCING 11.00am

SINGLES SEMI-FINAL

L. HARVEY-WILD V R. FAIRBANK-NIDEFFER
(TO FINISH)

SINGLES FINAL
NOT BEFORE 1.30pm

WINNER OF SEMI-FINAL V L. MCNEIL

FOLLOWED BY THE DOUBLES FINAL

COURT 1
COMMENCING 11.00am

DOUBLES SEMI-FINAL

J. NOVOTNA v A. SANCHEZ-VICARIO
L. SAVCHENKO-NEILAND   H. SUKOVA
(TO FINISH)

SECOND SEMI-FINAL NOT BEFORE 11.30am

M. J. FERNANDEZ v G. FERNANDEZ
Z. GARRISON   N. ZVEREVA

COURT 2
COMMENCING 11.00am

FINAL OF THE PLATE

K. ADAMS V C. RUBIN

TO BE ADVISED - NOT BEFORE 1.00pm

FINAL OF THE UNDER 21

K. HABSUDOVA V M. MALEEVA

PILKINGTON GLASS

INTERNATIONAL
LADIES TENNIS
CHAMPIONSHIPS

DEVONSHIRE PARK
EASTBOURNE

15 - 20 JUNE 1992

30p

ORDER OF PLAY &
RESULTS UPDATE

Eastbourne 1992. The order of play for the final day at Devonshire Park showing the impact of rain delays.

Wimbledon, 1992. The programme for the first day when I stood in the queue from early in the morning.

Ilkley 1992. The programme for the British Tour event where I spent a great week between Wimbledon and the US Open.

US Open, 1992. Watching Jim Grabb and Richey Reneberg win the men's doubles at Flushing Meadows.

Sydney, 1993. The week before the Australian Open. At White City in Sydney, wearing my Harry Hopman T-shirt.

Los Angeles, 1992. A fun mock-up from a shop in Hollywood. I was never an incredible tennis machine but it was nice to dream, in my Tennis Fantasies' tracksuit top.

Oldham, 2017. Commemorating the 30th Anniversary of Tennis Fantasies. I am surrounded by Roy Emerson, Dick Stockton, Charlie Pasarell, Brian Gottfried and Ross Case.

Cheltenham, 2014. Me with (right to left) my sister, Zoe, brother, Ben and mum, Sheila at her 90th birthday party. This book is testimony to mum and dad's love and support.

Bibliography
Recommended Tennis Books

Allaby D. (1981). *Wimbledon of the North: 100 Years at the Northern.* Manchester, UK: E.J. Morten.

Armitraj V. & Evans R. (1990). *Vijay! From Madras to Hollywood via Wimbledon.* London, UK: Libri Mundi.

Ashe A. & Amdur N. (1982) *Off the Court.* London, UK: Eyre Methuen Limited.

Ashe A. & Deford. F. (1975). *Arthur Ashe: Portrait in Motion.* Boston, MA: Houghton Mifflin Company.

Ashe A. & Rampersad A. (1993). *Days of Grace.* New York, NY: Ballantine Books.

Bellamy R. (1986). *Game, Set and Deadline.* London, UK: The Kingswood Press.

Berry E. (1992). *Tough Draw: The Path to Tennis Glory.* New York, NY: Henry Holt and Company, Inc.

Bodo P. (1995). *The Courts of Babylon: Tails of Greed in the Harsh New World of Professional Tennis.* New York, NY: Scribner.

Bollettieri N. & Schaap D. (1996). *My Aces, My Faults.* New York, NY: Avon Books.

Bowers C. (2002). *The Book of Tennis.* London, UK: Jeff Wayne Music Publishing Limited.

Burwash P. & Tullius J. (1981). *Peter Burwash's Tennis for Life.* New York, NY: Times Books.

Cash P. & Flatman B. (2002). *Uncovered: The Autobiography of Pat Cash.* Exeter, UK: Greenwater Publishing.

Collins B. (1990). *My Life With The Pros*. New York, NY: E.P. Dutton.

Collins B. & Hollander Z. (1994). *Bud Collins' Modern Encyclopaedia of Tennis*. Detroit, MI: Visible Ink Press.

Drucker J. (2004). *Jimmy Connors Saved My Life*. Toronto, ON: Sportclassic Books.

Evans R. (2017). *The Roving Eye: A Reporter's Love Affair with Paris, Politics & Sport*. London, UK: Clink Street.

Fein P. (2002). *Tennis Confidential: Today's Greatest Players, Matches, and Controversies*. Washington, DC: Brassey's, Inc.

Feinstein J. (1991). *Hard Courts: Real Life on the Professional Tennis Tours*. New York, NY: Villard Books.

Garrison Z. & Smith D. (2001). *Zina: My Life in Women's Tennis*. Berkeley, CA: Frog Limited.

Gillmeister H. (1998). *Tennis: A Cultural History*. London, UK: Leicester University Press.

Jones D. & Hodgson L. (2001). *The Life and Times of Lew Hoad, a Tennis Legend*. Peterborough, Cambridgeshire: DSM.

King B.J. & Deford F. (1982). *The Autobiography*. London, UK: Granada Publishing Limited.

Laver R. & Collins B. (1971). *The Education of a Tennis Player*. London, UK: Pelham Books.

Marble A. & Leatherman D. (1991). *Courting Danger*. New York, NY: St. Martin's Press.

Maskell D. & Barrett J. (1988). *From Where I Sit*. London, UK: Willow Books, William Collins Sons Company Limited.

Mewshaw M. (1993). *Ladies of the Court: Grace and Disgrace on the Women's Tennis Tour*. London, UK: Warner Books.

Mewshaw M. (1993). *Short Circuit: Six Months on the Men's Professional Tennis Tour*. New York, NY: Atheneum.

Mitchell B. (1999). *How My Mother Accidentally ... Tossed Out My Entire Baseball Card Collection and Other Sports Stories*. Berkeley, CA: North Atlantic Books.

Nastase I. & Beckerman D. (2004). *Mr Nastase: The Autobiography*. London, UK: CollinsWillow.

Newcombe J. (2002). *Newk: Life On and Off the Court*. Sydney, Australia: MacMillan Books.

Newcombe J. (2005). *No-one's Indestructible: Surviving Strokes and Avoiding Them*. Sydney, Australia: Pan MacMillan Books.

Perry F. (1984). *Fred Perry: An Autobiography*. London, UK: Arrow Books.

Riessen M. & Evans R. (1974). *Match Point*. London, UK: Pelham Books.

Scanlon B., Long C. & Long S. (2004). *Bad News for McEnroe*. New York, NY: St. Martin's Press.

Shriver P. & Adams S. & Deford F. (1987). *Passing Shots: Pam Shriver On Tour*. New York, NY: McGraw-Hill Book Company.

Stabiner K. (1986). *Courting Fame: The Hazardous Road to Women's Tennis Stardom.* London, UK: The Kingswood Press.

Tilden W.T. (2001). *The Art of Lawn Tennis. Reprint of 1922 edition.* Amsterdam, Netherlands: Fredonia Books.

Various. (1993). *Coaching Children in Sport: Principles and Practices.* Edited by Martin Lee. London, UK: E. & FN Spon.

Various. (1985). *For the Love of Tennis. Edited by Ronald Atkin on behalf of the Lawn Tennis Writer's Association.* London, UK: Stanley Paul and Company Limited.

Various. (1999). *Roller Skates and Rackets: The Story of Devonshire Park and Tennis in Eastbourne.* Seaford, East Sussex: S.S. Publications.

Various. (1999). *The Right Set.* Edited by Caryl Phillips. London, UK: Faber and Faber.

Index

A League of Their Own 227
Abdul, Paula 48
Adams, Chuck 181
Adams, David 184, 282
Adams, Katrina .. 95, 184, 250, 251, 283
Adams, Russ 203, 215, 311
Advantage International .. *See* Octagon
AELTC .... *See* Chapter 6
Agassi, Andre ... 49, 55, 71, 85, 87, 88, 123, 129, 132, 139, 141, 181, 186, 235, 253, 277, 297, 308
Agenor, Ronald 56, 60, 72, 124, 278
Ahl, Lucie 157
Airplane 238
Alderton, Terry 177
All-England Club .... *See* Chapter 6
Alvarez, Lili 52
American Express .... *See* Prologue
Anderson, Mal 197, 243
Andrews, Brian 22
Annacone, Paul 105
Aorangi Park 114, 116, 307
Apell, Jan 261
Appelmans, Sabine 72, 125, 174, 175, 181, 246, 249, 250, 252, 263, 283
Arendt, Nicole 251
Arias, Jimmy 45

Armitraj, Vijay 289, 309
Arsenal F.C. 17
Ashe, Arthur 44, 179, 180, 188, 299
Atkin, Ronald 340
Austin, Bunny 148
Austin, Tracey 99, 169, 308
Australasian Championships .... *See* Australian Open
Australian Hardcourt Championships 244
Australian Open *See* Chapter 13
Bahrain .... *See* Prologue
Bailey, Chris 172, 278
Bailey, James 291
Bank of England Sports Ground 18, 109
Baron's Court ...... *See* Queen's Club
Barrett, John 288
Basuki, Yayuk 95, 136
Bates, Jeremy 72, 93, 104, 105, 109, 124, 125, 129, 131, 135, 136, 278
Battrick, Gerald 147
Bauer, Mike 112
Beadle's About 229
Becker, Becker 55, 75, 93, 117, 123, 125, 129, 131, 139, 181, 185, 278, 310
Beckman, Charles 82, 88
Beecher, Colin 112
Benevista Tennis Centre 38

Benjamin, Camille 174, 279
Bentley, Rita 148
Bergstrom, Christian 261, 262, 278, 281, 284, 290
Berry, Eliot 298
Bevan, Rohun 37
Billingham, Caroline 112, 157
Birmingham City F.C. 20
Black Sabbath 275
Blackpool F.C. 17
Bloxham, Clifford 43, 307
BMW European Indoor 66
Bobkova, Radka 72
Bodo, Peter 298
Bollegraf, Manon . 85, 99, 136, 140, 184, 250, 251, 283
Bollettieri, Nick . 141, 195, 308
Bolton Abbey 160
Bonsignori, Federica 247, 248
Borg, Bjorn 43, 53, 301
Borneo, Belinda ... 95, 101, 136
Borotra, Jean 68
Bowery, Lesley 200
Bowes, Beverley 83
Bowie, David 275
Boyle, Mike 154
Bridges, Albert 90
Brioukhovets, Elena ... 72, 100
British Hard-Court Championships 67, 117
British Tour ...... *See* Chapter 6
Broad, Neil 108, 135, 136
Brooks, Norman 275
Brown, Amanda 97

Brown, Nick 135
Brown, Peter 22
Bruges 50, 189
Brugnon, Jacques 68
Bruguera, Sergi 55, 60, 71, 261, 262, 277, 284
Brussels 50
Bryan, Bob and Mike 274, 308
Bryan, Steve 122
Bucholtz, Butch 28
Budge, Donald 10
Bueno, Maria 27
Bungert, Wilhelm 15, 27
Bunn, Michael and Rita 34, 94, 302
Burgess Hill Town F.C. 37, 97
Burwash, Peter 44, 45, 158, 180
Butch Cassidy and the Sundance Kid 225
Byrne, Jenny 95
Cain, John 300
Callens, Els 133
Camporese, Omar 58, 59, 104, 135, 173, 264, 268
Canè, Paolo 58
Capriati, Jennifer ... 72, 76, 85, 130, 132, 140, 181, 225, 262, 263, 264, 268, 279, 284
Caratti, Christiano 58
Carillo, Mary 87
Carpenter, Harry 26
Carpenter, Vanessa 203
Carrigan, Clive 305

Casal, Sergio 44, 184, 282
Case, Ross...................310, 333
Cash, Pat.......................82, 124
Castle, Andrew .108, 172, 182
Cavendish family................97
Champion, Thierry......59, 129
Championships of New
 South Wales....................258
Chandos L.T.C......................27
Chang, Michael ..1, 60, 67, 78,
 104, 181, 185, 186, 326
Chatrier, Philippe 69
Chelsea F.C. 18
Cherkasov, Andrei79, 85, 104
Chesnakov, Andrei...........104
Cierro, Massimo..................71
Clark, Tony 37
Cliff Richard Challenge 44
Clifton, John.......................147
Coca Cola 33
Cochet, Henry 67, 69
Coetzer, Amanda...............175
Collins, Bud .77, 179, 303, 338
Collins, Rene......................247
Collins, Sandy............184, 283
Connell, Grant.............85, 135
Connolly, Maureen.....10, 259
Connors, Jimmy 43, 75, 76,
 93, 124, 169, 170, 171, 172,
 179, 281, 301
Contardi, Steve.175, 193, 195,
 201, 205, 206, 209, 213, 215,
 231, 311, 315
Coolhurst L.T.C..................148

Copenhagen 50
Cornell, Rob.........................44
Costa del Sol..................38, 40
Costa, Carlos .. 61, 63, 71, 123,
 151, 172, 261, 262, 281
Costi, Kyri... 33, 35, 36, 38, 39,
 40, 41, 42, 93, 189, 219, 221,
 302, 306
Courier, Jim.... 49, 55, 59, 60,
 63, 71, 84, 85, 88, 123, 129,
 172, 181, 185, 186, 277, 280,
 284, 290, 291, 308
Court, Margaret..... 10, 24, 27,
 217, 274, 286, 287, 300
Courting Fame 42, 125, 174,
 279
Cox, Mark 147
Coyne Long, Thelma........ 274
Cripps, Ben.. 25, 164, 301, 333
Cripps, Harry 37
Cripps, Sheila............. 192, *See*
 Chapter 1
Cripps, Terry... *See* Chapter 1
Cripps, Zoe... 25, 50, 164, 301,
 333
Crocodile Dundee 204
Croft, Annabel 44
Cunningham, Carrie 181
Curren, Kevin...... 75, 77, 124,
 158
Curtis, Peter....................... 147
Dahlman, Nanne 248
Dalton, Mark and Susie.. 241,
 302

Damm, Martin.................... 125
Danzig, Alison 8
Date, Kimiko 79, 99, 100, 125, 137, 138, 174, 175, 279
Davenport, Lindsay . 187, 250
David, Herman 116
Davidson, Owen .. 29, 41, 147, 200, 206
Davies, Mike...................... 147
Davis Cup ... 27, 40, 42, 44, 45, 56, 68, 85, 99, 147, 148, 197, 198, 199, 200, 201, 219, 220, 245, 246, 260, 267, 275, 288, 289
Davis, Ron.......................... 313
Davis, Scott................ 129, 135
de Jager, John-Laffnie 286, 291, 309
Deane, Angus 204
Dechaume-Balleret, Alexia 184, 248, 255
Delatte, Tracy 309
Demetriou, Harry 313, 314
Demongeot, Isabelle.... 81, 83, 136, 184, 281, 284
Dempsey, Charles............. 222
Denton, Steve 75, 158
Devonshire Park 98, 149
Devonshire Park F.C. 97
Devonshire Park L.T.C. 97
Devries, Steve.... 135, 282, 283
Dier, Jeremy......................... 38
Dinkins, David.................. 171
Djokovic, Novak 274

Dodd, Lottie 117
Donald, Allan..................... 98
Dow Classic 92, 94, 96, 99
Doyle, Grant..................... 261
Draper, Scott 308
Drobny, Jaroslav............... 148
Druckemiller, Bill 214
Drucker, Joel 311
Drysdale, Cliff.. 199, 215, 241, 287, 288, 301
Duke of Devonshire.......... *See* Cavendish Family
Durant, Kelly...................... 46
Durie, Jo .. 79, 95, 99, 100, 136, 167, 175
Durr, Francoise 139
Dylan, Bob......................... 275
Eastbourne International . *See* Devonshire Park L.T.C.
Eastbourne Town F.C. 97
Eaves, Wilberforce 258
Edberg, Stefan.. 44, 55, 71, 79, 85, 93, 122, 129, 132, 139, 151, 172, 173, 181, 185, 186, 188, 277, 284, 290, 291
Eden, Al 209, 312
Edgbaston Classic 94
Edgbaston Priory Club...... 94
Edgware Town F.C. 16
Edmondson, Mark 77
El Shafei, Ismail 26
Ellis, Marc......................... 315
Eltingh, Jacco.... 108, 140, 142, 186, 282, 297

Emerson, Roy ...198, 199, 243, 244, 260, 261, 273, 274, 333
Emmons, Jessica 251
Endo, Mana 79
Enquist, Thomas 261
Evans, Richard 51, 289, 303
Evert, Chris 53, 67, 99, 169, 308
Fairbank-Nideffer, Ros 77, 100, 101, 136, 181, 248, 251, 263, 283
Faul, Jo-Anne 112
Feaver, John 147
Federation Cup 72, 99, 133, 148, 157, 246, 249, 267
Federer, Roger .. 117, 169, 276, 301
Fein, Paul 298
Feinstein, John 298
Fendick, Patty 95, 132, 184, 262, 283, 287, 308
Fenway Park 190
Fernandez, Gigi 86, 89, 95, 100, 101, 130, 140, 142, 187, 282, 284, 287, 291
Fernandez, Mary Joe ... 79, 81, 99, 100, 101, 130, 181, 185, 186, 262, 284
Fernberger, Marilyn 207
Ferreira, Wayne 63, 93, 123, 135, 181, 261, 262, 264, 282, 284
Fieldsend, Jeremy 201
Filippini, Marcelo 79

Finchley C.C. 21, 32, 149
Finchley County School ... 17, 19, 27
Fitzgerald, John 83, 94, 111, 112, 123, 291
Flach, Ken 44, 135, 184
Flam, Herbie 98
Fleming, Peter 60, 87
Flinders Park .. See Australian Open
Florence 63, 65, 92
Florida Federal Open 42
Flushing Meadows .... See Chapter 8
Foltz, Shawn 42
Forget, Guy ... 55, 71, 125, 129, 131, 135, 139, 173, 185, 261, 262, 266
Foro Italico .... See Chapter 3
Frana, Javier 136
Fraser, Neil 198
Frazier, Amy 99, 262, 264, 268
French Open .... See Chapter 4
French, Paul 37
Frick, Paul 313, 315
Fromberg, Richard .. 173, 181, 261
Fuchs, Jennifer 137
Fulco-Villella, Bettina 262, 263
Fulwood, Nick 155
Furlan, Renzo 58, 59
Gagnon, Larry 45, 302

Galbraith, Patrick..... 109, 135, 184, 283
Garner, Chris 284
Garrison, Zina 81, 95, 99, 101, 125, 130, 132, 181, 185, 187, 262, 263, 281, 303
Gatting, Mike 21
Gerulaitis, Vitas 219
Gettysburg, battle of 190
Gibson, Althea 180, 259
Gilbert, Brad .71, 93, 104, 129, 172, 181, 236
Gilbert, Dana 236
Gimeno, Andres 28, 273
Golders Hill Park 25
Gomer, Sara 37, 44, 99, 137, 175
Gomez, Andres 221
Gonzales, Pancho .. 14, 28, 34, 273
Goolagong, Evonne 83
Gottfried, Brian 311, 333
Gould, Nick 155
Grabb, Jim ... 81, 134, 140, 142, 186, 282, 286, 287, 331
Graebner, Clark 14, 29
Graf, Steffi ... 10, 66, 67, 72, 79, 85, 86, 89, 125, 130, 132, 140, 175, 181, 185, 186, 235, 262, 278, 281, 290, 303
Graham, Debbie 247, 248, 279, 303
Grand Canyon 189, 191
Grand Slam 9

Grand Slam Cup 104, 129
Great Barrier Reef 241
Greatorex, Peter 154
Grossman, Ann 174, 262
Grunfeld, Amanda 72, 95, 99, 100, 125, 136, 157, 161
Gunthardt, Heinz 44
Gurney, Melissa 42
Gustafsson, Magnus 261
Haas, Tommy 308
Habsudova, Karina . 137, 248, 251
Haillet, Robert 71
Halard, Julie 77, 130, 246, 249, 250, 284, 290
Hamburg 50, 266
Hampstead C.C. 36
Hand, Paul 112, 155
Harford, Tanya 77
Harhuis, Paul 135, 186, 282
Harper, Peanut 112
Hart, Doris 259
Harvey Wild, Linda 100, 101, 174, 279
Helsinki 50
Henderson, Gary 155
Henman Hill 127
Henman, Tim 111, 155, 310
Hererra, Luis-Enrique 108
Hester, William 'Slew' 169
Hetherington, Jill 136, 287, 291
Hewitt, Richard 159
Hingis, Martina 225, 274

Hiraki, Rika....................... 112
Hlasek, Jacob .. 63, 71, 89, 123, 124, 129, 135, 140, 184, 267
Ho, Tommy........................ 181
Hoad, Lew...... 28, 29, 40, 113, 206
Hobbs, Anne...................... 182
Holm, Henrik ... 129, 132, 261, 262
Hooker, Ron........................ 21
Hopman, Harry.. *See* Chapter 10
Hopman, Nell.................... 224
Horvath, Kathleen 221
Hosking, Michael........ 48, 192
How to Teach Americans Cricket 98
Huber, Anke 130, 184, 262, 264, 268
Humphrey-Davies, Virginia 157
Hunt, Lamar 232
Hurricane Andrew 175
Hussein, Saddam...............*See* Prologue
Hutchins, Paul................... 148
Hutchins, Ross................... 148
Hy, Patricia 181, 185, 186
Ickringill, Simon....... 153, 155, 156, 158, 214, 304
Iles, Clay.............................. 37
IMG ... *See* McCormack, Mark
Inter-County Cup (County Week)....................... 96, 155

Invasion of the Body Snatchers 203
Iran-Iraq War .... *See* Prologue
Isherwood, Larry................ 38
Ison, David 112
Italian Open..... *See* Chapter 3
Ivanisevic, Goran. 55, 93, 129, 135, 139, 141, 181
Jaggard-Lai, Michelle...... 249, 250, 255, 262, 263, 303
Jarrett, Andrew................... 82
Jarryd, Anders...... 44, 94, 125, 278, 291
Jausovic, Mima 221
Javer, Monique... 99, 100, 125, 175, 278, 279
Jenson, Luke..................... 135
Jenson, Murphy 311
John, Elton 275
Johns, Peter....................... 146
Johns, Richard........... 302, 323
Jones, Ann........................... 94
Jones, Kelly 135, 186, 282, 284
Jordan, Kathy 182
Keating, Mike..................... 46
Kidowaki, Maya 100, 137
Kiene, Monique 251
Kijimuta, Akiko 79, 112
King Alfred School............. 25
King, Billie Jean...... 24, 27, 94, 200, 217, 259, 299
Kinnear, Kent............ 135, 282
Kirk, Darren 155
Kode-Kilsch, Claudia......... 94

Kodes, Jan 29
Koenig, Rob 309
Koevermans, Mark 135
Kooyong L.T.C. .... *See*
   Australian Open
Korda, Petr 60, 85, 88, 124,
   172
Kosta, John. 130, 183, 190, 301
Krajicek, Richard . 55, 79, 129,
   185, 261, 262
Kramer, Jack 147, 232, 234,
   235
Kratzmann, Mark 63, 280,
   286
Krickstein, Aaron.. 55, 79, 123
Kulmann, Caroline 184
Kulti, Nicklas 1, 78, 80, 85, 87,
   124, 173, 261, 262, 264
Kuwait .... *See* Prologue
La Guardia Airport .. 171, 312
Labat, Florencia 181, 184, 250,
   255, 262, 283
Lacoste, Rene 67
Lake, Valda 95, 100, 157
Larned, William 169
Larsen, Art 98, 258
Larsson, Magnus 129, 261
Laveissiere, Geraud 45
Laver, Rod .. 10, 13, 14, 28, 29,
   197, 198, 232, 236, 243, 273,
   276, 300
Lawhon, Mike ... 212, 214, 313
Leach, Rick. 135, 186, 282, 311

Leconte, Henri . 71, 79, 85, 86,
   88, 129
Led Zeppelin 275
Lee, Sammy 19
Lehmann, John 214
Leicester City F.C. 16, 17
Lendl, Ivan ... 87, 93, 129, 132,
   172, 181, 185, 186, 278
Lenglen, Suzanne 67
Liptons Championships.... 99
Little, Rich 234
Lively, Mary 127, 301
Liverpool F.C. 19, 22, 32, 132,
   322
Lloyd, David 147
Long, Colin 274
Longwood Club 168
Loosemore, Sarah 95, 136
Louis Armstrong Stadium
   167, 169, 170, 177, 185, 186,
   187, 299
Lozano, Jose 83
Luxembourg 50
Mabry, Clarence 193
Mabry, Terri 194, 215
Maclagan, Miles 112
MacNamee, Paul 221
Macpherson, David. 109, 135,
   282
Magers, Gretchen 135, 136
Majoli, Iva 308
Maleeva, Katerina 55, 72,
   130, 132, 140, 181, 283

Maleeva, Maggie......174, 181, 185, 186, 246, 250, 255, 278
Maleeva, Manuela 72, 79, 130, 181, 185, 186
Mallory, Molla................... 169
Manchester Open...............*See* Northern L.T.C.
Manchester United F.C...... 16
Mancini, Alberto..... 55, 60, 71
Mandarino, Edison............. 26
Mansdorf, Amos...... 61, 104, 124, 173, 262, 264, 268, 278, 303
Marchese, Cino.................... 52
Martin, Todd 181
Martinez, Conchita....89, 125, 174, 184, 245, 250, 255, 256, 267, 279, 284
Maskell, Dan.................. 92, 99
Masur, Wally 105, 108, 129, 173, 181, 261, 280
Matsuoka, Shuzo 93
Matthews, Lawrence........ 156
Matthews, Stanley Jr 147
Matthews, Steve..96, 304, 305
McCall, George.................. 273
McCarthy, Shannan..251, 255
McCormack, Mark.............. 52
McCormack, Steve.....62, 132, 302
McEnroe, John....... 87, 88, 93, 105, 124, 129, 131, 135, 139, 140, 141, 142, 150, 152, 171, 172, 178, 183, 184, 186, 277, 281, 289, 327
McEnroe, Patrick 85, 135, 282
McKinlay, Bob................... 310
McKinlay, Chuck................ 24
McMillan, Frew................... 13
McMurtry, Larry 310
McNeil, Lori ... 83, 89, 95, 100, 101, 124, 125, 130, 136, 137, 140, 184, 187, 262, 263, 268, 278, 281, 287
McPhee, John 62
McQuillan, Rachel... 136, 247, 250, 251, 255, 262
Medvedev, Andrei....... 76, 84
Medvedeva, Natalie.. 99, 100, 123
Meskhi, Leila............. 122, 125
Metreveli, Alex 259
Mewshaw, Michael.......... 298
Michibata, Glenn...... 135, 291
Middlesex C.C.C.... 20, 21, 32, 98, 323
Milan 51
Mill Hill C.C. 25
Milton Tennis Centre........*See* Chapter 11
Mitchell, Bob 98, 312
Monument Valley............. 192
Moore, Howard 224
Moore, Ray 311
Moran, Gertrude 'Gussie'.. 24
Mortimer, Angela............. 288

Morton, Tracy......81, 184, 251, 255, 283
Munich............................50, 77
Munson, Ken......................311
Murray, Andy........38, 93, 309
Musch, Barry......................241
Mussolini, Benito..........53, 54
Muster, Thomas...... 261, 262, 264, 268
Nadal, Rafa....................53, 67
Nargiso, Diego............58, 135
Nastase, Ilie ..31, 32, 289, 309, 339
Navratilova, Martina .. 53, 94, 99, 100, 117, 125, 130, 132, 136, 140, 174, 245, 274, 277, 283
New York......... *See* Chapter 8
Newcombe, John ... 15, 27, 53, 147, 176, 189, 193, 196, 197, 198, 200, 205, 207, 211, 260, 288, 307
Nijssen, Tom.....135, 136, 140, 282
Northern L.T.C..................103
Northern Lawn Tennis Championships..............*See* Northern L.T.C.
Norval, Piet................135, 282
Novacek, Karel..............55, 71
Novelo, Lupita...................184
Novotna, Jana.72, 83, 99, 101, 130, 136, 140, 142, 174, 187, 279

Nystrom, Joakim................82
Oakwood F.C......................32
Okker, Tom...........29, 53, 206
Olhovskiy, Andrei... 129, 184, 282
Oncins, Jaimie...................172
Ondruska, Marcus...........286
Orange L.T.C.....................168
Oremans, Miriam....140, 142, 251
Oslo......................................50
Paish, John........................147
Palafox, Tony....................185
Palmer, Jared....................135
Paradis-Magnon, Pascale 174
Pasarell, Charlie..... 13, 15, 34, 310, 333
Pate, David........................135
Patterson, Gerald..............275
Patty, Budge.......................71
Pavilion and Avenue L.T.C. 37
Paz, Mercedes...................184
PBI (Peter Burwash International)..................44
Pearce, Brad...... 61, 62, 81, 83, 108, 135, 184, 303, 325
Perez, Diego........................79
Pescosolido, Stefan.............58
Petchey, Mark .. 125, 136, 157, 172
Peters, Nigel........................48
Pfaf, Eva..............................81
Philadelphia C.C. 168

Phillips, Caryl 340
Pierce, Jim 82
Pierce, Mary 72, 82, 85, 125, 136, 174, 175, 181, 185, 279, 284
Pierce, Ray 43, 306
Pietrangeli, Nicola 71
Pimek, Libor 62
Pioline, Cedric 71, 125, 173, 262
Pistolesi, Claudio 58, 59
Plaza Hotel 166
Pleming, Louise 251
Po-Messerli, Kimberley 77, 251, 255
Porwick, Claudia 136, 281
Potter, Barbara 308
Pozzi, Gianluca 58, 93, 108, 173
Pratt, Nicole 250, 284
Priory L.T.C. 94
Procter and Gamble 33
Provis, Nicole ... 100, 136, 187, 281, 284, 285
Pullin, Julie 112
Queen's Club 92, 93, 94, 97, 145, 149, 258, 314
Queens Park Rangers F.C. 17, 18
Quist, Adrian 274
Radford, Kristine 95
Radlett Tennis and Squash Club 302
Radwanska, Agnieska 139

Ralston, Dennis 28, 29, 194, 258
Rattenbury, Adrian 305
Reggi, Rafaella 136
Rehe, Stephanie . 42, 174, 279, 283
Reinach, Elna 184
Reneberg, Richey 81, 133, 134, 140, 142, 186, 282, 331
Renshaw, William 117
Reynolds, Candy 77
Richardson, Andrew 135
Richardson, Julie 250, 251, 283
Richey, Nancy 29
Riessen, Marty ... 29, 201, 206, 215, 237, 289, 314, 315
Riggs, Bobby 217
Rinaldi, Kathy 136, 287
Rittner, Barbara .. 55, 130, 250, 251, 263, 264, 279
Robinson, Paul 155, 159
Roche, Tony. 53, 147, 211, 310
Roddick, Andy 228
Roger Taylor Tennis Centre 33
Rogers, Simon 2, 32, 166, 180, 301
Rogg, Howard .. 108, 204, 311, 313
Roland Garros. *See* Chapter 4
Rolling Stones 275
Rome .... *See* Chapter 3
Rose, Mervyn 274

Rosewall, Ken... 14, 15, 28, 29, 40, 197, 232, 273, 274, 308, 310
Rosewall, Wilma 308
Ross, Lionel 316
Rosset, Marc . 63, 89, 125, 129, 135, 184
Rostagno, Derek 129
Rottier, Stephanie 249, 250, 263
Round, Dorothy 259
Rubin, Chanda 185, 250
Rusedski, Greg .. 111, 112, 310
Russell, JoAnne 308
Sabaratnam, Frank 45, 172, 214
Sabatini, Gabriela .. 42, 54, 72, 86, 125, 130, 132, 136, 140, 181, 186, 259, 262, 264, 268, 278, 284, 290
Saceanu, Christian.... 125, 129
Saddlebrook .. *See* Chapter 10
Salmon, Julie....... 37, 100, 112, 136, 157
Salumaa, Sven 135, 282
Sampras, Pete ... 49, 84, 85, 93, 104, 129, 132, 139, 156, 169, 181, 185, 186, 188, 261, 262, 264, 268, 277, 278, 284, 290
Samuel, Albert 31
Sanchez Vicario, Arantxa . 86, 89, 101, 125, 135, 181, 184, 186, 187, 262, 263, 264, 284, 290, 291

Sanchez, Emilio 44, 60, 71, 122, 125, 135, 172, 184, 259, 262, 282
Sangster, Mike 27
Santana, Manolo 71, 310
Santoro, Fabrice ... 60, 72, 124, 278
Sapsford, Danny 93, 155, 156, 161, 172, 304
Savchenko-Neiland, Larissa 100, 101, 140, 142, 187, 250, 255
Saviano, Nick 308
Sawamatsu, Naoko 132
Schofield, Mark. 111, 155, 159
Schultz, Brenda 95, 99, 174
Schuurman, Renee 259
Sears, Nigel......................... 38
Sears, Richard 169
Segan, Marc 208
Seguso, Robert 44
Seixas, Vic 258
Seles, Monica.... 54, 67, 72, 76, 79, 85, 86, 89, 125, 130, 132, 140, 181, 185, 186, 187, 262, 266, 278, 290
Seymour, Jane 238
Shales, Jeremy 46
Shaw, Winnie 148
Shea Stadium 167
Shelton, Bryan...... 83, 89, 124, 129, 135, 137, 140, 184
Shields, Brooke 308

Shriver, Pam .94, 95, 100, 135, 136, 187, 262, 263, 264, 268, 279, 283, 284, 287, 291, 297
Siddall, Shirli-Ann 95, 99, 100, 125
Smith, Anne 75
Smith, Stan 49, 197
Smylie, Elizabeth 83, 100, 112, 136, 184, 262, 268, 283, 287, 291, 303
Sonenfield, Nick 32
South of England Championships .... See Devonshire Park L.T.C.
Southern Amateur League 32
Spence, Debbie 42
Sphairistike 115
Stabiner, Karen 42
Stadio Olimpico, Rome 55
Stankovic, Branislav 112
Stark, Jonathan 135, 282
Starr, Larry .202, 206, 210, 311
Steeb, Carl-Uwe 59, 84, 85, 181, 278
Stella Artois Championships 92
Stephenson, Alexandra 308
Stevens, Phil 316
Stevens, Shakin' 44
Stewart, Sherwood 311
Stich, Michael ...55, 61, 76, 79, 129, 132, 135, 139, 140, 142, 172, 183, 186, 278, 284, 290
Stockholm 50

Stockton, Dick 311, 333
Stolle, Fred 24, 28, 129, 199, 215, 241, 260, 273, 287, 288, 307
Stolle, Sandon 125, 261, 268
Stoltenberg, Jason 268
Stone, Allan 288
Strandlund, Maria 112, 251
Stringfellow, Mike 16, 17
Strnadova, Andrea .. 184, 249, 283, 287
Stubbs, Rennae... 95, 100, 136, 268, 287
Sugiyama, Ai 247
Suk, Cyril .. 135, 140, 142, 187, 282, 283
Sukova, Helena 55, 99, 101, 136, 174, 181, 185, 187, 262, 263, 278
Super Saturday 187
Sussex C.C.C. 37, 66, 96, 98
Sussex County League 37
Svensson, Jonas 173, 181, 261, 264
Swallow, Ken 38
Talbot, Byron 61, 62, 81, 83, 108, 135, 136, 179, 184, 282, 284, 303, 325
Tanner, Roscoe 31
Tarabini, Patricia 82, 136
Tarango, Jeff 105
Taroscy, Balazs 44
Tauziat, Natalie 72, 81, 85, 130, 132, 140, 175, 283

Taylor, Roger.... 13, 15, 23, 27, 29, 33, 34, 147, 199, 267, 306, 321
Teacher, Brian 308
Tebbutt, Michael....... 261, 262
Tennis Fantasies with John Newcombe and the Legends........ *See* Chapter 9
Tennis for Life .... *See* Burwash, Peter
The Woodies........... *See* Todd Woodbridge, Mark Woodforde
The Championships .... *See* Wimbledon
The Club at Harper's Point 176, 195, 311
The Four Musketeers 68
The Saffrons.................... 97, 98
The Somme.......... 7, 89, 90, 91
The Southdown Club.......... 37
This is Wimbledon............... 128
Tilden, Bill.. 24, 52, 53, 61, 169
Tinling, Ted 24
Tottenham Hotspur F.C. .. 17, 38
Tranmere Rovers F.C. 19
Trinity University men's tennis team 194
Truman, Christine 27
Truman, Nell...................... 148
Turnbull, Wendy 182
Ulrich, Torben.............. 26, 148

United States Professional Tennis Registry (USPTR) 304
University of Liverpool.... 19, 31, 132, 322
University of Manchester 157
University of Michigan .. 131, 190, 191
US Championships .... *See* Chapter 8
US Open............*See* Chapter 8
Vale de Lobo .... *See* Roger Taylor Tennis Centre
Valenti, Jack....... 310, 311, 313
van Lottum, Noelle . 250, 251, 255
Van Rensburg, Christo.... 135
Vanderbilt Club............ 36, 43
Venice............................. 63, 65
Verdun...................... 7, 89, 91
Vienna............................ 65, 66
Vilas, Guillermo .. 60, 79, 281, 311
Vines, Ellsworth 258
Visser, Danie.... 184, 282, 283, 286, 291
Volkov, Alexander 55, 85, 104, 122, 129, 277, 281
Wade, Andrew.................. 154
Wade, Virginia.............. 27, 99
Walden, Nick 34, 306
Wang, Shi-Ting 250, 255
Warder, Laurie. 109, 135, 282, 286, 291

Washington, Malivai 104, 108, 172, 185, 284
Waters, Ian 314
Werdel, Marianne 42, 125, 174
West Side Tennis Club 98, 168, 169, 275, 306
West Worthing L.T.C. 145, 151, 152, 178
Wheaton, David . 93, 104, 123, 129, 262, 264, 281
White City ...... *See* Chapter 12
White, Robin 135, 136
Whitefield, Katie 148
Whiteley, Richard 161
Whitlinger, Tami 112, 262, 263, 264
Wiesner, Judith .. 125, 130, 174
Wightman Cup 148, 288
Wilander, Mats 79, 273
Wilkerson, John 95
Wilkins, Alan 23
Wilkinson, Chris 93, 105, 125, 136
Williams, Serena 169, 274, 308
Williams, Venus 312
Wills, Helen 117
Wilson, Bobby 26, 148

Wimbledon ...... *See* Chapter 6
Winchmore Hill F.C. 32
Wingate F.C. 17
Witsken, Todd .. 105, 135, 184, 281
Wood, Clare 37, 66, 72, 80, 81, 82, 88, 95, 99, 100, 123, 125, 136, 167, 175, 179, 184, 247, 250, 251, 255, 262, 278, 279, 283, 303, 327
Woodbridge, Todd 81, 89, 136, 173, 184, 281, 291
Woodforde, Mark 81, 173, 181, 187, 212, 261, 311
World Lawn Tennis Professional Championships 28
Worple Road 10, 47, 114, 115, 311
Wrigley Field 190
Wynne Bolton, Nancy 274
Yorkshire C.C.C. 20, 23, 160
Youl, Simon 105
Yzaga, Jaime ... 56, 60, 72, 124, 278
Zurich 65, 66, 242
Zvereva, Natasha .. 86, 89, 95, 101, 130, 132, 140, 142, 187, 282, 287, 291, 292